Virginia Woolf's Essays

Virginia Woolf's Essays

Sketching the Past

Elena Gualtieri

Published by PALGRAVE
Houndmills, Basingstoke, Hampshire RG21 6XS and
175 Fifth Avenue, New York, N.Y. 10010
Companies and representatives throughout the world

PALGRAVE is the new global academic imprint of
St. Martin's Press LLC Scholarly and Reference Division and
Palgrave Publishers Ltd (formerly Macmillan Press Ltd).

Outside North America
ISBN 0–333–74931–6

In North America
ISBN 0–312–22791–4

This book is printed on paper suitable for recycling and made from fully managed and sustained forest sources.

A catalogue record for this book is available from the British Library.

Library of Congress Cataloging-in-Publication Data
Gualtieri, Elena, 1966–
Virginia Woolf's essays : sketching the past /Elena Gualtieri.
p.   cm.
Includes bibliographical references and index.
ISBN 0–312–22791–4 (cloth)
1. Woolf, Virginia, 1882–1941—Prose.   2. Literature and history––Great Britain—History—20th century.   3. Feminism and literature––England—History—20th century.   4. Women and literature—England––History—20th century.   5. English essays—20th century—History and criticism.   6. Criticism—England—History—20th century.
7. Autobiography.   8. Essay.   I. Title
PR6045.O72Z67   1999
824'.912—dc21   99–43172
                                                            CIP

10   9   8   7   6   5   4
08   07   06   05   04   03   02

Printed and bound in Great Britain by
Antony Rowe Ltd, Chippenham, Wiltshire

Per Tula e Franco
Voor Corné

Contents

Acknowledgements

This book was originally written as a doctoral thesis at the University of Sussex. My first debt of gratitude goes to Rachel Bowlby, who supervised my work on the thesis with an unfailing critical eye and with clear respect for my own critical positions. Peter Nicholls examined the thesis and has ever since given generously of his advice, support and encyclopedic knowledge of modernism. Hermione Lee's suggestions on shaping the thesis into a book have also been very valuable. Thanks are also due to Mrs Elizabeth Inglis of the University of Sussex Library for the continuous help throughout the years in which this project was developed.

Among friends and family, thanks go to Davide Peró and Elisabetta Zontini for helping, listening and laughing at my obsessions; to my parents for sustaining and loving me despite the distance; and to Corné Kros, who gave unstintingly of everything he had, and then some more.

A shorter version of Chapter 2 appeared in *Textual Practice*, 12:1 (1998): 49–67, © Routledge. Acknowledgements are due to *Textual Practice* and to the publisher for permission to reprint.

Acknowledgements for permission to reprint from *The Essays of Virginia Woolf*, ed. Andrew McNeillie, vols i–iv (London: Hogarth, 1986–), are due to the executors of the Virginia Woolf estate, the title, the editor and the publishers; for permission to reprint from *The Crowded Dance of Modern Life*, ed. Rachel Bowlby (Harmondsworth: Penguin, 1992), to the Society of Authors as the Literary Representative of the Estate of Virginia Woolf.

The jacket shows a sketch of Hogarth House by Richard Kennedy, which is taken from his brochure for the exhibition that accompanied the publication of his *A Boy at the Hogarth Press* (London: Whittington, 1972). Kind permission to reprint the sketch was generously given by Mrs Olive M. Kennedy, for which I warmly thank her.

List of Abbreviations

CD	*The Crowded Dance of Modern Life*
CE 1, 2, 3, 4	*Collected Essays*
CR 2	*The Common Reader: Second Series*
D 1, 2, 3, 4, 5	*The Diary of Virginia Woolf*
E 1, 2, 3, 4	*The Essays of Virginia Woolf*
L 1, 2, 3, 4, 5, 6	*The Letters of Virginia Woolf*
MB	*Moments of Being*
O	*Orlando*
PA	*A Passionate Apprentice*
RO	*A Room of One's Own*
SF	*The Complete Shorter Fiction of Virginia Woolf*
TG	*Three Guineas*
WE	*A Woman's Essays*

Introduction: Virginia Woolf, European Essayist

In 1923 Virginia Woolf was forty-one years old, living in Richmond, and had already published three novels: *The Voyage Out* (1915), *Night and Day* (1919) and *Jacob's Room* (1922). She was also a regular reviewer for the *Times Literary Supplement* and other major literary journals, including the *Nation & Athenaeum*, where on 1 December 1923 she published 'Mr Bennett and Mrs Brown', one of the best-known of her essays and usually considered to be her literary manifesto. 'Mr Bennett and Mrs Brown' was written in response to Arnold Bennett's criticism of *Jacob's Room*, which Bennett claimed showed Woolf's incapacity to create characters that could 'survive in the mind'.[1] Rattled, as usual, by hostile reviews, Woolf returned to Bennett's comments in a diary entry of June 1923, where she set out to 'say something about my writing' (*D* 2, 248) following her reading of extracts from Katherine Mansfield's journals in the introduction to *The Doves' Nest and Other Stories* (1923).

Woolf's relationship to Mansfield was notoriously and, by her own admission, extremely competitive, with Woolf often measuring the value and achievement of her own writing against the standards laid out by Mansfield either in conversation with Woolf or in her published work. In this particular diary entry, Woolf takes up Mansfield's notion that writing should be *'deeply felt'* to question the integrity of her own creations. It is an act of self-scrutiny that leads her back to the issue of character raised by Bennett's review, as she admits:

> It is true that I dont have that 'reality' gift. I insubstantise, wilfully to some extent, distrusting reality – its cheapness. But to go further, have I the power of conveying the true reality? Or do I write essays about myself?
>
> (*D* 2, 248)

In the way in which it links together essay-writing, autobiography and Woolf's experiments with the form of the modern novel, this diary entry is central to the conception of this book. It shows Woolf entertaining the kind of self-doubt which is banned from the pages of her public reply to Bennett's criticism, where she confidently announces the coming of 'one of the most important, the most illustrious, the most epoch-making' eras of literary history (*E* 3, 388). And yet, the very availability of this private commentary calls up hordes of questions about literary and historical documents and the ways in which their respective domains are to be defined. In Woolf's case perhaps more than for any other woman writer of this century, the respective roles of private and public documents have been clearly scrambled as the most personal and intimate circumstances of her life have become the subject of a sizeable publishing industry that appeals to a wide spectrum of readers, both specialised and non.

If the context of reading of this diary entry shows a clear disturbance of lines of division between different kinds of writings, so its content charts a clear crossing over of boundaries between apparently 'natural' definitions of different literary styles and periods. It moves away from a simplistic Bennett vs. Woolf, Edwardian vs. Georgian, realist vs. modernist opposition to concede a certain element of common understanding between terms of which we are used of thinking as in stark contrast to each other and to all intents and purposes irreconcilable. Woolf admits that Bennett's charge is to some extent justified, that she does not have 'that "reality" gift', but at the same time also points out that her deficiency is in fact the product of a choice, of a sense of discrimination between the given of experience (reality in inverted commas) and that which has to be sought after (the artistic representation of another kind of reality). Classifying the first as 'cheap' and the second, by implication, as precious, Woolf's remarks about the true nature of reality are also made to prefigure, albeit unwittingly, some of the charges of snobbism and limited social range that were to be brought against both her personally and her work from the 1930s onwards.

It is interesting in this context that the question of literary form and, specifically, of the essay surfaces here both as an element in the opposition between different kinds of reality and as a step further in the line of reasoning followed by Woolf's reflections. On the one hand, 'writing essays about oneself' is seen as a de-valued kind of activity by comparison with the pursuit of the true type of reality that figures here as the most valuable of the two occupations. While the comparison might suggest a certain similarity of positions between 'cheap' reality and essay-writing, it is also nevertheless quite clear that for Woolf the question of the essay exceeds the terms of her opposition to Bennett's materialism and of the simple historical paradigm that would cast modernism as the antithesis of realism. As Woolf warns, the ultimate risk lies for her not in an improbable fall into base materialism but rather in the final dissolution of what remains of objective reality into boundless autobiography.

In the space of a few lines, then, this entry encompasses both the scope of Woolf's artistic and intellectual ambitions and her sense of the risks and the problems associated with her projects. The movement described by her line of reasoning here mimics quite closely that of the Hegelian dialectic, whereby an initial splitting into two of 'reality' opens the way for the subsequent transcendence of those splits into a new synthesis or art form. As always with Woolf, however, the third movement of the dialectic appears here only as a question and a problem, but never as a solution.[2] From this point of view, the essay then figures in Woolf's own conception as the symbol of a failed synthesis, as the recycling of the given of experience into its own transcendence.

The understanding of the essay that emerges from this quotation reveals Woolf as being suspended between two different conceptions of the genre. On the one hand there is the tendency to see the essay as a second-order literary phenomenon that is concerned with autobiographical questions rather than more philosophical issues such as the true representation of 'reality'. In this sense, Woolf's observations occupy the same space as Mr Ramsay's agonising analysis of his own achievements in *To the Lighthouse*, which his son Andrew reflects by comparing his father's pursuit of 'the nature of reality' to 'think[ing] of a kitchen table... when you're not there'.[3] The homely character of Andrew's example might be read as yet another version of Woolf's assertion of the 'cheapness' of reality and her preference for more insubstantial forms of inquiry. In this case, Woolf's association of the essay with the kind of reality pursued by Mr Ramsay finds its place within a specifically English tradition of thinking about the genre as a 'minor', marginalised form of literature which is the purview of *amateurs* and leisured gentlemen.[4]

This conception of the essay as *belles lettres*, as a form of writing exclusively interested in the pursuit of style and good form has also guided the reception of Woolf's critical writings in the postwar years. Although during her lifetime the essays enjoyed a wider and, in Leonard Woolf's term, 'more catholic' (*CE* Editorial Preface) appreciation than Woolf's novels, in the years which followed her death and up to the late

1960s this situation was reversed, as critics began to focus almost exclusively on her activity as a novelist and relegated the essays to the traditional role of 'minor' genre, dutifully included in studies of her work, but dismissed as more imperfect and less challenging than her fiction.[5]

But this isolation of the essay to the margins of the canon of Woolf's work also finds a point of resistance in the second line of thinking outlined in the diary entry of 1923. As Woolf turns to examine the status of her own work within the development of literary history, the essay is offered as a possible source of disturbance of a historical paradigm which would see the 'old post-Dostoevsky argument' (*D* 2, 248) about character in fiction superseded by a better representation of character in a sort of progressive move towards the best possible literature. This is a remarkably un-English conception of the genre which associates it not so much with leisurely pursuits and the exercise of style for style's sake, but rather with a different way of thinking about history and modernity. In this sense, the essay becomes an interruption to progress and, at the same time, signals the emergence of a type of literary history that questions the identification of modernity with the culmination of progress.

This other conception of the genre aligns Woolf's thinking in matters of literary historiography with a Continental tradition of commentary upon the essay that has found its most sophisticated exponents among Continental Marxists such as Lukács and Adorno. Both Lukács and Adorno saw in the genre one of the paradoxes and puzzles of modernity, a form of writing that was at one and the same time the product of a determinate time and place and yet approaching the conditions of pure discourse. This conception of the essay as a type of discourse that disturbs established boundaries between different kinds of writing was first articulated by Lukács in his introductory chapter to *Soul and Form* (1911). Lukács insisted that the essence of the essay lies precisely in its ability to bring together modes of being and of thinking that are commonly thought of as being in opposition to each other. He admits that the aesthetic and the epistemological domain relate to two different forms of consciousness (the thing itself and the concept), produce two different types of expression (the image and meaning), and two different ontologies (that of giving form, or creation, and that of inquiry, or intersubjective relationship). Yet he claims that as a modern genre still in its prehistory the essay presents features from both sides of the distinction. It asks the fundamental ontological questions, 'what is life, what is man, what is destiny?', but provides them not with 'the answers of science or, at purer heights, those of philosophy' but with a form, a 'symbol'.

As the form given to the ontological questions, the essay partakes then of both modes of being and therefore makes problematic any clear-cut opposition between cognition and aesthetic experience. For Lukács, the essay articulates knowledge as the experiencing of wholeness that in Kant's terms only belongs to the aesthetic moment. As this kind of cognitive experience seals together subject and object, the essay cannot belong to science or philosophy, even though it shares with them the ontology of inquiry. To articulate 'intellectuality, conceptuality as sensed experience, as immediate reality, as spontaneous principle of existence' criticism must both be form and address itself to the forms of art.[6] In Lukács's argument, then, the essay as criticism does not stand in opposition to the essay as *belles lettres* but rather represents the realisation of the essence of the genre. The definition of the essay as a well-written piece of prose which is commonly associated with the English tradition signals some kind of understanding of the essence of the genre but fails to articulate its wider implications. As form, the essay attempts to bridge the gulf between knowledge and experience by giving knowledge the form of aesthetic experience. Rather than producing knowledge the way that science does, the essay creates a form where knowledge can be experienced as art.

Lukács's analysis of the genre reflects then the blurring of boundaries in the search for new forms of writing that is articulated by Woolf in the diary entry of 1923. The parallel becomes even more striking when Lukács's argument is enlarged to take into consideration the type of subjectivity inscribed in the essay and its relation to the form of the novel. In *The Observing Self* (1988), Graham Good follows Lukács in arguing that the essay emerges from the cultural revolution of the Renaissance in reaction to the scholasticism that had characterised medieval knowledge. To the culture of commentary and authority the essay prefers an appeal to personal experience that aligns it to the empiricism of the 'new' science. Unlike modern science, however, the essay does not lead this experience back into the folds of systematic knowledge, but attempts to make a faithful reproduction of singularity and uniqueness. Close to other autobiographical genres in its drive towards capturing the self on the page, the form of the essay is distinguished from them by its relation to temporality. For Good, diary and autobiography structure their representation of the self along chronological or narrative sequences, while the essay mimics in its very form the experience of a scattered and only loosely connected self. Thus, if the essay offers no general rules and truths, Good nevertheless insists that, as a genre, it does put forth a claim for the truthful representation of the general experience of selfhood, so that 'the essayist's personality' becomes 'an example ... of an "actually existing" individual and the unorganized "wholeness" of his experience'.[7]

In the essay, experience appears then not just as the raw material from which writing is moulded but also as the product of writing itself. With the essay, experience acquires a form and a shape, even though that form and shape remain much looser than those of highly formalised genres such as tragedy or poetry. Good argues that the formlessness and pliability that characterise both essay and novel are the marks of their roots in bourgeois individualism, where the uniqueness of personal experience does not tolerate compression into any schema or pattern. Following Ian Watt's analysis of the rise of the novel in English culture, Good argues that the episodic character of early examples of the genre marks a break with the strictly codified rules of medieval and Renaissance romance in the attempt to give a more truthful representation of individual experience. As an inversion of the knightly quest, the picaresque novel offers the story of an individual's education through experience of the world rather than scholastic learning. But while the form of the novel subsequently crystallised into the *Bildungsroman* of the nineteenth century, Good argues that the essay has preserved a radical resistance to the imposition of any system upon the representation of individual experience.

While the novel has become, then, the locus of schemas and formulas to which experience is made to conform, the form of the essay lets experience itself shape the text. But, since experience is as much a product of essay-writing as its source, the essay as a genre makes problematic any appeal to the notion of an unmediated, transparent experience. Good recognises this much, but argues that to see something as constructed is not necessarily to deny its reality. He argues that, although the essay constructs and shapes experience in a certain way, the refusal to resolve that experience into a system of knowledge amounts to a commitment to retain the fundamental formlessness of personal experience. For Good, the essay thus becomes the most suitable form with which to combat both the homogenisation of individual consciousness by mass culture and the systematic reduction of that consciousness to an abstract entity in the theories of the human sciences.

In its coupling of mass culture and modern science as destructive of individual freedom, Good's analysis of subjectivity in the essay shows to be strongly indebted to Adorno's and Horkheimer's critique of the Enlightenment project. In the influential *Dialectic of Enlightenment* (1944), Adorno and Horkheimer had argued that the separation of facts and values that founded the modern project harboured in itself the possibility of both freedom and domination. Adorno saw in the development of mass culture a continuation of the total domination of consciousness by capitalist power structures and equated this domination with the subjugation of materiality and the object to the concept. Thus the effects of mass culture and advanced capitalism on individual consciousness are in line with the kind of identity-thinking that Adorno claims has characterised the history of Western metaphysics since its beginning. Identity-thinking is the mode of consciousness that corresponds to the structuring of human relations in capitalist societies. Adorno follows Marx in arguing that the relation between the worker and the capitalist appears as a property of the commodity produced by the worker under the guise of surplus value. In capitalist societies, surplus value is what makes it possible to exchange commodities through the mediating instance of money. But what appears as the property of the commodity is in fact the intrinsic human essence of the worker that is being sold off to the capitalist as labour.

For Adorno, the alienation of human consciousness produced by capitalist relations of production is at the foundation of a fetishistic relation to objects. In capitalist societies, objects are perceived either as resources to be exploited or as commodities. This endowing of the object with properties that do not belong to it is also reproduced, according to Adorno, in that mode of consciousness that he calls identity-thinking. Identity-thinking consists in an endless reduction of the particular and of the differences between things to their universal idea or concept. This domination of the particular by the universal amounts to the annihilation of the otherness of the object carried out by the observing or dominating subject. This reduction of the object to an instrument of the subject structures the relation to materiality inscribed by modern technology and corresponds to the domination of individual consciousness by the totality of the capitalist structure of production. The only form of consciousness that escapes such total domination is, according to Adorno, non-identity thinking, that is, that mode of thinking that breaks up the appearance of absolute equivalence between, on the one hand, different objects and, on the other, objects and concepts.

Non-identity thinking is made possible by the contradictions implicit in capitalist societies and, in particular, by the dialectic of the Enlightenment. The separation of fact and value that liberated science from morality and enabled the development of the technology necessary to the production of capital also sanctioned the fundamental non-identity of concept and object that had previously been covered over by scholasticism. The legitimation of experience and direct observation as a ground for the critique of authority thus uncovered the lack of an absolute adequacy between the order of things and the order of words. Adorno argues that this other side of the dialectic of the Enlightenment founds the very possibility of freedom and emancipation by revealing the inadequacy and limits of identity-thinking. As this freedom remains in a dialectical relation to the principle of domination, it can only be a limited or negative kind of freedom, rather than the full realisation of human potential envisaged by the notion of (utopic) emancipation.

As Gillian Rose argues in *The Melancholy Science* (1978), the essay represents for Adorno the form that remains most faithful to non-identity thinking as it refuses to resolve thought into either a logical argument or a story-line.[8] For Adorno, the essay presents the relation between concepts as a constellation rather than a derivation from first principles. Unlike Lukács, however, Adorno does not align the particular configuration offered by the essay to art rather than science. He remarks that to see the essay as art is in fact to reinforce the hegemony of the scientific model of knowledge as the only valid one. As an instance of non-identity thinking, the essay does not endow objects with properties that do not belong to them, nor does it bend materiality to make it fit into a hierarchical structuring of thought. Because of its attention to the irreducibility of the particular, 'the essay has something like an aesthetic autonomy that is easily accused of being simply derived from art, although it is distinguished from art by its medium, concepts, and by its claim to a truth devoid of aesthetic semblance'.[9]

In Adorno's work, the essay thus functions as the privileged vehicle of non-identity thinking and negative dialectics. As Gillian Rose remarks, Adorno's search for a form of consciousness and thought that would not be liable to assimilation by the totalizing drive characteristic of capitalism led him to develop a style of writing that, by its very difficulty and impenetrability, resisted the possibility of being traced back into the imperialism of equivalence. Rather than developing systems of thought, Adorno preferred to elaborate his critique in the form of fragments, aphorisms and essays. His analysis of scientific knowledge and practices as the most evident realisation of the domination of the object by the subject led him to reject the notion of method and substitute that of style. This choice was also in agreement with Adorno's contention that art and artistic practice represent the only locus of resistance to the impending totalization of consciousness by capitalism.

Adorno's style is thus often seen as performing the resistance against reification he theorises. Rose has described the chiasmus as the fundamental structure of this style. The intersection of sentences so that the second sentence inverts the word order of the first one may be seen as a plastic rendering of the workings of negative dialectics in writing but, as Rose remarks, has also made Adorno's thought liable to being reduced to a series of sound-bites. The ironic fate of Adorno's attempt to escape commodification can be explained by the disjunction between essay and aphorism that is often overlooked in his writing. This disjunction corresponds to a theoretical problem in Adorno's thought. As we saw earlier, although Adorno claims that the essay represents a form of non-identity thinking and therefore the other side of the dialectic of freedom and subjugation, his reliance on Walter Benjamin's concept of constellation also reveals a tendency to propose the other side of the dialectic as an alternative in itself to the reification of thought effected by identity thinking. Adorno's theory of the essay therefore hovers uneasily between a purely dialectical understanding of history and the temptation to set up an alternative metaphysics.

This alternation between dialectic and metaphysics has been described by John Snyder in *Prospects of Power* (1991) as the fundamental difference between the French and the English tradition of essay-writing. According to Snyder, Montaigne's and Bacon's essays differ in their relationship to temporality: while Bacon's aphoristic writing aims to crystallise time into eternity, Montaigne's essays simply substitute the temporality of the private for the macro-time of public office and politics. Snyder observes that the essay springs from an historical situation of retreat from public life into a sort of exile that is usually located in the countryside. This situation of retreat marks the essay as the locus of freedom from the occupation and preoccupation of public life and leaves writing free to roam over any topic without having to resolve its thoughts into a system. The essay thus gives shape to an alternative dimension that is completely autonomous from that of action and history, the dimension of discourse itself: 'The essay is self-reflexive discursivity, the proper function of which is to declare a private politics of liberation from history by generating a verbal state, the state of verbality.'[10]

For Snyder, the essay then replaces the legal and administrative framework of the modern state with a form of discourse whose only aim is the generation of the parallel and autonomous dimension of pure verbality.

He argues that for Montaigne the essay functioned as an opportunity for liberating the self from the strictures and determinations of history by providing an arena where the self can be continuously re-fashioned and re-generated.[11] As Graham Good argues in *The Observing Self*, the essay emerges out of the split between the order of words and the order of things that occurred during the Renaissance, but does not align itself with either the empiricist or the scholastic position. Rather than determining the epistemological superiority of either ontology, the essay creates a world and a self out of words and thus endows language with the power to generate a different order of reality. This reality remains in a shifting or changing relation to the reality of history and politics. In Montaigne, the relation of private to public sphere is non-antagonistic and ruled by co-existence rather than conflict, as conflict itself belongs to the particular historical situation Montaigne is trying to escape. In Bacon, the ambition of the genre is enlarged to make it an instrument of the essayist's own claims to status in history, that is, the essay is conceived as a monument to the man who aspires to direct and control his fortune: 'Bacon looks not for continuity of actions *in* writing, but for suspension from time altogether, from politics or time as power, through recourse to a supposedly timeless discourse *about* things political'.[12]

Bacon's ambition to elevate himself above the accidents of time and history produces the aphoristic style as a means of stopping the movement of history in language. While Montaigne's essays are characterised by a movement of digression that constitutes self and object as a set of possibilities, Bacon's aphorisms crystallise that movement into an alternation of thesis and antithesis that shapes thought as nuggets or gems of wisdom. The point-like character of Bacon's writing makes his pronouncements therefore much easier to quote than Montaigne's fluid discourses. As sound-bites, Bacon's sentences can indeed achieve an independence from the situation of their formulation that approaches the eternal character of monuments. Although structured by an antithetic movement, as a whole his sentences present themselves as syntheses, as the ultimate realisation of the course of history. 'The aim of this second step [the synthesis]', Snyder points out, 'is to make the essay itself, as aphoristic language, "follow the example of time"' and thus 'maneuver out of the apparent stasis of determinist time'.[13]

For Snyder, then, the essay arises out of the historical situation of retreat from the public world of politics and history but does not determine or fix the relation of the private sphere it generates to the public world it leaves. This amounts to saying that the essay is in effect an exploration of the meaning of that historical situation of retreat from which it springs. In Montaigne's case, this retreat comes to signify a refusal to engage in the bloody conflicts of religion that characterise his historical moment. It therefore founds the private sphere as the *absence* of conflict where the emblematic form of relationship to the other is friendship. In Bacon's writing, the sphere of discourse is forced to enter into competition with that of actions and history and attempts to establish itself as the truly transcendental realm of existence. Because history is understood by Bacon as what lasts rather than what passes, discourse is then made to take the place of history, to imitate the stasis of a history that does not pass but stays. Thus, the form of the aphorism takes the generating power of discourse to build a sphere of existence that is liberated from the accidents of historical being and, therefore, eternal. While in Montaigne writing is parallel to history, in Bacon it hovers above it.

As Snyder remarks, it is not surprising to find that women writers in general and feminist critics in particular have often engaged with the essay as a form for their exploration of the intersections between private and public, personal and political. Although the essay founds the split between the two spheres that has been so forcefully contested by feminists, it also endows the personal or private sphere with the kind of autonomy from history that makes possible such a contestation. Snyder concedes that 'among the genres, the essay has never dominated', but also insists that it is the only genre capable of 'accommodat[ing] ... those deepest rhythms of the kind of personal transformation that is also completely political.' As instances of this kind of exploration Snyder cites both Woolf and Adrienne Rich, though adding that their essay-prose tends to swerve towards 'the perfection of stasis'.[14] In this, he claims, British and American feminists tend to follow the tradition outlined by Bacon rather than Montaigne's attempt to liberate the self from history.[15]

Snyder claims that Montaigne's essay might in fact be the most appropriate genre for feminism precisely because it invests language with the power to generate different selves and worlds. As a genre, Montaigne's essay would therefore enact a synthesis of language and sexuality that counters the Cartesian split between mind and body which feminism has radically criticised. But as this synthesis is predicated upon a situation of retreat from public life, the choice of the essay as *the* genre of feminism ends up by reinforcing rather than challenging the private/public split. While the essay might be the only genre that makes possible an exploration of the personal as political, it still cannot accommodate an analysis of the public side of the political, that is, of institutions. The historical occasion of the essay limits its intervention in history to a series of isolated pockets of digression from the main course of history. In this sense, the essay does not and cannot offer a real challenge to the linearity of either logic or historical plots. Hence, what Snyder sees as Woolf's and Rich's swerve towards metaphysics testifies to the difficulty of finding alternative ways of writing history that would not fall out of history altogether.

This dilemma and the problems it raises for feminist critics and writers is also in evidence in the history of the feminist reception of Woolf's essays. Although the essays and the questions of genre they raise have only recently become the focus of explicit investigation in feminist studies of Woolf's work, it was the intervention of feminist criticism itself that opened up the canon of her work to a complete re-evaluation. The attention to issues of sexual difference that animated the 'new' readings of Woolf that began to appear towards the end of the 1960s and the early 1970s brought to the forefront the notion of androgyny and, with it, texts such as *A Room* (1929) which had previously been confined to the niche dedicated to Woolf's 'feminist pamphlets' and thus isolated from the rest of her writing.[16] This foregrounding of *A Room* at the centre of Woolf's work carried with it the possibility of re-thinking from scratch the role of her non-fictional writings and their relation to her novels. This possibility was realised by Michèle Barrett in 1979 with the publication of *Women and Writing*, a selection of Woolf's most outspokenly feminist essays. Although Barrett preserved Leonard Woolf's clear-cut distinction between essays and novels as two essentially separate and very different forms of writing in Woolf's *oeuvre*, in her introduction she argued for a reversal of their respective positions in the canon, claiming that Woolf's essays and critical writings offered a far more empowering model for feminist critics than the aesthetics of impersonality pursued by Woolf in her fictional work.

Published at the end of a momentous decade that saw the appearance in print of Quentin Bell's official biography of Woolf (1972), of her letters (1975–84) and then of her diaries (1977–84),[17] *Women and Writing* explicitly took issue with the kind of images and representations that were being projected by the controversies surrounding the representation of Woolf's private life and the interpretation of her work based on it. In her introduction, Barrett argued that the essays countered the twin images of madwoman and delicate Bloomsbury aesthete that were current at the time with that of an intellectually powerful woman capable of providing both 'a general theoretical account of women's literary work' and 'a detailed critical assessment of many individual authors'.[18] According to Barrett, the essays showed a clearly defined attempt at elaborating a materialist analysis of the history of women's oppression that was at odds with Woolf's sustained belief in the autonomous character of artistic expression. She claimed that this opposition between Woolf's modernist and feminist commitments had been generally overlooked by feminist studies of her work, which had rather preferred to characterise her *oeuvre* as a drive towards the unification of opposites.[19]

While to Barrett the importance of the essays lay in the revised reading of Woolf's work they could provide, until very recently Woolf studies had generally left unheeded her suggestion of a link between two questions: the compatibility of Woolf's feminist and modernist commitments and the issue of genre in her work. In fact, one of the most influential intervention in the history of feminist debates around Woolf, Toril Moi's *Sexual/Textual Politics* (1985), effectively reversed Barrett's suggestion to argue that *A Room* itself should be read not so much as a blueprint for feminist criticism but rather as a modernist text akin to her novels in its rhetorical and textual strategies. Moi famously criticised Elaine Showalter's dismissal of *A Room* in *A Literature of Their Own* (1979), where Showalter had condemned Woolf's celebration of the androgynous ideal as a 'flight' from the pains and conflicts of the experience of womanhood and embodiment in patriarchal society.[20] Moi replied that, like many other Anglo-American feminists, Showalter had failed to realise the value of Woolf's work for the deconstruction of polarised gender positions through the '*textual practice*' of her writing rather than just its content, adding that 'that practice is of course much more marked in the novels than in most of her essays'.[21] Crucially, then, her argument rested on reading *A Room* not so much as a programme or manifesto for the development of feminist criticism but as a modernist text whose fictional strategies carried out a radical destabilisation of gendered identities.[22]

This valorisation of the fictional character of *A Room* as the locus of its feminist critique showed that Moi was implicitly working on the basis of a hierarchical disposition of different kinds of discourse where fiction dominated as the genre both of modernism and of feminism, while the essay was associated with a 'naive' kind of reading that privileged content over form. This unexamined distinction became the focus of explicit investigation in Rachel Bowlby's monograph on Woolf, first published in 1988 and then re-issued in an expanded version in 1997. *Feminist Destinations* opened with an extended reading of 'Mr Bennett and Mrs Brown', arguing that Woolf's importance to the development of feminist criticism lied not so much in her privileging of fiction over other genres, but rather in the way in which Woolf's writing set out to undermine the very distinctions between them.

Intended as the first comprehensive study of Woolf's work in the light of literary theory, *Feminist Destinations* was immediately concerned with providing new readings of very well-known texts, from *Mrs Dalloway* (1925) and *To the Lighthouse* (1927) to *Three Guineas* (1938) and *Between the Acts* (1941). Bowlby returned, though, to the question of Woolf's essays a few years later, in her introduction to the Penguin edition of two selected volumes of essays, which were brought out as part of a series marking Woolf's temporary exit from copyright in 1991. Penguin's inclusion of the essays in its series on Woolf indicated an enlargement of the canon that was both aided and confirmed by the publication of the first four volumes of Andrew McNeillie's *The Essays of Virginia Woolf*. McNeillie's edition of the essays started to appear in 1986 and will, when completed, mark the end of the process of attribution, publication, collection and referencing of Woolf's writings that seals a writer's acceptance into the canon of English literature. His introductions have underscored this process of canonisation by refusing to take a polemical stance and focusing rather on the historical outline of Woolf's career as an essayist and reviewer both in its own right and in relation to her fiction.

In a move that parallels the progressive canonisation of Woolf's essays signalled by McNeillie's edition, the two Penguin volumes, *A Woman's Essays* (1992) and *The Crowded Dance of Modern Life* (1993), set out to make the essays more available to a larger public, while at the same time attempting to reject the opposition of popular to elitist, lowbrow to highbrow that has relegated them to the role of minor work.'[23] Focusing upon the way in which these oppositions translate into a separation of Woolf the novelist from Woolf the essayist and of her modernism from her feminism, Bowlby argued in her introductions that Woolf's own writings both invite and undermine the establishment of a definitive hierarchy between the different kinds of writings in which she engaged. She remarked that while Woolf tended to see writing for money as incompatible with the demands of artistic creation, she also considered it as one of the first instruments of financial and psychological emancipation for women. Conversely, Woolf was very keen upon restricting the space for polemics and arguments to the form of the essay, which, in her hands, often transforms itself into a fictional account.

The instability of the distinctions between essay and fiction suggested by Woolf also undermines, according to Bowlby, any attempt at defining the confines of Woolf's feminist and modernist commitments. The first dedicated to women and writing and the second to the experience of modern living, the Penguin volumes are meant to illustrate that, in Bowlby's words, 'the two topics for which Woolf's essays have been known – modern writing and feminism – are intimately connected, as modern writing daughters work out the strength of their ties, or lack of ties, to mothers, fathers and patrons of all sorts' (*WE*, xiv). Rejecting Barrett's split between feminist politics and modernist aesthetics, Bowlby insists that the question of women's space and place is translated by Woolf into the question of which forms and which genres might be best suited to women's writing. Unlike the novel, which for Woolf represented the possibility of experimenting with new forms and shapes, the essay remained for her attached to the paternal figure and therefore became the arena where the relationship between tradition and modernity was explored. Far from standing in opposition to each other then, Woolf's essays and novels can be seen for Bowlby to articulate complementary aspects of the same project: to tell stories left untold and represent new forms of consciousness.

In its stress upon the radical instability of hierarchical formations within Woolf's writing Bowlby's work has been instrumental to opening up Woolf studies to a wide range of critical and historical approaches. Like Moi before her, Bowlby set out to dismantle the kind of impassable oppositions that have regulated the reading of Woolf's work as either a modernist or a feminist, an essayist or a novelist, a refined aesthete or a committed socialist revolutionary. In linking the existence of these oppositions to questions of literary historiography and of genre, Moi and Bowlby have strongly contributed to steering the course of Woolf studies towards the question of the essay as one of the crucial points of intersection between gender and genre, between literature and its cultural and historical context.

The second half of the 1990s has in fact seen the appearance of a cluster of monographs exclusively dedicated to Woolf's activity as a cultural critic, journalist, reviewer and literary historian. Beth Carole Rosenberg's *Virginia Woolf and Samuel Johnson* (1995), Juliette Dusinberre's *Virginia Woolf's Renaissance* (1997), Leila Brosnan's *Reading Virginia Woolf's Essays and Journalism* (1997), the articles collected in *Virginia Woolf and the Essay* (1997) have all effected a widening of the frames of reference deployed to read Woolf's non-fictional writings. They have enlarged both the historical context of Woolf studies, which now includes the Renaissance and the eighteenth century in addition to the more familiar early twentieth century, and their critical pool, which has brought authors such as Bakhtin and his theory of the dialogic character of language at the centre of many of these readings of Woolf's essayistic practice.[24]

The focus on the dialogic nature of Woolf's essay-writing that is typical of these studies has tended to ally her work with the Montaignian tradition, with its stress on the importance of friendship and the humility of a writing persona identified by the tag 'Que scais-je?'.[25] Although this might indicate a return to a belletristic conception of the essay as an exercise in style that is devoid of true content, the Bakhtinian notion of the dialogic in writing has in fact worked to radicalise the 'familiar' or 'personal' essay as practised by Woolf. Defined in these recent studies as a profoundly democratic practise capable of destabilising hierarchies of power, Bakhtin's dialogic has helped to translate Woolf's focus on the conversational character of her essay-writing into an instrument for the feminist critique of more traditional models of the construction and transmission of knowledge. As dialogue, Woolf's essays are therefore seen as explicit contestations of the dominance of the authoritative 'I', for which they substitute a provisional formation which, like Montaigne's 'Que scais-je?', does not offer meaning as truth but as the result of an intersubjective process of reading and writing.

This view of the essay as an anti-authoritarian form of writing that privileges process rather than result has, as we saw, its origin in the work of Lukács and Adorno and in their analysis of the nature of knowledge in post-Enlightenment, capitalist societies. Its re-emergence in recent feminist studies of Woolf's essays indicates a convergence of critical frames that places her activity as an essayist at the intersection between a feminist critique of patriarchal power structures and a Marxist analysis of the ideological formations of capitalism. But this intersection in its turn raises important questions about the suitability of the essay itself and of Woolf's understanding and practising of it for the articulation of a type of literary history that could be defined as specifically feminist. Juliette Dusinberre's recent study of Woolf's readings of Renaissance literature suggests in its very subtitle, *Woman Reader or Common Reader?*, that the tendency to identify the essay as such with feminist critique makes it in fact quite difficult to differentiate between the 'woman reader' and the 'common reader' in their strategies of dissent and disarticulation of the discourses of authority, whether patriarchal or otherwise.

The privileging of the essay as a fragmentary and unsystematic genre that is common to feminist studies of Woolf's critical writings and to Marxist theories of the genre also brings with it important questions about the possibility of writing history at all, about the very idea of history as a viable concept. If, as we saw with Lukács and Adorno, the essay can be understood as an essentially modernist genre that resists the pull towards continuity and follows instead a digressive logic, what kind of history can it write and what would the relationship between an essayistic history and other types of history be like? This is a question that returns constantly in Woolf's work but which also finds no resolution or clear-cut answers there. In this, Woolf's essayistic practice comes perhaps closer to the kind of 'Essayism' described by Robert Musil in *The Man Without Qualities*, a novel which alternates narrative and discursive reflection in much the same way as Woolf's *The Pargiters* was supposed to do. Defined by Musil as a way of 'living hypothetically' or in the realm of the possible, 'Essayism' is offered to his readers as a 'Utopian idea' to be opposed to the increased rationalisation of the modern world, a form of living and of writing that is dispersive and without an organising centre.[26] Like many of the protagonists of Woolf's novels from Jacob Flanders to Orlando, Musil's Ulrich refuses to shape his life into the coherent narrative of the *Bildungsroman* and chooses instead the provisional, more circumscribed formation of a collection of separate moments and points of view.

Although the notion of Essayism as described by Musil has far more critical currency in Continental Europe than in Britain and America, these parallels between Musil's and Woolf's work suggest that a shift in the context of reading Woolf's work towards European modernism might also bring with it a change of perspective on the essay, highlighting its role as a site of reflection on the problem of modernity as a historiographic concept. My aim in this book is to investigate whether a modernist understanding of the genre as Essayism is compatible with Woolf's practice as one of the first feminist historians of literature. This means analysing Woolf's essay-writing in the light of the theories of the essay elaborated in Continental Europe, but also, at the same time, using Woolf's own essayistic practice to question the boundaries that define the difference between 'Continental Essayism' and the English essay. From the well-established opposition between Bacon's and Montaigne's writings to more recent attempts to differentiate between 'essayistic' mode and the essay as a genre,[27] this split between two understandings of the genre has long regulated its critical study. The question that remains to be asked is whether this distinction continues to be valid when sexual difference and gender identities intervene as significant elements in the history of the essay.

Chapter 1 will present a sort of prehistory of Woolf's involvement with the genre by charting her beginnings as an essayist and reviewer, while at the same time raising questions about what it means to read those beginnings now, in the light of Woolf's unique position in the history of feminist criticism. Drawing on Woolf's own interrogation of the notion of continuity and interruption in literary history, this chapter focuses its attention on the two most prominent characteristics of her early writings. It stresses the fluidity of generic boundaries between Woolf's early journals, her essays and her short stories, calling into question her own insistence on a rigid distinction between private (and uncensored) forms of writing and public ones marked by editorial intervention. It also traces, though, Woolf's developing sense of the *lacunae* or gaps that punctuate the smooth narrative of historiographic institutions such as the *Dictionary of National Biography* and which she identified with a series of marginal figures, first called the 'eccentrics', then the 'obscure' and, ultimately, 'Anon'.

These two sides of Woolf's writing practice, her essayism and her interest in the marginal figures of literary history and biography, can also be identified in her reconstruction of the history of the essay. As we shall see in Chapter 2, Woolf outlined a tradition of essay-writing that run from Montaigne to the Edwardians, stressing the genre's affiliation with a form of autobiography that offers a non-narrative alternative to traditional biography. It is in this sense that she most cherished the essay as the first of modernist forms in its fragmentary, unresolved and preliminary character. But this interpretation of the modernism of the essay comes into conflict in Woolf's writing with her perception of the modernity of the genre, which she saw as indissolubly linked to the emergence of mass readership, consumer culture and narcissism. Thus Woolf's ambivalence toward the essay shows in fact the existence of a split that is also at the heart of Adorno's understanding of the genre. For both writers the essay functions both as a modernist form that might offer an alternative to the relentless drive forward of the dialectic and, at the same time, as one of the foremost participants in the process of commodification of thought they associated with the spread of mass media and consumer society.

These two poles of Woolf's understanding of the genre correspond to her own implicit distinction between the literary essay and journalism and are the defining limits of her own practice as an essayist. This binary distribution of her position on the essay was disturbed, though, by the issue of sexual difference and gender roles which, as we shall see in Chapter 3, forced Woolf to consider the connection between writing for money and women's emancipation. Although Woolf is often celebrated as the champion of women's professional involvement with literature, her representation of the relationship between women writers and working women reveals in fact a constant attempt to differentiate between the two. Chapter 3 will focus in particular on the relationship between audience and speaker inscribed in some of Woolf's most famous speeches, from *A Room* to 'Professions for Women', and will compare it to her representation of the audience's point of view in 'Memories of a Working Women's Guild'. It will then turn on to *Three Guineas* to analyse how Woolf renounced any attempt at reconciling women writers and working women in the late 1930s and how this renunciation produced a radical restriction of her intended audience to 'the daughters of educated men who do not need to earn their living'. At the rhetorical level, this inscription of the split between women writers and working women breaks apart the synthesis of argument and fiction that Woolf had produced in *A Room* and 'Professions for Women' and which had found its figurative expression in the image of the woman novelist fishing along the banks of the imagination. This splitting-up process can be witnessed in the pages of *Three Guineas*, where words and images are separated by a gap that is as profound as the gulf that divides the daughters of educated men from their brothers and fathers.

Chapter 4 continues the analysis of the relationship between text and image that was initiated by the use of the Spanish photographs in *Three Guineas* by focusing first on Woolf's memoirs, 'A Sketch of the Past', and then on *Orlando*. The inclusion of these works within a study of the essays indicates both the extreme flexibility of the genre itself and the ways in which the historiographic concerns that animated Woolf's critical writings were not confined to them but tended to spill over into other, often unclassifiable texts. Woolf's extensive use of visual metaphors can in fact only be understood in the light of the reflections on the form of the sketch which organise her memoirs, where the sketch is seen as Woolf's own way of, as she puts it, 'marking the past'. Her explanations of this tendency are, as it is appropriate for the memoirs, autobiographical, indicating once again the emergence of that anxiety about the dangers of 'writing essays about oneself' that we saw in the diary entry for June 1923. What is crucial, though, is that this anxiety which in the diary entry referred to the status of modernist fiction, in the memoirs becomes an anxiety about the permanence of memory and its veracity.

Orlando in its turn shows how those anxieties were made productive for Woolf by defining a new genre of writing, the fictional (auto)biography. It is read here as a re-inscription of Woolf's own personal history within the larger *tableau* of the history of literature in a way that conflates the distinctions between private and public, shared and individual that will become so troublesome for Woolf in the 1930s and early 1940s. This chapter focuses on the ways in which *Orlando* plays against each other the conventions of different genres and discourses – biography, historical romance and fiction – and yet manages to retain as operative some of the constitutive features of those genres. In particular, it argues that *Orlando* uses the trope of marriage to contain and limit the significance of Woolf's own relationship to Vita Sackville-West, which the book translates from lesbianism into androgyny in order to make it compatible with heterosexuality as a legal institution.

Chapter 5 then turns to analyse Woolf's more explicit reflections on questions of historiography by returning to *A Room* and its privileging of fictional rather than historiographic discourse. This chapter reveals the other side of the erosion of generic boundaries performed by Woolf in her writing and shows how Woolf actively relished the possibility of re-inventing history in 'Lives of the Obscure' as an occasion for hinting at and suggesting those things which she felt could not be said directly or outside the boundaries of fictional discourse. It is as the chronicler of the 'obscure' and of women's forgotten lives that Woolf has perhaps been identified more clearly as the founding pioneer of feminist literary history. But her own analysis of the way in which her historical imagination works in 'A Sketch of the Past' also indicates that Woolf perceived this recourse to fiction as problematic, often dismissing the little cameos that resulted from it as the symptoms of an artistic failure.

This is one of the least well-known sides of Woolf's work but, as I explain in Chapter 5, a fundamental addition to any attempt at understanding her contribution to debates about the possibility of writing a specifically feminist type of literary history. Woolf's ambivalence towards the kind of textual strategies she deployed throughout her career and for which she is often celebrated as 'the mother of us all'[28] by feminist critics emerges only in some of the most marginal of her critical writings and especially in the essays that reflect upon the relationship between painting and literature. These writings reveal her discomfort with a purely formalist understanding of art that is intrinsically linked to the intervention of class structures within English literature. In fact the imagination on which Woolf relies to bring back to life the forgotten and marginal figures of history is here revealed as a hopelessly limited faculty whose arena of intervention is strictly defined by the artist's position within a class-system that Woolf describes as a cluster of 'glass boxes', invisible and yet isolating.

This failure of the imagination in transcending its own historical situation represents a critique of the kind of classicist aesthetic that guided Woolf's diffidence towards the autobiographical impulse and her chastisement of Charlotte Brontë's thinly disguised identification with Jane Eyre. It explains the difficulties encountered by Woolf and by her feminist supporters in articulating the intersection between issues of class and of gender in her work,[29] but also reveals Woolf as keenly aware of the sociological inflections carried by any form of writing, at least as a reader if not always as a writer. When feminism and history meet in Woolf's non-fiction, the question of class is always there, underlying many of her chosen strategies of argumentation and shaping the very angle of vision from which history is perceived and re-written. This hidden and yet always present thorn in the side might in fact be the most important of Woolf's legacies to feminist criticism itself.

1
Eccentric Histories

Virginia Woolf Practising

Virginia Woolf started her career as a professional writer in December 1904, with the publication of a cluster of articles that appeared in the women's page of the *Guardian*, a clerical weekly.[1] She was then Virginia Stephen, aged 22, and just recovering from the nervous breakdown that followed the death of her father in February of that year. Her introduction to the *Guardian* had been fostered by her friend Violet Dickinson, who put her in touch with Mrs Lyttleton, the editor of the women's page. Between 1904 and 1907 Stephen[2] contributed more than thirty articles to the *Guardian* on a disparate range of subjects and books. She wrote personal essays on the death of her dog and on laughter, reviews of Jane Carlyle's letters and Henry James's essays, an obituary of Caroline Emelia Stephen, her 'Quaker' aunt, and the review of a 'how-to-do' manual for aspiring young writers, reviews of biographical studies and of 'light' contemporary novels.

Writing for this 'pretty dull clerical newspaper' (*E* 1, xii) exercised Stephen, who often complains in her letters of Mrs Lyttelton's editorial interventions and of the need to mould her own writing to suit the moralising tone of the paper and the expectations of its readers, which she dubbed 'the Parsonesses' (*L* 1, 178). Her contributions to the paper dwindled as she developed her association with the *Times Literary Supplement*, which was to become the main outlet for her journalism throughout her life. Her first article for the *TLS* appeared in 1905, after she had been introduced to Bruce Richmond, the editor, in the course of a dinner party given by friends of Violet Dickinson's in January 1905. Initially her contributions to the *TLS* consisted mainly of short notices that were made up of a very quick summary of the content of the book and a few words of evaluation. Between 1905 and 1906 she wrote over a dozen of these, serving a kind of apprenticeship in the paper which soon led her to be commissioned longer articles on prominent literary figures such as Wordsworth ('Wordsworth and the Lakes', 1906, *E* 1, 105–9), Sidney ('Philip Sidney', 1907, 139–43), Shelley ('Shelley and Elizabeth Hitchener', 1908, 174–8), Christina Rossetti ('Letters of Christina Rossetti', 1908, 225–7), and Gissing ('The Novels of George Gissing', 1912, 355–62).[3]

But this attention to established authors was complemented by other articles on biographies, memoirs and letters of more minor figures, some of which appeared in the *TLS* but most of which were published in 'The Book on the Table' series of the *Cornhill Magazine*, of which Leslie Stephen had himself been an editor from 1871 to 1882. Throughout 1908 Virginia Stephen alternated with Lady Robert Cecil, with whom she shared the series, in writing for the *Cornhill* on books which should have been chosen by them but were, as Andrew McNeillie points out, in fact often imposed on them by Reginald Smith, the editor of the *Cornhill*. Stephen wrote six articles for 'The Book on the Table', reviewing memoirs ('The Memoirs of Sarah Bernhardt', *E* 1, 164–71; 'The Memoirs of Lady Dorothy Neville', 178–83), biography ('John Delane', 188–94; 'A Week at the White House', 204–10; 'Louise de La Vallière', 215–20), and journals ('The Journal of Elizabeth Lady Holland', 230–9). In 1909 she submitted to Smith 'Memoirs of a Novelist' (*SF*, 69–79), where she pretended to review the non-existent biography of a fictional character. The fictional review was rejected by Smith and signalled the end of her association with the *Cornhill*.

Besides writing for the *Guardian*, the *TLS* and the *Cornhill* Stephen occasionally contributed articles to other journals, from the *Academy & Literature*, which in 1905 published her first signed article ('The Decay of Essay-writing', *E* 1, 24–7), to the *National Review*, which accepted 'Street Music' in the same year but then never employed her again, to the *Speaker*, which published three of her articles in 1906. From 1909 to 1912, though, she wrote exclusively for the *TLS* but not in the same volume as in previous years. 1905, 1906, 1908 and 1909 were the most prolific years of the early part of her career as a literary journalist, yielding respectively 35, 21, 19 and 16 articles each. From 1910 to 1912 she produced only 7 articles, partly due to a recurrence of her mental illness but mainly because she was busy re-writing and revising her first novel, *The Voyage Out*, which was submitted to Duckworth in 1912 but whose publication was delayed by Woolf's illness until 1915.

In many ways, the year 1912 works, then, as a sort of *caesura* in Woolf's career and personal life, a pause which is also a break changing the places where the accents fall in our reading of her work.[4] It marks a change of name from the Virginia Stephen of articles and reviews to the Virginia Woolf of novels, short stories and feminist pamphlets. This change in the status of her signature as an author corresponds to a change of legal status from 'spinster' (as registered in her marriage certificate) to married woman, from daughter of Leslie Stephen to wife of 'a penniless Jew' (*L* 1, 500), as she put it in her letters announcing her engagement to Leonard. It is also the beginning, though, of a protracted period of mental illness during which she is said to have suffered of hallucinations, mania, depression, violent revulsion of her husband first, then of her nurses, as well as making a serious attempt at taking her own life. By bringing together marriage, authorship and 'madness' this year signals also the symbolic beginning of a certain way of reading Woolf that concentrates specifically on questions of sexual difference and sexuality, writing and repression, madness and femininity.[5]

But if 1912 can be seen as the beginning of a life and career that we have come to recognise as Woolf's own, this leaves open the question of how should we read the work that preceded her emergence as, in Rachel Bowlby's phrase, the 'exemplary woman writer' of the modernist period.[6] Her early childhood and adolescence, with their traumatic losses and intimations of child abuse, have been extensively investigated and become part of the critical knowledge that informs the reading of her work.[7] But the period from 1904 to 1912 remains uneasily suspended between the 'life' and the 'work', a hybrid that appears to have no connotations of its own and tends to be subsumed under the early history of the 'Bloomsbury Group'. Hermione Lee's recent biography of Woolf, for instance, fragments this period into a series of changes and experiments in the attempt to break up the chronological sequence of conventional biography into a series of thematic lines. This stress on the birth of Bloomsbury represents also Woolf's own preferred self-narrative, which will become a few years later part of the mythology surrounding the group and Woolf's relations to it.[8] That this was her own narrative does not, however, necessarily bind her readers to its acceptance as the only possible one or even as an account of events 'as they happened'.

The temptation when faced with such an amorphous and unremarked time is of course to reverse the terms of discussions and claim for it a significance that is both historical and theoretical, a sort of 'blind spot' in the reception of Woolf's work that needs to be brought to light, examined and removed. In this reversal of current critical paradigms that privilege the work of later years, Woolf's early years as a professional writer might come to be seen as the germs of her future developments. They all show the beginning of her interest in the tangential and obscure figures of literary history, the development of that ironic twist that is typical of her critical *persona*, the blend of autobiographical and critical elements that were to characterise her later essays. If her short notices for the *TLS* and the *Guardian* give, by their nature, little indications of the directions her writing will take, longer pieces such as 'The Sister of Frederic the Great' (1906; *E* 1, 87–91) or 'Lady Fanshawe's Memoirs' (1907; *E* 1, 143–7) are full of echoes of Woolf's more mature prose and reflect many of the questions and points of view that in later years will guide her approach to history and her investigation of women's place within it.

This search for the beginnings of 'Virginia Woolf' as we have come to know her can in fact be extended as far back as her composition of the family newspaper, *Hyde Park Gates News*, which Leila Brosnan has analysed as evidence of Woolf's early consciousness of 'the theoretical and practical implications of writing essays . . . as well as professional journalism'.[9] Other, recent studies of Woolf's essays and criticism also share this stress on the essential continuity of her writing career, linking together beginnings and ends under the aegis of Woolf's continuous interest in the intersection between literary history and gender.[10] This approach has the obvious advantage of confirming our current views of who 'Virginia Woolf' was and what constitutes her importance for feminist literary criticism. But precisely because of its reassuring character, it raises important questions about the scopes and methods of feminist criticism and its role in establishing Woolf as a literary and cultural icon.

Some of the questions about literary canons, aesthetic values and gender issues which are now explicitly and implicitly raised by feminist readings of her early writings were familiar to Woolf herself in her practice as a critic and reviewer. Intensely preoccupied with the process that determines the value of a writer's work, Woolf often found a way of articulating her concerns by writing and thinking about another kind of literary icon, the Jane Austen whom she felt had been quite literally canonised by the male critical establishment of her day. In her 1922 review of a posthumous edition of Austen's first work, *Love and Freindship*, Woolf set out to warn her readers against the dangers of being suffocated by the smothering embrace of received critical opinion, which she compares to the comforting layers of bedclothes on a cold summer night, reassuring and yet excessive. 'All over England for the past ten or twenty years,' Woolf continues, 'the reputation of Jane Austen has been accumulating on top of us like these same quilts and blankets' ('Jane Austen Practising', *E* 3, 331), to the point where any attempt at reading her work without being influenced by her growing reputation has come to require 'a frightful effort' (332).

Love and Freindship provides for Woolf precisely the opportunity of sliding off from underneath the oppressive weight of idolatry and reading 'Jane Austen before she was the great Jane Austen of mythology' (332). This vision of Austen 'practising' the rudiments of her art represents then a chance to dig beneath the brilliant, perfected surface of her masterpieces, revealing that, as Woolf will put it in a later essay, she 'was no conjuror after all' ('Jane Austen', 1925, *E* 4, 149), toiling on version after version of her stories until her sentences acquired that apparently effortless elegance which Woolf herself was later to celebrate in *A Room*. In the 1922 essay, though, this promise of a different critical angle on Austen's work is not delivered, as Woolf concedes that, even as 'a girl of seventeen', Austen was 'not writing to amuse the schoolroom' (*E* 3, 332), but was already 'trying over a few bars of the music for *Pride and Prejudice* and *Emma*' (334). Woolf admits that this kind of reading back into Austen's early work the seeds of her later ones might be the effect of her canonisation as 'the most perfect artist in English literature' (332). Yet she insists that Austen's 'music' has remained untouched by her elevation to iconic status and can still be heard over and above the chorus of approbation provided by 'the elderly and distinguished', by 'the clergy and the squirearchy' (331).

The language and practices of criticism, and especially of academic criticism, have changed considerably since Woolf's time, so that it is now unlikely to find a critic setting out in search of the beginnings of Woolf's 'music'. But the sense of continuity, of persistence of voice that is embodied in Woolf's metaphor keeps on guiding our reading of her disparate and heterogeneous *oeuvre*. Even critics such as Rachel Bowlby, who have argued for the radical irreducibility of Woolf's work to any one single scheme of thought, have admitted that the 'gesture of deification' is nearly impossible to resist and goes by its very nature with the history of Woolf's reception.[11] Others still have suggested that Woolf's canonisation is a direct result of reading her work through certain kinds of critical frames, of historico-empirical and Anglo-American extraction. To these they have opposed alternative (mainly French) types of feminist theory as the foundation for a different kind of Woolf criticism that would be capable of attending to those uncomfortable, uncomforting moments in her writing where her identity as 'the mother of us all' becomes difficult to sustain.[12]

In her critique of Jane Marcus's insistence on staging Woolf as the origin of feminist criticism, Bette London has suggested that the places of discomfort in the iconic celebration of Woolf's work might be located precisely in the question of the continuity of her voice over and against the interruptions and disjunctions that characterise her writing and the history of its reception. She points out that there are many points in Woolf's own work, both in the novels and in her critical essays, where the notion of voice itself comes under investigation as a far from natural construct whose relationship to identity is heavily structured by sexual difference. Encapsulated in the poetics of 'not speaking out', Woolf's interrogation of the notion of voice is for London a form of 'resistance to the appropriation of one's words' which nevertheless 'remains incomplete, poised precariously between subversive mastery and submissive consent',[13] a gesture towards feminist critique which, at the same time, refrains from articulating the exact positioning of that critique *vis-à-vis* the notion of authority.

The precarious character of Woolf's critical strategy is, as London points out, perhaps best illustrated by her often-cited comments about the connection between 'tea-table training' and her criticism. Looking back upon the early part of her career towards the end of her life, Woolf lamented in her memoirs, 'When I read my old *Literary Supplement* articles, I lay the blame for their suavity, their politeness, their sidelong approach, to my tea-table training. I see myself not reviewing a book, but handing a plate of buns to shy young men...' Having established this parallel that casts the manners and mores of upper middle class Victorian society as a negative influence on her own critical writings, Woolf nevertheless proceeds then to undermine her own statement, adding that she is 'not sure' whether that kind of training is 'a disadvantage in writing'. 'The surface manner,' Woolf goes on, in fact 'allows one, as I have often found, to slip in things that would be inaudible if one marched straight up and spoke out loud' (*MB*, 150).

London's reading of this passage as exemplary of the kind of problems bequeathed by Woolf to feminist criticism has been more recently revised by Leila Brosnan in *Reading Virginia Woolf's Essays and Journalism* (1997), the first critical monograph to analyse Woolf's non-fiction from a feminist perspective[14]. Following the development of Woolf's prose style from the family newspaper to her career as a professional literary journalist, Brosnan has argued that Woolf's 'sidelong approach' took shape through a life-long engagement with the demands and expectations of her editors, which led her to deploy 'a language of duplicity, a double-voiced ability' to fit 'her complex and often condemnatory meanings...under the cover of superficial respectability'.[15] For Brosnan, then, although Woolf's essayistic style is itself split between the surface of her pronouncements and their actual meaning, its continuity through time is guaranteed by her relentless fight against the strictures of censorship, both overt and covert, and of propriety.

In stressing the effects of censorship upon the development of a critical *persona* marked by irony and satire, Brosnan's interpretation of Woolf's critical practice echoes the young writer's own record of clashes with the 'official eye' (*L* 1, 178), that is, with editors who tried to influence her reviews, censored specific uses of words, cut her pieces down without consultation or rejected her work as not 'academic' (188). Faced with such obtuseness, Virginia Stephen vented her frustration in her private writings, where she can often be found parodying the 'fluent, rounded style' of her published essays and contrasting it with the 'curt and mordant' manner of her letters (198). This self-consciousness about the different sides of her writing *persona* gives then a different picture from the one Woolf will provide more than thirty years later in her comments about tea-table training. It shows Virginia Stephen distancing herself from the restrictions and conventions required by contemporary reviewing practices, which she treats as if they were a mask behind which her true self and opinions remained untouched.

This separation between private and public forms of writing explains the somewhat old-fashioned character of her early essays. Pieces such as 'Street Music' (1905; *E* 1, 27–32) or 'The Value of Laughter' (58–60) are well-written in a conventional, Edwardian way, with sentences rolling smoothly after each other, exemplifying the kind of 'suavity' and concentration on the surface of writing which Woolf was quick to condemn in other essayists.[16] In reading them now, outside of their original historical context and against the background of her identification with a markedly modernist and feminist type of writing, we are reminded of the fact that at the time when she started writing most of the works we consider to be central to the modernist canon lay still unpublished and, indeed, unwritten.[17] Of Woolf's future friends and associates, only E. M. Forster was already active as a novelist at the time, with the publication of *Where Angels Fear to Tread* in 1905. D. H. Lawrence, with whom Woolf will later recognise a certain affinity of intents, only published *Sons and Lovers* in 1913, while Conrad, whose *Nostromo* appeared in 1904, was discounted by Woolf on the grounds of his nationality. On the other hand, the writers who were being published around this time included precisely that triumvirate of Edwardians who will famously become the targets of Woolf's criticism in 'Mr Bennett and Mrs Brown': H. G. Wells's *Kipps* appeared in 1905, John Galsworthy published *The Man of Property* the following year, while Bennett's *Anna of the Five Towns* had appeared in 1901 and *The Old Wives' Tale* was published in 1908.

This historical and cultural situation of transition, of pre-modern and post-Victorian literature and culture is clearly perceptible in the 'absurdly formal'[18] tone and style of the early essays, which are in many ways closer to those of Woolf's Victorian progenitors than to the ironies and seduction of, say, *A Room*. It explains Woolf's discomfort, more than thirty years later, at the sight of her youthful self, as well as the link she establishes between her own essay-writing and a culture and tradition that elsewhere she emphatically rejected as not her own. And yet, the reluctance to dismiss that kind of double-writing that is in evidence in the memoirs also indicates an understanding of the dynamic between private and public statements, indirection and direction that is more subtle and complicated than the opposition between the 'curt and mordant' manner and the 'fluid, rounded style' she set up in her early letters.

This more subtle interaction between different styles and forms is also reflected in Woolf's writing practice, which shows that in the early stages of her career she was not always working within the parameters of genre but rather wrote through and across a variety of texts, from the autobiographical to the epistolary to the descriptive to the journalistic. Stephen's diaries, letters, travel journals and short stories are in fact characterised by such an extreme fluidity of generic boundaries that their identification with any of the chosen categories must per force remain precarious and a matter of argument. Her early journals, for instance, are very different from the confessional, intimate kind of diary that she was to start writing in 1915. They are rather exercise books, where Stephen tried a variety of forms and voices, alternating descriptive pieces to self-reflection to journalistic spoofs.[19] This record of a painstaking apprenticeship in professional writing constituted for Stephen a reservoir of potential articles into which she dipped quite often, modelling her published essays onto descriptions of travels and visits that had already been sketched out in the journals or reported in her letters.[20]

But the most sustained and most visible of these generic cross-overs – and the one which was later to become one of the distinguishing features of her work – was not that between journals and journalism but rather that between fiction, which at this stage in Stephen's career meant mainly short stories, and essay-writing. The earliest of the short stories date back to 1906 and were composed during Stephen's stay in Norfolk. The style and subject of these four stories, ['Phyllis and Rosamond'], ['The Mysterious Case of Miss V.'], ['The Journal of Mistress Joan Martyn'], ['A Dialogue Upon Mount Pentelicus'] (*SF*, 17–68), clearly indicate that at this point Stephen was relying on her two-year experience as a writer of essays to forge her path into the writing of fiction. All of the stories are introduced by a discursive paragraph that eases the reader into the story rather than presenting him or her with one of those abrupt beginnings in *media res* that are characteristic of Woolf's later prose. These introductions address the reader as a 'you' in a way that transgresses the fundamental differentiation between narrative and discourse in terms of the disposition of the positions of address.[21] As a consequence, the narrator does not occupy the conventional position of the omniscient observer, but becomes herself almost a character in the story, much in the same way as Elia or Sir Roger de Coverley work as fictional *personae* in Charles Lamb's essays (1820–33) or Addison's and Steele's *Spectator* articles (1711–14).

The exchange between fiction and essay-writing, though, never worked just in one direction for Woolf. In fact it was only after she started writing *Melymbrosia* sometime in 1908 that what we have come to recognise as her characteristic essayistic *persona* begins to emerge. Essays such as 'The Memoirs of Lady Dorothy Neville' (1908; *E* 1, 178–83), 'Château and Country Life' (1908; 222–4), 'The Duke and Duchess of Newcastle' (1911; 345–51) show Stephen appropriating for her critical writing the freedom of invention and expression that fiction had taught her. Unlike the 1906 short stories, which were introduced by a discursive or analytical preamble, these later essays open up with a fictional scene that carries with it a sense of immediacy which was not there in her earlier essays and which helps her to establish a sense of intimacy with her readers that bypasses the formalities of literary and critical conventions.

The mixture of fictional and analytic discourse that is typical of these essays, and their tendency to establish a sense of dialogue with their readers, show that Stephen's development as a writer of essays was quite consciously modelled on the Platonic dialogues. In a review of Vernon Lee's essays on culture and aesthetics, Stephen described the structure of the dialogues as a progressive ascent through 'pages of questions and answers' to 'the constructive part' of the argument, which is normally given not through analysis but as 'a myth or in the words of some wise woman' ('Art and Life', 1909, 279).[22] This stress on the fictional or mythological character of the Platonic dialogue reflected Stephen's dislike of the analytical mode of writing as exemplified by her father's writings, which she felt lacked 'imagination' (*L* 1, 285). But the fact that Stephen at this time saw fiction as a sort of counterpart to the driest forms of literary criticism also indicates the extent to which she herself remained unclear about the future direction of her career when she started publishing essays and reviews. In fact for some time before she started writing *Melymbrosia* in 1908, her declared ambition was to write history rather than fiction (190), but a kind of history which she was striving to infuse, like Miss Merridew in ['The Journal of Mistress Joan Martyn'], with the breath of living life rather than with the hard contours of facts. As she progressively invested more and more into the writing of fiction, though, the project of writing history was pushed to the background and, although Woolf will return to it many times during her lifetime, 'the real historical work' (*L* 1, 202) which she first envisaged in 1905 will remain the great unfinished project of her career.

Traces of this unrealised project can be found scattered throughout Woolf's critical work. After writing *The Voyage Out* (1915) and *Night and Day* (1919), in 1919 she started to consider a book of criticism which was initially conceived not as a collection of critical essays, but as a more connected overview of English literature, from its pre-history to the present day. Today the remnants of this project, and the difficulties which for Woolf were associated with it, are still visible in 'Reading' (1919; *E* 3, 141–61), an essay which was never published during Woolf's lifetime or in Leonard's editions. 'Reading' weaves together different temporal planes, from the passage of time within a day to the course of human life from childhood to maturity and old age, interlacing these different stages with the history of English literature. According to Andrew McNeillie, it represents the first germ of the critical book that was eventually to become the first *Common Reader* (xvi). It shows Woolf trying to grapple with the difficulties raised by attempting to tell the story of the development of literature in a country where 'the art of speech came late', making it impossible to access its pre-Renaissance literature through language and dialogue. As a consequence of this absence, the landscape of this period is perceived by Woolf as a sort of silent film, with 'knights and ladies' wearing 'apricot . . . dresses' and 'gilt crimson' and moving with the hieratic gestures of picture portraits: 'it is, after all, a question of seeing them' (143).[23]

This separation between sight on one side and speech on the other was for Woolf a historiographic problem which required the moulding of a critical language and form capable of articulating the silences of literary history. In 'Reading' the problem is not so much resolved as given a formulation, as Woolf attempts to convey at one and the same time both the historical narrative of the development of English literature and the experience of reading the sources on which that narrative is based. In the course of the years, this attempt at keeping the broader picture in the background will progressively be abandoned and Woolf will come to rely more and more upon the immediacy of the reading experience as a way of enabling the historical imagination to bypass the obstacle presented by the fact that 'speech came late to England'. In this, she looks back upon a whole tradition of Victorian and late Victorian historiography, which believed that history must be absorbed through the act of the imagination, must in fact be relived in order to be comprehended.[24] This conviction leads her to try and establish with her readers the same sense of intimacy that pervades her own relationship to books, which, as she often remarks in the essays, are not so much objects as subjects, friends and confidants.[25]

The process of forging a critical language imbued with intimacy and immediacy was, however, far from straightforward and led Woolf to experiment with a variety of solutions before she arrived at the idea of the common reader as its realisation. Throughout the early 1920s she kept on experimenting with different forms and languages for her critical writings, much in the same way as she tried out different ways of writing fiction through the short stories that subsequently led to *Jacob's Room* (1922) and *Mrs Dalloway* (1925). During this period Woolf became increasingly self-conscious about the interaction of analytical and fictional discourse she had identified in Plato, often including within her pieces explicit comparisons between their respective domains. The most sustained of these comparisons occurred perhaps in 'Byron and Mr Briggs' (1922; *E* 3, 473–99), the draft of the introductory essay to her projected book on reading which will later metamorphose into the first *Common Reader*.[26]

Like the earlier 'Memoirs of a Novelist', 'Byron and Mr Briggs' is framed as the fictional review of an equally fictional book, *The Flame of Youth*, a contemporary first novel which the narrator is preparing to evaluate. Within this frame Woolf inserts a number of scenes of reading centred around a variety of texts, from Byron's letters to an anonymous medieval poem. Each of these scenes is meant to illustrate the difference between the book lover's approach to literature, exemplified by the Mr Briggs of the title, and that of the scholar or critic. Claiming that the reviewer's task is to convey the common reader's experience rather than that of the critic's, Woolf defines it as a reading which is done 'according to the needs of the moment' (*E* 3, 492) and goes from book to book in search of complementary feelings that, when put side by side, 'form a nucleus' which then grows into 'a vast body of emotions which increases according to our capacity to feel' (488). Through this stress upon the common reader's need to 'make a whole' (482), reading is then compared to the activity of making up stories about people one over-hears while travelling on a train, a piecing together of enigmatic scraps of language and meaning into a coherent story that might or might not be an accurate reflection of the facts.

Woolf will return to the image of the train carriage a few months later in the more famous 'Mr Bennett and Mrs Brown', where the experience of observing one's fellow passengers is explicitly offered as a metaphor for novel-writing. The intervention of the comparison between reading as a critical activity and the scene in the railway carriage in 'Byron and Mr Briggs' indicates then that at this point in time she was striving to define a form of criticism that would effectively be indistinguishable from the writing of fiction. In this, 'Byron and Mr Briggs' looks forward to some of Woolf's more extreme experiments with the mixture of essay and fiction which she will attempt in many of her better-known works. It is peopled with fictional characters from her early and later novels (Terence Hewet, Clarissa Dalloway) and alternates fictional scenes and critical commentary in a way which anticipates *The Pargiters*, the essay-novel which Woolf will start about ten years later, but never finish. Closer in time, the dramatisation of different critical and readerly posi-tions through the dialogue between Mr Briggs and the narrator/reviewer has echoes both of Stephen's earlier pieces, from the short story ['A Dialogue upon Mount Pentelicus'] (1906; *SF*, 63–8) to the essay 'A Talk About Memoirs' (1920; *E* 3, 180–6), and of the later, and seminal, essay 'Mr Conrad: A Conversation' (1923; *E* 3, 376–80).

By Woolf's own account, 'Mr Conrad: A Conversation' represents a turning-point in her search for an alternative form of criticism that would cross over the distinction between essay and fiction and thus give voice to what the form of the essay on its own could not articulate. The article appeared in the *Nation & Athenaeum* in September 1923, and was used by Woolf to test the viability of her own version of the Platonic dialogues, where the argument of the essay is constructed through the exchange between two fictional characters. It features Penelope Otway, whom Woolf describes as 'the oldest unmarried daughter' who 'had always, since the age of seven, been engaged in reading the classics' (376), and her friend David Lowe, who has received a more traditional, institutional kind of education. Like a female version of Socrates, Penelope challenges her friend's obsolete and fixed ideas about the right of modern writers to aspire to the status of a 'classic' and makes a compelling case for enlisting Conrad among them. Penelope Otway is herself a figure who will become increasingly familiar to the readers of Woolf's fiction, a sort of early incarnation of Eleanor Pargiter who functions in this dialogue as the antagonist of received opinion and traditional truths and the champion of individuality and first-hand experience. Like Mr Briggs before her, she represents yet another embodiment of that idea of the common reader which, in one form or another, returns with insistence throughout Woolf's critical writings of the early 1920s.

The links between 'Mr Conrad: A Conversation' and the first *Common Reader* are confirmed by a diary entry, where Woolf reports her reaction to the reception of the article and, at the same time, announces the discovery of the idea of the common reader for her book of criticism. Taken aback by the lack of response elicited by the Conrad article, which she claims '[n]o one has mentioned', Woolf resolves to turn it into a positive spur, and comments that '[a] cold douche should be taken (and generally is) before beginning a book', as it 'has the effect of making me more definite and outspoken in my style'. The net result of what Woolf sees as the failure of the article on Conrad is then to push her straight into the writing of that critical book which she had been projecting throughout the early 1920s. 'At any rate,' she announces in the same entry, 'I began for the 5th but last time, I swear, what is now to be called The Common Reader' (*D* 2, 265).

This bold announcement of the birth of the *Common Reader* on 5 September 1923 represents in fact the culmination of a process of reflection on and experimentation with the forms of criticism that had occupied Woolf since at least 1919. It shows that the idea of the common reader as the thread that links together different aspects of Woolf's critical practice emerged as a compromise solution between more traditional forms of criticism on the one hand and Woolf's more extreme experimentations on the other. A few weeks before announcing her final choice, Woolf had in fact rejected the collection of essays as 'an inartistic method' and had sketched out in the diary the outline of a book of criticism that differed widely from the format of the first *Common Reader*. Searching for a 'device' or technique that would turn the fragmentary character of unrelated essays into a well-structured whole, Woolf toyed with the idea of enclosing her essays within the fictional frame of an 'Otway conversation'[27] taking place among 'a family which reads the papers'. 'The main advantage' of such a 'device', she remarked, 'would be that I could then comment, & add what I had had to leave out, or failed to get in' (*D* 2, 261), indicating once more that the intervention of fiction within a critical discourse would work on two different levels at the same time. It would provide the fragmentary and scattered pieces of her critical vision with a more unified form, while at the same time giving her the space and the means of going beyond the 'suavity' and 'surface manner' of her *TLS* leaders.

But as Woolf went on to acknowledge, this was a rather ambitious project that 'might run away with me; it will take time' (261), subtracting energies from the writing of fiction which was engrossing her at this time. The plan was therefore rejected, the *Common Reader* was conceived and realised in its place, and for the rest of the 1920s Woolf showed no sign of still considering problematic the issue of the relationship between essay and fiction in her criticism. More preoccupied with experiments around the form of the elegy (for *To the Lighthouse* (1927)), of biography (in *Orlando* (1928)) and of the dramatic monologue (in *The Waves* (1931)), Woolf will only return to reflect upon the interaction of essay and fiction in texts such as *A Room* (1929), but, especially, in *The Pargiters* (1931–33), where she attempted to devise the form of the 'essay-novel' to accommodate her insights into women's relationship to history and politics. That she will abandon that project too suggests that the question of the relationship between essay and fiction represented for Woolf a returning problem which she felt compelled to address but to which she could not find a satisfactory solution.

Eccentrics, Obscure and Anon

The search for a different form of criticism that would combine fiction and essays was motivated for Woolf by the desire to give a voice to those parts of literary history that could not find a representation in conventional accounts. In 'Reading' the silences of literary history had been identified by Woolf with a sort of prehistory that could be captured visually but not in writing. In her project for an 'Otway conversation' those spaces or gaps were most explicitly linked to a distinction between private and public spheres, between the kind of intimate conversation that takes place around a family reading the newspapers and the voice of official criticism as embodied by Woolf's own articles for the *TLS*. But at the same time as Woolf was occupied with her experiments in the form of conversations between fictional characters, she was articulating a different way of bringing into her criticism what was usually marginalised and excluded from literary history. This consisted in shifting the focus of interest from the question of which form to give to her criticism to the issue of which personalities and whose work should be deemed worthy of critical attention.

The two processes were in fact always connected in Woolf's work, as the question of whom to include in her account of literary history automatically called up for her the issue of how to articulate the voices that had previously been excluded or marginalised by it. The dilemma was already there in 'Mr Conrad: A Conversation', where the fictional dialogue was used by Woolf to question the construction of the canon of English literature and the hierarchy of values that gives the status of classics only to dead authors. Its most explicit articulation, though, is to be found in Woolf's writings on less prominent and more marginal figures than Conrad, whom she variously called 'the eccentrics' or 'the obscure'. Although the two terms alternated in a chronological sequence in Woolf's writings, her deployment of them shows considerable areas where their meanings overlap, as well as points of differentiation. Between them the eccentrics and the obscure encompass some of the most crucial stages in Woolf's thinking about historiographic questions and will lead her to formulate the idea of Anon as a point of intersection between historiography and sexual difference.

In Woolf's earliest diaries and letters the problem of the literary canon and of the aesthetic and cultural values that define it is generally called up implicitly through her fascination with figures who cannot be easily accommodated into pre-existing schemes. In a 1912 letter to Lytton Strachey, who was himself intensely interested in questions of biography and history, she asserted that 'the most interesting thing to observe' from a historical point of view are not the 'distinguished spirits' such as Donne, Meredith or E. M. Forster 'but the humble ones, the slightly touched, the eccentric' (*L* 1, 499). Although this letter is important for the way in which it connects eccentricity to madness (the 'slightly touched'), it does not represent her earliest definition of the eccentrics. In 1910, her essay on Lady Hester Stanhope had made clear that the label had been appropriated from the *Dictionary of National Biography* whose writers, as she puts it, 'have a pleasant way of summing up a life, before they write it, in one word, thus – "Stanhope, Lady Hester Lucy (1770–1839), eccentric"' (*E* 1, 325). Woolf's parodic appropriation of the official definition serves to highlight the element of prejudice and bias that is inscribed in the label, so that the life is summed up before it is written, its value fixed before it can be told. At the same time, though, the essay works to reverse those values which would have Lady

Stanhope cursorily dismissed as a 'slightly touched' noblewoman and uses her example to question the limits of a historiographic practice that is bent upon encasing people into pigeonholes.

In her writings about these figures Woolf insists that the pigeonhole marked 'eccentrics' is the least stable of all of them, calling into question the very possibility of categorising lives and people with absolute certainty, in a final verdict. In 'The Eccentrics' she makes clear that this most precarious of identities cannot be faked by assuming the external signs of recognisably unorthodox behaviour, such as 'walk[ing] up and down the Tottenham Court Road wrapped in a towel in imitation of the Greek' (1919; *E* 3, 38). The essence of eccentricity in fact lies for Woolf in the lack of self-consciousness, in the inability to see oneself as reflected by others, so that 'all true eccentrics... never for a moment... believe themselves to be eccentric' (38). It is a lack that places the eccentric in a complete misalignement with the rest of the world, which they consider to be 'cramped and malformed and spiritually decrepit, while they alone have lived their lives according to the dictates of nature' (38).

Unable and unwilling to subscribe to the rules of human society, the eccentrics represent then for Woolf the intervention of a natural, unfettered form of identity into a highly codified and regulated world. Defined by the rest of society as an exception, they see themselves as the rule perverted by the artificial and assumed identities of the social world. They thus come to embody a hyperbolic realisation of the notion of individuality, which stresses the uniqueness and inimitability of identity in a way that paradoxically highlights its susceptibility to categorisation, to becoming a type and a caricature of individuality itself. As Woolf points out, 'a touch of the ridiculous' always seems to accompany the 'sublimity' of the eccentric's life. Lady Stanhope's decision to ride a horse 'in the trousers of a Turkish gentleman', for instance, was undermined by her maid's insistence on retaining the standards of English life even if she was 'dressed in man's clothes [and] expected to ride like a man' (*E* 1, 327). Margaret Cavendish's appearances in London were greeted by a crowd of laughing boys and courtiers, whose jeers were then recorded for posterity in the biting mockery of Pepys's diaries ('The Duchess of Newcastle', 1911; *E* 1, 349). Woolf's own mockery is much gentler, recognising the Duchess's desire for recognition and her somewhat anachronistic position (she lived 'either too late or too soon' (348)). Only later will it become a curt dismissal relegating 'harebrained, fantastical Margaret of Newcastle' (*RO*, 79) and all the other 'solitary great ladies' (82) to the pre-history of the tradition of women's writing she will outline in *A Room*.

The space in time and thinking that separates Woolf's early interest in the eccentrics and their marginalisation in *A Room* marks a change of focus in her historiographic projects. Woolf's insistence in 1929 that the history of women's writing can only be said to have started with the advent of the middle-class, income-generating Aphra Behn is meant to empower a wider category of women but carries with it the price of excising from that history the great aristocratic women she had earlier described as prime examples of eccentricity.[28] In its turn this shift of emphasis from the aristocracy to the middle classes underlines the connection between eccentricity and class location that is essential to Woolf's understanding of the term. When writing about Lady Stanhope and the Duchess of Newcastle in the early 1910s, Woolf had clearly identified in their nobility a necessary precondition for their eccentric behaviour and choices, to the point of turning the two terms into near-synonyms. Lady Stanhope's and the Duchess's aristocratic birth are described as placing them above the sets of rules that govern the life of their contemporaries and form the foundations of their deep belief in their own individuality. Lady Stanhope is said by Woolf to have 'had a conviction of the rights of the aristocracy, and ordered her life from an eminence which made her conduct almost sublime' (*E* 1, 326). Similarly, Margaret Cavendish's shortcomings as a writer, the fanciful character of her imagery and the lack of logic in her disquisitions, are imputed to 'the irresponsibility of the child and the arrogance of a Duchess' (*E* 4, 84).

Although not all of the figures that Woolf treats as belonging to the eccentrics are aristocrats, there is a clear sense that her definition of eccentricity overlaps significantly with her understanding of what it means to belong to an aristocratic family. Describing her early meetings with Lady Bath and her daughters, Woolf wrote in 1936 that what made nobility attractive to her was its ability to 'breed...confidence' (*MB*, 208) and its consequent 'indifference to public opinion' (207). Because of this disregard for the kind of social conventions that regulated the life of her upper middle class existence in Kensington, aristocrats represent for Woolf 'human nature in its uncropped, unpruned natural state.... the aristocrat is freer, more natural, more eccentric than we are' (208). As with her essay on Lady Stanhope and her life in the Middle East, there are clear echoes here of the freedom of travel and manner that characterise the life of Woolf's fictional version of the eccentric aristocrat, Orlando.

But this connection between eccentricity and nobility also brings out the peculiar dialectic of permanence and evanescence, belonging and individualism which structures the identity of the eccentric for Woolf. After all, the unthinking and unconscious self-assurance that characterises nobility emerges, as Woolf is quick to point out, from the permanence of their state, from the 'land...and country houses' (208) to which the nobility is wedded and which imprints their identity as firmly as the land is shaped by their presence. This sense of permanence was typical of Woolf's understanding of the nobility and found perhaps its clearest representation in Orlando's near-eternal existence. Historically, though, it has been analysed as part of the British aristocracy's own strategy of legitimation, emerging between the end of the eighteenth and the beginning of the nineteenth century, at a time when, as David Cannadine has pointed out, the upper classes found themselves engaged in a process of radical renewal and re-shaping of their own position within the burgeoning British Empire.[29]

If eccentricity represents, then, for Woolf the expression of an extreme individualism that is unfettered by the constrictions of middle-class conventions, it is nevertheless steeped in another type of group identity, that of the family and of the land. Notions of Englishness and of belonging are as deeply implicated in Woolf's understanding of eccentricity as the idea of marginalisation from the historical process. Reviewing an account of the history of the Legh's in 1917, Woolf remarked on the effect that family letters have on the historical perspective. They show 'the indifference of contemporaries to events which to us seem of the greatest, perhaps of the only, importance' (*E* 2, 98). This different type of history has to do more with 'men and women in the mass' (*E* 1, 241) than with the biographies of great men, as Woolf puts it in *Jacob's Room* (1922). It is silenced in the historical records that privilege actions and events over the *longue durée*[30], the sense of continuity through time which for Woolf was embodied in a community deeply rooted to a specific place.

This connection between eccentrics, continuity, place and national identity explains Woolf's desire, as she expressed it in a diary entry of 1915, to write 'one day...a book of "Eccentrics"' that was to have included 'Mrs Grote....Lady Hester Stanhope. Margaret Fuller. Duchess of Newcastle. Aunt Julia?' (*D* 1, 23). Like many other of Woolf's historical projects, the book was never realised and today we only have fragments of its conception in essays such as 'The Eccentrics', which mentions all of the figures listed by Woolf in the 1915 diary entry as instances of offbeat, unconvential lives that 'must not be forgotten' (*E* 3, 40). Woolf, though, appears to have herself forgotten about them, since apart from the essays on Lady Stanhope and Margaret Cavendish which she had already written before the 1915 diary entry, she subsequently returned to only one of the figures listed there, the 'aunt Julia' whose inclusion among the eccentrics was marked by doubt.

'Julia Margaret Cameron' (*E* 4, 375–86) appeared in 1926 as the introduction to a volume of Victorian photographs published by the Hogarth Press. In it, Woolf described her maternal great-aunt as an eccentric, over-generous woman living at the heart of a circle of Victorian notables which included Tennyson, Watts, Burne-Jones and Henry Taylor, who called it 'Pattledom' in reference to the Pattle sisters of whom Cameron was one (377). The essay opens with the well-known family story of Cameron's father, whose corpse is said to have burst open of its coffin during its transport from India to England, revealing the 'indomitable vitality' which also characterises Cameron in Woolf's portrait. But Woolf also insists that Cameron's inheritance was as much marked by her father's spirit as by her mother, a French noblewoman descended from a page of Marie Antoinette who impressed in her daughters 'her love of beauty and her distaste for the cold and formal conventions of English society' (376).

This heritage of eccentricity, conviviality and disregard for social conventions can be seen to have marked not just Cameron's life, but also Woolf's own, forming some of the precedent for the formation of the Bloomsbury Group in its insistence on the importance of art and beauty as well as in its experimentation with alternative life-styles. In her biography of Woolf, Hermione Lee has suggested that the pre-Raphaelite, mid-Victorian environment of Little Holland House where Woolf's own mother grew up might be a more appropriate 'spiritual ancestor' to Bloomsbury than the Clapham sect, which is more usually seen as its most immediate predecessor.[31] Woolf was herself keenly aware of the role played by this environment in the constitution of her mother's character and life. In her 1940 memoirs, she described it as 'a summer afternoon world', where people sat in the garden sipping tea while Watts painted and Tennyson read poetry aloud (*MB*, 87). Although Woolf acknowledges that the picture is derived from the memoirs of that time she read in the course of her adult life, she also remembers being taken as a child to the spot where the house used to be and observing her mother as she 'gave a little spring forward, clapped her hands, and cried "That was where it was!" as if a fairyland had disappeared' (87). For Woolf, Little Holland House came then to symbolise a period of extreme happiness in her mother's life, a sort of Eden on earth that preceded her widowhood and the aura of mourning and sadness that will characterise her own memories of Julia.

The dynamic of luminosity and obscurity that structures Woolf's description of her mother's world in the memoirs also suggests some of the paths through which her interest in eccentricity transformed itself into a focus upon the forgotten and obscure. The projected book on the eccentrics was in fact superseded in the 1920s by an exploration of the other side of the radical individualism she had celebrated in her essays on eccentric figures. Obscurity and anonymity took the place of eccentricity in the course of a gradual process that demonstrated that the semantic catch of the two sets of terms, eccentrics and obscure, did overlap significantly in Woolf's understanding. As early as 1906 she had in fact already dramatised the interplay between the two concepts in one of her first short stories '[The Journal of Mistress Joan Martyn]', whose main narrator, Miss Merridew, is herself presented as the type of the eccentric 'learned lady', who has renounced family and traditional feminine attachments in order to pursue her interest in the early history of England. As with all eccentrics in Woolf, Miss Merridew has run foul of the authorities, in this case the professional historians, who have sternly criticised her approach and methods as unscholarly. As Woolf will do years later in 'Lives of the Obscure' (1925; *E* 4, 118–45), Miss Merridew acknowledges that the criticism is justified, as she has often used her imagination to fill in the gaps left open by the historical record and thus bring to life those aspects of the past that would otherwise have remained beyond the purchase of contemporary readers.[32]

But if Miss Merridew's approach is itself moulded on Woolf's own, she is also shown to have a certain romanticised and antiquarian interest in the past that is implicitly criticised by the attitude of Mr Martyn, the owner of the fifteenth-century journal which represents Miss Merridew's invaluable discovery. Slowly but surely Miss Merridew comes to realise that there is an enormous gulf between her own interest in Mr Martyn's family history and the way in which Mr Martyn himself relates to that history. For him, his ancestors and the objects they have left behind are not segregated into a past that is cut off from the present, but are living presences with whom he converses, surrounding his daily activities and his sense of his own history like a sort of halo, a 'clear and equable light' that is 'not romantic' but 'very sober' (*SF*, 43–4).[33]

In many ways Woolf's later shift from eccentricity to obscurity is embodied in the difference in attitudes that separates Mr Martyn from Miss Merridew. The transformation undergone by Miss Merridew in the course of the story charts the progress from a figure of eccentricity (and self-mockery) to a point of understanding and identification with the author of the precious journals, the Mistress Joan Martyn of the title whose account of everyday life in fifteenth-century Norfolk forms the second part of the story. As the journal is supposed to be Miss Merridew's transcription of the original manuscript, Miss Merridew herself comes to work within the story both as a figure of eccentricity and as the pioneer of that kind of fictional or imaginative reconstruction of the past that will subsequently be undertaken by Woolf in her own work on the obscure. The intersection between the two terms that is charted by this early story is also demonstrated by the fact that 'Eleanor Ormerod', which will appear as one of the three obscure featured in the first *Common Reader*, was initially announced by Woolf in her 1919 diary as a follow up to 'The Eccentrics' which, like the previous essay, was to be offered to the *Athenaeum* (*D* 1, 260). In fact, 'Miss Ormerod' never appeared in the *Athenaeum* and was only published in America in the *Dial* five years later.[34]

This shift from the eccentrics to the obscure also made more explicit the dialectic of untrammelled individualism and group identity which, as we saw, linked the eccentrics to the aristocracy in Woolf's conception of the term. Her interest in forgotten lives and the writings recording them brought Woolf to question the hierarchy of values that structures literary history. She warned that the 'smaller books' where the lives of the obscure are embalmed must be read with more, not less, effort than the great ones, which 'we take ... on trust' ('A Vanished Generation', 1908, *E* 1, 239). What they yield in reward for their readers' labour are 'sights and voices ... living things ... some vague region' which are not illuminated by 'the sharp circle of light cast by one pair of eyes' but rather by 'a whole radiance' that transcends that of individual vision (240). This process of undermining the individual as the centre of historical writing also breaks up that sense of continuity with the past that links the eccentric to the aristocracy, thus allowing Woolf to concentrate on the discontinuous character of the historical experience and of its records. In this sense the obscure offer for Woolf the possibility of making more explicit the critical slant that was attached to her interest in the eccentrics. They signal a process of revision of the terms in which literary history itself is written and on which literary honours are awarded. This revision provides a negative answer to the questions Woolf had placed at the end of 'The Eccentrics', on whether biography should be made up of 'good books devoted to good men' (*E* 3, 40).

Woolf's interest in the obscure informs then not just her reading of marginalised figures but also that of the acknowledged 'greats' of the history of English literature. As a critic and historian of literature Woolf used the 'smaller books' to put into context and draw out the particular significance of the masterpieces, but also to illustrate the invisible links that join the latter to their social and historical context. This contextualization was especially necessary whenever Woolf found herself writing about the earlier periods of English literature, which she felt to be particularly remote to the modern reader because of the lack of documentation depicting the every-day life of, say, medieval England. When writing about Chaucer for the *Common Reader*, Woolf decided in fact to use the letters of the Pastons from the fifteenth century to envelop her reading of his poetry but also to contrast it with the everyday reality of his contemporary 'common reader' (1925; *E* 4, 20–38).

The Pastons' letters offer evidence for Woolf of the constitution of the medieval world for its average, unexalted inhabitants, who lived cramped, toiling, harsh lives with the idea of death never very far from their minds. Her reflections on Chaucer's poetry and its relation to the world that emerges from the Pastons' letters are inserted as a break in the smooth narrative that tells of the succession of various generations in the family. Woolf creates for her readers the picture of the first Sir John's son and heir who, after the death of his father, could be found reading Chaucer 'in broad daylight . . . on the hard chair in the comfortless room with the wind lifting the carpet and the smoke stinging his eyes' (26). What we have come to see as an innocuous act, Woolf suggests, signals in fact a very deep historical change. The son's rejection of his father's hard-working, unadorned way of life marks the end of the medieval era and the emergence from that 'hard outer shell' of 'something sensitive, appreciative, and pleasure-loving' (25).

Chaucer embodies for Woolf precisely that moment in history when the burden of survival is lifted and a lighter kind of humanity begins to take shape. She speculates that 'he must have heard' the same language of the Pastons' letters, 'matter of fact, unmetaphorical, far better fitted for narrative than for analysis'. But to this 'very stiff material' (35) Chaucer brought the gift of transformation of the poet, 'the architect's power' which took the various elements that made up the Pastons' lives and shaped them into a 'better order' (32). His individuality is that of the poet, who marks a particular point in history through his work and is in his turn marked by it. But the individuality of his fifteenth-century reader is swamped under the collective identity of the Pastons, whose letters 'heap up in mounds of insignificant and often dismal dust the innumerable trivialities of daily life', the contingency of human existence which should be swept away by the wind of change and yet has more permanence than the solid stone of Caister Castle, of which 'only ruined walls remain' (20).

'The Pastons and Chaucer' traces the outline of an understanding of the dynamic between social and literary history that we have come to recognise as distinctively Woolf's own. It was summarised in *A Room* by the famous assertion that 'masterpieces are not single and solitary births', but rather 'the outcome of many years of thinking in common, of thinking by the body of the people' (*RO*, 85). For Woolf, the production of great works of art is always nourished by the unrecognised and yet steadfast toil of a silent majority, which prepares the ground for the emergence of those exceptional creations. In this sense, masterpieces share with the eccentrics their position as exceptions to the rule which is always, in Woolf's interpretation, tempered by a sense of what they owe to the background of anonymous faces and lives that went before them.

The change of terminology in Woolf's projected historical work from the eccentric to the obscure signals then also a shift of focus from exceptional individualities and characters who cannot be assimilated to anything other than themselves to figures who are so embedded in communal textures that their contours become indistinguishable from the historical background. This transformation of terminology is also marked by an increasing awareness of the ways in which sexual difference and gender identities appear to determine the positions occupied by these figures in relation to a centre that for Woolf remained relentlessly structured by patriarchal power. Although Woolf's list of eccentrics in the 1915 diary is made up exclusively of women, eccentricity never became for her as explicit a tool of feminist critique as the notion of the obscure or, later, as that of Anon. There was always a composite side to the tag of eccentric which helped to normalise the exceptions or the subversives by situating them in relation to a well-established centre. The connection between eccentricity and nobility did not help either, as it prevented its deployment in the service of the emancipation of the middle class woman which Woolf advocated in *A Room*. As she remarks of Lady Winchelsea, 'men, of course, are not snobs...but they appreciate with sympathy for the most part the efforts of a countess to write verse. One would expect to find a lady of title meeting with far greater encouragement than an unknown Miss Austen or a Miss Brontë at that time [seventeenth century] would have met with' (*RO*, 75).

The importance of the unknown Miss Brontë or Miss Austen for Woolf lied precisely in their being representative of an average rather than an exception. As such they provided an *a posteriori* argument on the basis of which she could claim for women the authorship of anonymous or unsigned literary works. Women writers who adopted male pseudonyms during the nineteenth century proved, in Woolf's eyes, how difficult it was for them to expose themselves to the criticism and censure of their contemporaries. For 'Currer Bell, George Sand, George Eliot' anonymity represented 'the relic of the sense of chastity' (65) that maintained their link with a history of oppression but also with a tradition which Woolf speculates might date as far back as the beginning of English literature: 'Anon, who wrote so many poems without signing them, was often a woman' (63).

Merely a hint or a suggestion in *A Room*, about ten years later this hypothesis about the origins of vernacular literature became the guiding theme of Woolf's project for a continuous history of English literature, which she called 'a Common History book' (*D* 5, 318). As with the two *Common Readers* that preceded it, this later historical project emphasised the multiple meanings of 'common'. For Woolf the term indicated not just the low extraction of the figures which replaced the eccentrics or of the readers to whom she addressed herself. 'Common' also suggested the sense of something shared, the foundation of a community, in a way that joins this later stress on anonymity to the interest in questions of permanence – both geographical and historical – that ran through Woolf's fascination with the nobility.[35] This transformation of commonness into communality can best be witnessed in *Between the Acts* (1941),[36] the novel Woolf was in the process of finishing when she started jotting down notes on her Common History book. The 'orts, scraps and fragments' that form the background of the novel's actions would, in other contexts, be read as mere gossip, senseless conversations or doggerel. Within *Between the Acts*, though, they become the glue that holds together a community whose history stretches back to the beginning of written records.

The emphasis on group identities marked by the mundane and everyday that is characteristic of Woolf's last novel also transpires from the surviving manuscripts of her plans for writing a Common History book. First conceived in September 1940, the book took shape quite rapidly. By November of that year Woolf had begun to draft an introductory essay which she called 'Anon'; the following essay, provisionally called 'The Reader', was left incomplete at the time of her death in March 1941.[37] As the editor of Woolf's last two essays, Brenda Silver has remarked that the preliminary notes made by Woolf for the Common History book reveal quite clearly her persistent attraction for the idea of writing a continuous history of English literature, but also her distrust for what she called the 'text book' approach which privileges '"periods"' rather than 'the genuine scent – the idea of the moment'.[38] This distrust for the academic and the scholarly was evident in the titles Woolf chose for her projected book, *Reading at Random* and *Turning the Page*, which both underline her belief in an unsystematic and informal approach to literary history that proceeds by hints, suggestions and intuitions rather than by pre-ordained categories or classifications. Equally, as the method of 'reading at random' reverses the traditional procedures of historical research, so the substance of Woolf's historical enquiry would have encompassed precisely those aspects of literary production that are often overlooked or marginalised in traditional accounts of the development of English literature.

Woolf's interest in the anonymity of early literary productions and in the question of post-Renaissance authorship were by this time inescapably linked with the analysis of the history of suppression and silencing that characterised women's condition. Her aim in *A Room* had been to exploit this connection by reclaiming for women the collective authorship of unsigned literature. But, as Woolf's notes indicate, by the time she came to write 'Anon', this connection between women and obscurity had been enlarged to encompass the general condition of literary production in the times before the invention of the printing press, when literature arose out of a collective instinct for singing that preceded the separation of reader from writer and of public from author. This earlier, pre-modern and almost pre-historical condition also corresponded for Woolf to a time of undifferentiated creative urges that did not distinguish between 'stone, wool, words, paint' but simply got themselves expressed in whatever medium was available.[39]

For Woolf, then, the idea of anonymity, and especially of anonymous literature, brought together a series of issues that had informed her reflections on the nature of history throughout her writing career. It worked as a figure or a metaphor for that alternative way of writing and thinking about history, literature and sexual difference that she had attempted to articulate in a more piecemeal fashion in the critical essays that preceded this project. Anonymity symbolised the unity of public and private, of different artistic forms and media for which Woolf had been striving in the attempt to heal what she perceived to be the painful splits endured by the modern subject.[40] As such, it designated for Woolf also the pre-history of English literature and of individual psychology, a sort of collective unconscious which, as Silver remarks, got articulated and expressed in the artistic works of a society or community.[41] As this collective unconscious, anonymity also enabled Woolf to reverse at a figural or imaginative level the historical condition of obscurity and silence that had traditionally been women's lot into a positive source of artistic creativity and underlying permanence.

Although Woolf's projected revision of English literary history in the name of anonymity was terminated by her suicide on 28 March 1941, there are strong indications that the incomplete character of the surviving fragments is not just accidental but reflects fundamental problems in the conception of the book. As Silver points out, it is clear that Woolf encountered considerable difficulties in linking up the overview of the anonymous origins of literature she gives in 'Anon' with the description of the emergence of the modern audience she had planned for 'The Reader'.[42] The problematic character of the transition from the pre-historical to history proper exercised Woolf so much that, as Silver remarks, it remains unclear whether her last, uncompleted book of criticism was to preserve the sense of narrative continuity she outlined in her preparatory notes for *Reading at Random* or would rather have turned into the third volume of *The Common Reader*.[43] Paradoxically, and perhaps even rather sadly, the book that was going to join together the scattered pieces of Woolf's critical vision remains itself the most enigmatic of all those fragments.

2
The Essay as Form

The Essay as Autobiography

The interest in questions of marginality that characterises Woolf's focus on eccentrics, obscure and Anon also marks her reading of the history of the essay as a genre. Woolf wrote extensively both on the essay and on specific essayists throughout her career, starting in 1905 with the 'Decay of Essay-writing' and up to her essay on De Quincey published in the second *Common Reader* (1932). Her approach to the history and to the nature of the genre was always marked by an attempt to identify within what she saw as a male tradition an alternative line of descent to which she could affiliate herself. This she outlined by stressing the connection between the essay and autobiography, but a type of autobiography which she insisted was essentially non-narrative and presented the self as a conglomeration of moments of perception and reflection. In reading the essay as an autobiographical genre Woolf thus defined a form of writing that could bring together criticism and the private experience of reading in an intimate kind of historiography that allowed her to speak of and through the gaps which narrative sequence had conspired to close off.

'Almost all essays,' Woolf wrote in 1905, at the very beginning of her career as a critic and reviewer, 'begin with a capital I – "I think", "I feel" – and when you have said that, it is clear that you are not writing history or philosophy or biography or anything but an essay, which may be brilliant or profound, which may deal with the immortality of the soul, or the rheumatism in your left shoulder, but is primarily an expression of personal opinion' (*E* 1, 25). Categorical and yet not too exclusive, this definition of the essay represents Woolf's first attempt at marking out the boundaries of a genre she wrote in throughout her life. It occurs in

'The Decay of Essay-writing', a discussion of the Edwardian essay which was cut by half and shorn of its original title, 'A Plague of Essays', in a series of heavy-handed editorial interventions that exasperated Woolf. Even so, this essay presents many points of agreement with her later pronouncements on the genre, arguing that the Edwardian essay represents a betrayal and a perversion of the original and essential character of the genre. For Woolf, the essay was born with Montaigne, 'the first of the moderns' (25), to satisfy the need for self-expression, but has become in modern times a vehicle of vanity and exhibitionism, encouraging its writers to indulge their taste for a good turn of phrase without providing any food for thought. She warns that this sundering of form and content has led to the formulation of ill-informed and superficial judgements upon aesthetic matters that are the written equivalent of small talk. Expounding on the merits or faults of art is not, Woolf insists, the topic most suited to the 'peculiar form' that is typical of the essay (25). The freedom and ease of writing characteristic of the genre should rather be taken as a rare opportunity for exploring and bringing to light what other genres cannot or do not want to expose. 'If men and women must write,' she intimates, they should 'leave the great mysteries of art and literature unassailed' and concentrate instead on 'themselves' (26) as the subject matter most appropriate to the form of the essay.

Both self-portrait and book of the self, the autobiographical essay Woolf here offers as an ideal to strive for effectively returns the genre to its origins in Montaigne's writing. Reviewing a new edition of the *Essais* in 1924, Woolf opened her article with the picture of Montaigne standing in front of the King of Sicily's self-portrait and lamenting the impossibility of reproducing the same effect in writing ('Montaigne', *E* 4, 71–81). She argued that in the original conception of the genre Montaigne had reversed the hierarchy of values typical of the Edwardian essay by placing the simplicity of direct self-expression at a far higher level of achievement than the sophistication of style or 'good writing'. In his search for self-revelation, Montaigne devised a form of writing that escaped from the strictures of literary and scholarly conventions, but also flew in the face of received opinions and moral doctrines by revealing a soul 'so complex, so indefinite, corresponding so little to the version that does duty for her in public that a man might spend his life merely in trying to run her to earth' (73).[1]

Mysterious and impossible to grasp, the self portrayed by Montaigne exposed the existence of a private dimension running parallel to that of public life but which until then had remained obscure and inaccessible.

While a definitive blow to the knowledge accumulated by tradition, the opening up of this hitherto unknown dimension was for Woolf indispensable to the development of modern literature. As she argues both in 'On Not Knowing Greek' (1925; *E* 4, 38–53) and in 'The Elizabethan Lumber Room' (1925; *E* 4, 53–61), the passage from the universality of poetry to the particularity of prose marked a significant change in the whole history of Western literature. Woolf remarks that in the case of Greek literature the transition took place as smoothly and as naturally as the change from summer to winter or from outdoor to indoor activities. Stripped of its chorality, the dramatic structure of Greek tragedy was simply transferred into Plato's dialogues to follow the paths of Socratic reasoning. While a necessary stage in the development of prose-writing, this unproblematic transition from tragedy to philosophy was for Woolf in marked contrast with the far more momentous change that occurred in English literature in the seventeenth century.

Like Classical Greece, Elizabethan England had found in tragedy the best embodiment of its spirit and culture; unlike Greece, however, it had been granted no Plato to extract a fully mature prose out of its dramatic poetry. While well-suited to a fiery imagination and the staging of universal passions, the atmosphere of the Elizabethan playhouse was naturally inimical to the development of a more private, more finely attuned language. Stiff and dignified at best, riotous and undisciplined at worst, Elizabethan prose had none of the elegance and the subtle modulations that characterise Montaigne's contemporary *Essais*. Without a language fit for the complexities of introspection and intimacy, even Elizabethan letters and diaries fail to give any indication of their writers' personalities. As Woolf writes of Gabriel Harvey's sister, 'Nothing, one feels, would have been easier for Mercy than to read her lover a fine discourse upon the vanity of grandeur, the loveliness of chastity, the vicissitudes of fortunes. But of emotion as between one particular Mercy and one particular Philip, there is no trace' ('The Strange Elizabethans', 1932; *CR* 2, 14).

Ignoring Bacon and his contribution to the development of English prose writing, Woolf claims that the first English author to introduce the language of self-consciousness and intimacy into his writing was Sir Thomas Browne, who wrote in the middle of the seventeenth century and therefore at least a generation later than Bacon. Like Plato in Greece, Browne succeeded in shifting the focus of English literature from 'the publicity of the stage and the perpetual presence of a second person' inward to 'that growing consciousness of one's self, that brooding in solitude over the mysteries of the soul' which had been pioneered

by Montaigne in French ('The Elizabethan Lumber Room', *E* 4, 58). A
medical doctor trained in Italy and France, Browne represents for Woolf
a figure of transition in more than one sense. He straddled the old
culture of authority and submission and Bacon's new experimental
science, but was also for her a sort of pioneer in the landscape of
seventeenth-century literature, exploring the wilderness within that
had been left untouched by the geographical discoveries of the Renaissance ('Reading', 1919; *E* 3, 141–61). Because he was the first to lay his
eyes upon the region of the self, Browne managed for Woolf to preserve
the candour and innocence of discovery which she argues have since
been thwarted by awkwardness and vanity: 'The littleness of egotism has
not yet attacked the health of his interest in himself. I am charitable, I
am brave, I am averse from nothing . . . I, I, I – how we have lost the
secret of saying that!' (156).

As the first to leave such an indelible impression of himself in writing,
Browne had also opened up for Woolf one of the most crucial questions
in the history of literature:

> In short, Sir Thomas Browne brings in the whole question, which is
> afterwards to become of such importance, of knowing one's own
> author. Somewhere, everywhere, now hidden, now apparent in what-
> ever is written down is the form of a human being. If we seek to know
> him, are we idly occupied, as when, listening to a speaker, we begin to
> speculate about his age and habits, whether he is married, has chil-
> dren, and lives in Hampstead? It is a question to be asked, and not
> one to be answered.
>
> (156)

Emerging from the development of a literature in prose, the opening of
this question represents for Woolf a turning-point in the history of
literature which irrevocably separates the moderns from the classics.
She argues that the discovery of introspection in literature brought
along a marked change in the experience of reading, which shifted
from the public character of theatrical performances to the privacy of
the individual book. This more intimate kind of reading has made the
modern reader 'accustomed to find himself in direct communication
with the writer' (158) and therefore at a loss when faced with a book that
offers no foothold for establishing the same kind of relationship.
Trained by the psychological novel or the biography, even a reader as
gifted as Woolf must confess her inability to enter fully the world of the
classics, where the focus is not on the individual self but on the

universality of the human condition. Thus, if, as we saw with Montaigne, the introduction of the self in writing opens up the dimension of privacy, it does so at the expense of shutting off any access to transcendence.

Both Browne and Montainge are seen by Woolf as developing an alternative to history, a purely subjective form of writing that in its turn initiates a completely different kind of history, allowing the reader to inhabit a continuous present, to enter into intimate contact with his/her authors in a way that is made impossible by the transcendental impersonality of the classics. For Woolf the transient is what remains, enabling readers to re-experience the writing anew and thus connect to the past; the transcendental or universal is what cuts the readers off from that past, consigning it, if not to oblivion, certainly to the dryness and boredom of the classroom or the lecture theatre.

As an autobiographical genre, then, the essay works for Woolf both to enable a more direct apprehension of the past and, at the same time, to initiate modernity as a new condition that is marked by a focus on subjectivity as the new universal trait. As she points out in 'The Modern Essay' (1922; *E* 4, 216–27), this is a genre that has transformed the writer's self from something that lies outside literature into its controlling force. As a formless form, the essay has no structural equivalent of the fictional plot or the poetic rhyme to inform and sustain the vision expressed by its authors. It is thus left open to the twin dangers of empty form and unprocessed matter, so that the very informality or formlessness of the genre paradoxically require from its practitioners a degree of artistry that is unparalleled by other genres. As Woolf intimates, 'there is no room for the impurities of literature in an essay. Somehow or other, by dint of labour or bounty of nature, the essay must be pure – pure like water or pure like wine, but pure from dullness, deadness, and deposits of extraneous matter' (217–18). It is an uncompromising demand for perfection which recalls the genre's association with *belles lettres*, making of the essay the centrepiece of a conception of prose that puts the achievement of elegance and poise above everything else.

But Woolf laments that this restrictive definition of what constitutes 'good writing' is rooted in the controlled perfection of Addison's essays and has led to a purely imitative understanding of style. She claims that in the English tradition style has not been taken to designate the welding of self and writing effected by Montaigne's essays, but rather indicates a standard of formal perfection which is divorced from the substance of writing. Taken to its extreme, this position leads to the absolute achievement of Max Beerbohm, who, as Woolf herself acknowledges, invests his own self with such a consummate artistry that 'we do not know whether there is any relation between Max the essayist and Mr Beerbohm the man' (220–21). Beerbohm is credited by Woolf with the merit of having restored the essay to its eighteenth-century prototype, making the Victorian essay both less gloomy and more intimate. Known to his readers by his first name, Beerbohm has re-introduced into the essay its most characteristic element, 'that self which, while it is essential to literature, is also its most dangerous antagonist' (221). But the relationship of self and writing is not equal in Beerbohm's essays; being a dandy, he cannot allow the self or the life outside literature to spoil the writing but focuses all his energies on transforming life itself into an art object.

As Woolf points out in an earlier review of Beerbohm's writings ('The Limits of Perfection', 1919; *E* 3, 124–6), turning life into art deprives art itself of the nourishment it draws from life, preserving it in a splendid and yet deadening isolation. As a genre of small pretensions, the essay has for Woolf a very restricted brief, whereby its only purpose is the bestowal of pleasure: 'Vague as all definitions are, a good essay must have this permanent quality about it; it must draw its curtain round us, but it must be a curtain that shuts us in, not out' ('The Modern Essay', *E* 4, 224). Like a shield against pain and discomfort, the essay wraps its readers up in an atmosphere of secluded intimacy that excludes the outside world. While meant to bring about a more intense appreciation of life, this seclusion often threatens to result in a substitution of life by art.

To the tradition of mastery and control over life exemplified by the eighteenth-century essay and its epigones, Woolf opposes the exuberance and excesses of Romantic autobiography. Thomas De Quincey is her favourite essayist as the only writer in the history of English literature who attempted to push prose beyond the limits of eighteenth-century elegance.[2] As Woolf acknowledges in her essay on *The English Mail Coach* (1906; *E* 1, 365–8), De Quincey's style is nowhere as neat and harmonious as that of Walter Pater or Robert Louis Stevenson, who are traditionally understood to represent the peak of English prose-writing. He has none of the urbanity and composure of their style, is excessive and unruly, with a tendency to see 'everything a size too large', using 'words which are also a size too large' to articulate his overwhelming visions (366). While making him incapable of dealing with the prosaic nature of facts, these very defects are for Woolf what gives his writing its individual flavour. Endowed with the outlook of a poet and the ear of a musician, De Quincey stretches language beyond the limits of reason and measure to accommodate the 'beautiful sights and strange emotions [which] created waves of sound in his brain before they shaped themselves into articulate words' (367).

But Woolf also points out that De Quincey's attempt to translate into prose some of the qualities that are usually associated with poetry exposed him to the criticism of those who demand a strict separation between the two forms of writing. In 'Impassioned Prose' (1926; *E* 4, 361–9) she argues that in the English literary tradition prose has traditionally been identified with the writing of fiction, where it has been heavily influenced by the demand for verisimilitude. She claims that fiction works by leaving implicit the universal theme and concentrating instead on the particulars, the details of everyday life. It therefore transforms what poetry attempts to articulate into the narrative line, embedding the universal theme 'so deep beneath page after page and chapter after chapter that the single word when it is spoken is enough to start an explosion' (362). The method of fiction goes then against that of poetic prose, which attempts to bring the universal breath that animates poetry into the prosaic world of everyday life.

De Quincey's development of his 'impassioned prose' was, as Woolf admits, besieged by considerable difficulties. As a man plagued by dreams and visions, De Quincey had to find not only a language in which to convey his visions, but also a form in which they could subsist as prose poetry. Woolf warns that '[a] prose writer may dream dreams and see visions, but they cannot be allowed to lie scattered, single, solitary upon the page. So spaced out they die' (363). The link De Quincey provided to hold his visions together was himself, albeit a self that, as Woolf remarks, remains quite aloof and never becomes as intimate as that of other essayists. It is only in his autobiographical writings that De Quincey's extravagant gifts find their match in scenes remembered from the past and so far away in time that they take on the appearance of dreams. As these sketches blur the distinction between fact and vision, dream and reality, they manage to give voice to a part of human life which Woolf claims is usually left unsaid in traditional kinds of biographical writings.[3]

Yet, although De Quincey found in autobiography the mode of writing best suited to his individual talents, he was not perhaps himself the subject most appropriate for the kind of autobiography he advocated. Woolf points out in 'De Quincey's Autobiography' (1932; *CR* 2, 132–9) that his insistence upon the value of the inner, subjective life showed up the limits of the English tradition of biographical writing but did not in itself lead him to write the perfect autobiography. Too biased towards the subjective life, De Quincey lacked for Woolf that attention to outward reality that is indispensable to (auto)biographical writing. 'To tell the whole story of a life,' Woolf insists, 'the two levels of existence ... the rapid passage of events and actions; the slow opening up of single and solemn moments of concentrated emotions' must both 'be recorded' (139). As autobiography, De Quincey's prose writing encounters the problem that, for Woolf, haunts all biographical writing: the need to reconcile the factual and the symbolic level, the inner and the outer life, the subjective and the objective approach.[4]

In 'The Art of Biography' (1939; *CD*, 144–51), Woolf associates these two levels of existence with two modes of writing, one mere chronological account of events and the other a principle of selection and moulding. The difficulty of writing biography lies in combining the two kinds of writing into a single unity capable of conveying the whole truth about the life of the individual, both the literal and the metaphorical one. Like the essay, biography is charged with the difficult task of communicating the impression of personality in writing; unlike the essay, biography must develop this impression through the conventions of narrative, what Woolf calls the 'fiction' of biographical writing. As autobiography, the essay occupies simply the position of the sketch rather than that of the full-blown picture, an unresolved collection of 'moments of being'[5] that belong to the pre-history of narrative.

The definition and history of the 'personal' essay outlined by Woolf in her criticism assimilates the genre to a form of writing about the self that is not organised into a narrative. Part sketch and part epiphany, the essay participated in and perhaps even initiated for Woolf a momentous change in the history of literature, when prose took the place of poetry as the dominant literary form and the cult of the author marked the end of impersonal literature. While she conceded that this shift was fundamental to the development of a literature in prose and therefore of the form of the novel, Woolf nevertheless claimed that its significance was not restricted to fiction, but had important consequences for the whole question of the relation between art and life, literature and experience. In the English tradition she lamented the fact that the eighteenth-century ideals of harmony and measure had become identified with the mainstream of prose writing at the expense of the excesses and surplus of life. The ultimate outcome of this strand of writing was to turn the self into an art form, thus defusing precisely what in the self challenges art.

Looking for a form of writing that would not assimilate life to aesthetic experience, Woolf discovered the rich seventeenth-century prose of Browne and the visionary style of the Romantic De Quincey. Sharing a distance from eighteenth-century literature and culture, Browne and De Quincey symbolise for Woolf a kind of writing that does not rest content with its own measured achievements but is continuously stretched beyond its own limits, reaching out to the regions where nobody has ever been before. As Andrew McNeillie has remarked, the preference expressed by Woolf for poetic rather than prosaic essayists reflects in fact the kind of writing she herself experimented with in works such as *To the Lighthouse* (1927) and, especially, *The Waves* (1931) (*E* 4, xix). Her alternative version of the history of the essay can thus be seen to unearth a submerged current of English prose writing which functions as a literary precedent for her own search for an antidote to narrative in the writing of fiction.[6]

Common Readers and Modern Audiences

But Woolf's attempts to rewrite the history of the essay as an essentially modern and modernist genre were also accompanied by another, far less positive view of the modernity of the essay, which stressed its connection with the expansion of readership and the consequent commercialisation of literary practices. This link between the essay and a more negative conception of modernity is especially noticeable when her analysis of the history of the genre shifts from the question of subjectivity and authorship to that of reception. This shift from essayist to reader was most famously articulated by Woolf through the notion of the common reader, which she borrowed from Samuel Johnson's *Life of Gray*. The shift signals Woolf's continued preoccupation with the epistemological break marked by the emergence of the reader in the history of English literature. It also represents, though, her response to the commodification of literature, a resistance to resolving every aspect of modern life into an overarching narrative which, at the same time, gestures towards the possibility of a common history to be shared among non-professional readers.

The extent to which Woolf rewrote the Johnsonian notion as a point of resistance to modernity can be gauged by comparing her own definition to its acknowledged source. In the *Life of Gray* Johnson first deployed the idea of the common reader as an ironical weapon to deflate Gray's pretensions to literary distinction. He invoked it towards the end of his discussion of Gray's work to mark a sharp discrepancy between the poet's own self-perception and the public recognition of his worth. Casting himself as a voice of dissent from the kind of learned commendations which Gray's work has received from professional critics and men of letters, Johnson rejected most of that work as obscure and selected only the 'Elegy Written in a Country Churchyard' as an example of genuine achievement:

> in the character of [Gray's] *Elegy* I rejoice to concur with the common reader; for by the common sense of readers uncorrupted with literary prejudices, after all the refinements of subtility and the dogmatism of learning, must be finally decided all claim to poetical honours. The *Church-yard* abounds with images which find a mirror in every mind, and with sentiments to which every bosom returns an echo.[7]

This aligning of the critical judgement with that of the wider, non-specialised public constitutes an unexpected move on Johnson's part. It marks a gap between a restricted circle of readers who have arrogated for themselves the role of arbiters of taste and a more public and open readership that is the repository of universal values. It thus signals the end of the old system of patronage where the intended readership tended to coincide with the actual one and heralds the beginning of a much closer relation between the writer and the market. Faced with the conflation of social and literary privilege which supported the patronage system, Johnson invoked the idea of the common reader as the professional writer's alternative and, ultimately, more definitive source of legitimation.

In this sense, Johnson's notion of the common reader can be seen to lie at the intersection of a series of important and related changes in the history of literature. It marks the transition from writing as a vocation to writing as a profession, signalling the intrusion of the market and its values into literary matters. This intrusion in its turn requires a radical rethinking of the idea of literary and aesthetic values themselves and, with them, of the very principles upon which the literary tradition rests. Suffered by Johnson initially as a loss and then only subsequently accepted as a source of independence from aristocratic patrons, this turning-point in the history of literature came to be seen by Woolf in equally ambivalent terms, at times as a source of freedom (especially for women)[8] and at times as a form of imprisonment and enslavement for writers and readers alike.

The first and more positive set of associations elicited by the idea of the common reader emerges in the short definition Woolf offered in the way of an introduction to her first collection of essays. There, she stressed both the humble character and the mediating nature of her ideal reader, whom she envisaged as a sort of third term, escaping the two extremes of either inaccessible scholarship or mindless consumption:

> The common reader – she wrote – ... differs from the critic and the scholar. He is worse educated, and nature has not gifted him so generously. He reads for his own pleasure rather than to impart knowledge or correct the opinions of others. Above all, he is guided by an instinct to create for himself, out of whatever odds and ends he can come by, some kind of whole – a portrait of a man, a sketch of an age, a theory of the art of writing.
>
> (1925; *E* 4, 17)

An amateur rather than a professional, the common reader symbolises for Woolf the limits and opportunities of an education acquired within the home rather than in public institutions. His or her reading is carried out in rooms 'too humble to be called libraries, yet full of books' (17); his or her interest in literature is intensely private and almost secretive, characterised by the strong anonymity already implicit in the name. He or she is defective and undisciplined as a critic, but at least has managed to preserve that enthusiasm and personal involvement in the activity of reading which is often lacking in those who practise criticism as a profession.

Not surprisingly, perhaps, this definition of the common reader ends up by mirroring Woolf's own critical practice, describing a form of criticism that is grounded in the indissoluble unity of reader and writer rather than in the authority of learning and scholarly pursuits. Woolf's interpretation of the idea of the common reader develops along the lines of an opposition between amateurs and self-taught individuals on the one hand, and professional figures and public institutions on the other which returns Johnson's idea to the system of oppositions that it was originally meant to scramble. While Johnson had aligned his own critical judgement with that of the common reader, Woolf reconstructed the latter as the critic's own antithesis.[9] But such a clear demarcation of territory became for Woolf more a source of discomfort than one of reassurance, as it compelled her time and again to look for ways of bridging the split not just between critic and amateur, but also between her idealised public and the reality of a mass audience which she saw as its negation.

In 'The Patron and the Crocus' (1925; *E* 4, 212–25), the split between the ideal and the abject audience is translated in fact into a split between modern writers and readers. In her attempt to reconcile patronage and market values, Woolf makes a plea for the establishment of a more immediate and more indissoluble link between modern writers and their readers. In her definition, the modern reading public occupies very much the position of the aristocratic patron of the arts, who 'is not merely the paymaster, but also in a very subtle and insidious way the instigator and inspirer of what is written'. Woolf argues that the history of English literature shows writer and patron in a relationship of strong interdependence, with each age having its own chosen public to write for. In the modern age, this one-to-one 'alliance' (212) has been dissolved and fragmented, as writers find themselves supplied with an unending variety and quantity of different reading groups, each with its own interests and values.

Under these conditions, the relationship of writers to their readers is altered and substituted by the coupling of items as discordant as those of the title: the writer disappears and his or her place is taken by the object of writing, 'the first crocus in Kensington Gardens' (215). The appearance of the crocus as the object of the writer's inspiration signals also a splitting of the ideal unity of 'paymaster' and 'instigator' which Woolf defined as characteristic of the modern patron at the beginning of this article. The splitting in its turn deforms the relationship of writer to public into one of either superiority and disdain (as in the case of Samuel Butler, George Meredith and Henry James) or subservience and servility (as in the case of journalists and critics who write for the Press). But to the alternative of either inferiority or superiority, Woolf prefers the ideal of an absolutely equal relationship between readers and writers where the two are Siamese twins soldered into a symbiotic bond:

> [The patron] must make us feel that a single crocus, if it be a real crocus, is enough for him; that he does not want to be lectured, elevated, instructed, or improved; that he is sorry that he bullied Carlyle into vociferation, Tennyson into idyllics, and Ruskin into insanity; that he is now ready to efface himself or assert himself as his writers require; that he is bound to them by a more than maternal tie; that they are twins indeed, one dying if the other dies, one flourishing if the other flourishes . . .
>
> (215)[10]

Although the image proposed here is that of an egalitarian relationship between readers and writers, the distribution of the positions of address within this essay is far less than symmetrical. 'The Patron and the

Crocus' opens up as a sort of indirect response to a request of advice by 'young men and women beginning to write' (*E* 4, 212) which is formulated in the third person. It is in this person that we are offered a dispassionate overview of the history of the relationship between writers and their audiences in English literature and an analysis of the plight of the superior writer on the one hand and of the servile journalist on the other. But as Woolf comes to consider the question of the ideal patron/ public, her speaking persona suddenly switches to the first person plural to address the public in the collective voice of the modern writer: 'for whom should we write?' she asks (212).

In the course of the essay she progressively loses her equanimous stance as her historical analysis of Elizabethan, eighteenth-century and Victorian patrons turns into an impassioned plea for help and sustenance. The public becomes then the object of the writer's demands ('The patron we want . . . is one who will help us to preserve our flowers from decay', Woolf commands (214)) and the relationship between peers first evoked in the essay is turned into a one-sided contract. Placed under an enormous amount of obligations, the public figures here only as the recipient of the writers' injunctions (he must be ready to 'efface himself or assert himself' at will), so that the writer can take up the position of dominating subject dictating the terms and conditions of the relationship.

Resembling very closely the common reader, the ideal of the patron as both master and muse, tied to the writer by indissoluble bonds is here revealed as the writer's own fantasy of revenge and mastery upon a public that stubbornly refuses to shape itself in the writer's image and therefore makes the latter's dependence upon that public painfully clear. This other, more secret story revealed by the changes in perspective and speaking persona in 'The Patron and the Crocus' is also matched by the far from complimentary representations of the reading public Woolf offers in some of her less well-known essays. Because of its connection to journalism, Woolf tends to see the essay as the form that is most readily influenced by changes in the distribution and consumption of newspapers and magazines and therefore by changes in the size and composition of its readership. While at times such changes are perceived to be for the best, it is more usual for Woolf to stress the negative effects of an excessive encroachment of market demands upon literary activities, especially as far as the twentieth century is concerned. Oversized audiences seem for Woolf to go with a loss of autonomy and independence which corrupts and contaminates the purity of the literary product and, in particular, of the essay as a form.

Woolf's reviews of twentieth-century literary journalism are thus often accompanied by terrifying and violent images of consumption and enslavement which are at odds with the general temperament of her writing, well-known for its ironies and subtle innuendoes. She often tended to perceive literary journalism not just as incompatible with 'proper' literature but effectively as a possible source of contamination for the purity of the literary product. Her intense feelings of dislike and antagonism towards literary journalism typically found their expression in her reviews of contemporary books of essays, which she alternately censures either as meaningless ('Bad Writers', 1918; *E* 2, 326–9; 'Patmore's Criticism', 1921; *E* 3, 308–9) or, in a more sinister fashion, as disgusting and repulsive ('The Modern Essay', 1925; *E* 4, 216–7). Churned out by men who are chained to the writing desk as if they were in a labour camp, these collections of essays are aimed at a public that is seen by Woolf as a tyrannical master whose desires are not easily satisfied:

> Books of essays somehow have the tendency to make us feel autocratic and oriental. We are conscious of retinues of slaves. Numbers of them have had their heads cut off and been thrown into the moat for failing to please us already; but Solomon Eagle [the *nom de plume* of John Squire, then literary editor of the *New Statesman*] amuses the Sultan; he has made the Sultan laugh; therefore we grant him permission to go on living on condition that he makes us laugh every night before we go to sleep for ever and ever.
>
> ('Bad Writers', *E* 2, 327)

Compelled to spin tales and tell stories for dear life, modern essayists occupy the uneasy position of Scheherazade, faced with a public they have to keep happy and satisfied through constant feeding. The essayists are thus placed in a feminised position as victims of the tyrannical whims and unwieldy appetites of the public, a sort of overgrown child Woolf brands as monstrous and even inhuman.

Both passive and aggressive at the same time, this unwieldy modern audience is for Woolf totally deprived of a mind of its own but rather governed either by its animal instincts or, more ominously, by the wishes and interests of those in authority. As enslaved in its turn as the essayists it dominates, the public is represented as the crucial link in a chain of oppression that is ultimately brought to bear upon both readers and writers:

The order of the serious sixpenny weekly paper must originally have been evolved like the now almost extinct order of the meats and the sweets, in deference to some demand of the public appetite. It is a rule that after the politics we come to the lighter form of the essay and so to the reviews; and as this order is never upset, it must have been devised either for our pleasure or for our good.

('A Book of Essays', 1918; *E* 2, 212)

Here, the parallel between meals and weekly papers underscores the sense of force-feeding which for Woolf often accompanies the reading of contemporary literary journalism. At the same time, the idea that the traditional ordering of the courses is somehow 'extinct' attaches a certain obsolescence to the weekly paper itself and its religious observance of a long-established tradition. In this panorama of submission and conformity, Woolf confesses herself as a deviant and transgressive agent who, like a prototypical modern reader, undoes the natural and immutable quality of the existing order by refusing to swallow the propaganda dished out through the essay and preferring rather to speculate upon advertisements as if they were short-stories. As she distances herself from the rest of the modern reading public on the commuter train, Woolf spares a sisterly thought of empathy for the conditions under which modern essayists work, picturing a quite literal motion of disgust and rejection 'as our gorge rises at the thought of all the turns and twists and devices which some fellow-creature is going through in order to persuade us to swallow a fragment of the truth without recognising it' (212).

Presented from within Woolf's own essays and reviews, these pictures of enslaved writers and infantilised audiences raise serious questions about the reviewer's and essayist's integrity, and are therefore in danger of backfiring onto Woolf's own contributions to the writing of literary history and criticism. Woolf attempted to address the problem of the critic's integrity in the face of market relations through a proposal for the reforming of the activity of reviewing she put forth in a 1939 essay. 'Reviewing' (*CE* 2, 204–17) opens with the striking image of a London shop window, where women mending trousers and other items of clothing are exposed to the voyeuristic gaze of a crowd gathered outside the shop. Woolf compares the working conditions of these women to those of the modern writers, who are compelled to carry out their tasks under the watchful eyes and sharp commentaries of critics and reviewers. She argues that these conditions are detrimental to the writing of literature, as they stimulate the writers' vanity and their desire for money but leave untouched their aesthetic values or opinions.

This inauspicious and deleterious situation has arisen for Woolf as a direct result of the spread of publications and journalism that is characteristic of modern times. She points out that reviewing developed in the eighteenth century with the growth of newspaper publishing, but was soon separated into the two different activities of criticism (which 'dealt with the past and with principles' (205)), and reviewing proper, which concentrated upon contemporary literary production. As the distinction between the two activities deepened, the reviewer of the nineteenth century came to wield a considerable amount of power over both the public and the writers themselves, since a good or bad review could determine the fate of a book without appeal.

Woolf claims that in recent times the reviewers' enormous power of influence has been eroded by a tenfold increase in the number of reviews a book normally receives. Faced with this multiplication of demand, the contemporary reviewer has become a more modest figure who struggles under the conflicting pull of very different briefs. On the one hand, there are the commercial interests of publishers and the public's need for information; on the other, there is the critics' longing to speak to the writers and the writers' desire for the critics' honest opinion of their work. While the first set of interests fulfils a very public function, the second can only be damaged by the glare of publicity and requires the protection of secrecy and privacy.[11] As Woolf intimates, 'shut doors and windows; pull the curtains. Ensure that no fame accrues or money; and still it is a matter of the very great interest to a writer to know what an honest and intelligent reader thinks about his work' (*CE* 2, 211).

Because of this conflict between the private character of the writer/ critic dialogue and the need for publicity and advertisement, Woolf proposes at this point to differentiate between the two sets of functions and interests by splitting up what is still considered as reviewing into two separate activities. To satisfy the needs of both publishers and public alike, Woolf envisages a system of description and pricing of the literary product aimed at eliding any remaining differences between books and commodities. Reviewing will then be assimilated to working on an assembly line, where 'a competent official armed with scissors and paste' will provide a summary of the book under review and/or cut out a few extracts from it, to which 'what is left of the reviewer' will add a mark for approval or disapproval (209).

In contrast to the mechanical and almost proletarian quality of this 'Gutter and Stamp production' (209), the activity of the critic is instead portrayed by Woolf as an equivalent of the profession *par excellence*, that of the medical doctor:

> Let the reviewers then abolish themselves or what relic remains of them, as reviewers, and resurrect themselves as doctors ... The writer then would submit his work to the judge of his choice; an appointment would be made; an interview arranged. In strict privacy, and with some formality – the fee, however, would be enough to ensure that the interview did not degenerate into tea-table gossip – doctor and writer would meet; and for an hour they would consult upon the book in question.
>
> (212)

The figure Woolf proposes should be paid for this transaction between writer and critic is that of three guineas, the conventional figure for professional consultations at the time, but also the title of one of her most famous essays. A shorter version of 'Reviewing' in fact appears in the third section of *Three Guineas* (1938) as a footnote to Woolf's discussion of writing for money as a form of intellectual prostitution (*TG*, 400– 1, n. 10).

In 'Reviewing' itself the thorny question of the relationship between writing and market demands is solved by confining the reviewer to the role of little more than a skilled worker, an automaton in fact whose job could just as easily be performed by a machine. This relegation of the reviewer to an inferior order of being effectively manages to preserve the critic in a situation of integrity, and independence from literary journalism, that allies writer and critic in a very secluded and exclusive bond. Overturning the power relationships inscribed by the image of the shop-window, Woolf's proposal now implicitly places the journalists in the position formerly occupied by the working women, while writers and critics – both members of the same class, as Woolf points out – can retire to the back of the shop and out of the inquisitive public eye. Protected by 'the darkness of the workshop', the writer would not be exposed to the gaze of 'a horde of reviewers pressing their noses to the glass and commenting to a curious crowd upon each stitch' (*CE* 2, 213). The reviewer in his turn would be able to concentrate on the book and 'the writer's needs' and thus stop 'cutting shop window capers to amuse the public and to advertise his skill' (214).

In Woolf's account, though, it is the shop window itself that disappears, leaving in its place the vision of a more harmonious set of relations between author, reviewer and the public. Without the distorting reflections produced by the system of 'the shop window' and 'the looking-glass', the author will be transformed from an object of derision to simply 'an obscure workman doing his job' and will thus gain in the eye of the public the respect that is due to honest workmanship (214). In this way the hoped-for removal of the shop window signals the opening up of a space where traditional boundaries between writers, readers and critics can be transgressed. Woolf speculates that the introduction of the Gutter and Stamp production might free up the space for the emergence of a new Montaigne or a Matthew Arnold, liberating that repressed talent which at the moment cannot find its expression because of pressures of time, money and space. But this crossing over of the reviewer into writer's territory does not bring with it a radical overhaul of the system of values that sustains her representation of the shop window, where to be a worker is to be valued while to be a spectator is to be reviled. The reviewer might transform him or herself into a writer, but there is no space in Woolf's representation for the other parallel movement that would see the writer turning into the consumer of other people's productivity.

This asymmetrical distribution of positions in Woolf's proposals for the reform of reviewing was first noticed by Leonard Woolf, who appended a note of his own to her essay when it was first published as a Hogarth Pamphlet. Moved to add to his wife's 'ingenious suggestion' (216) his own interpretation of the history of literary journalism, Leonard Woolf argued that reviewing and criticism already were quite distinct activities and therefore did not need to be further separated and differentiated. He traced the birth of the reviewer back to the end of the patronage system and argued with Goldsmith that the shift from patron to paying public had effectively been for the best. Within this new system, Leonard insisted, the task of the reviewer had always been one of information and advice to the public rather than of inspired criticism for the author. As he put it, 'the reviewer, unlike the critic, in 999 cases out of 1,000 has nothing to say to the author; he is talking to the reader' (216).

Re-inscribing the split between critic and reviewer that Woolf had first opened up and then closed off again, Leonard thus claimed to be speaking from the reviewer's own point of view in response to an article which he felt had been written in protection of the author's interests. Appropriating for the reviewer the status of honest and modest workman that Woolf had wished for the author, Leonard shifted the locus of contradiction from within the office of reviewing to the predicament of the artist in modern society. Torn by the opposite claims of art and money, the modern author might crave for genuine criticism but is effectively dependent on the reviewer for the generation of his or her income. The source of the author's dissatisfaction with the reviewer lies, Leonard implied, not so much in the shortcomings of the latter, as in this relationship of power on one side and dependence on the other, whereby 'if [the author] wants to sell his books to the great reading public and the circulating libraries, he will still need the reviewer – and that is why he will probably, like Tennyson and Dickens, continue to abuse the reviewer when the review is not favourable' (217).

By pitting himself against his wife as the voice of the reviewer, Leonard thus quite literally added an extra dimension to the split between reader and writer which Woolf had attempted to address and heal through the ideal of the common reader and the image of the patron. Conceived as a substitute for Woolf's more ambitious project of blending essay and fiction in a new form of literary criticism, the common reader holds her critical essays together by relocating them in the privacy of leisure and home which screens from sight Woolf's own professional involvement in journalism. Through this retreat into the privacy of her own rooms and away from public sight, Woolf tried to place her criticism within the tradition of the personal essay that goes back to Montaigne rather than within the analytical and rationalistic kind of writing she identified with her father's own literary practice (and of which Leonard's note is itself an example).[12] But in choosing Montaigne as her predecessor, Woolf left open and unresolved the issue of the writer's relation to the public sphere and, consequently, also of the relation between her career as an essayist and reviewer on the one hand and as a novelist on the other.

Against this background of insistent splittings in two and complementary attempts at healing the rifts, Leonard's note signals an enlargement and redefinition of the problem. Implicitly, it adds the dimension of sexual difference as a third term in the set of oppositions analysed and enacted by Woolf in her writings. In translating the opposition of professional to amateur into the split between private and public, the idea of the common reader establishes a connection between the problem of practising literature as a profession and the issues of sexual politics which characterise Woolf's most famous writings, but are somewhat absent from her discussion of the essay as a genre and of journalism as such. From the demand of privacy and an autonomous space put forth in *A Room* (1929) to the separatist tendencies of the Society of Outsiders she advocates in *Three Guineas* (1938), the question of private and public spaces is for Woolf inseparable from the problem of women's roles in and through history. In 'Reviewing' itself, the question is posed in terms of a parallel between the women working as trouser menders and the writers of what Woolf calls 'imaginative literature' (204), suggesting an essential compatibility between writing and women's roles. But as the essay proceeds, the working women fall quite literally out of the picture together with the system of the shop window which defines their roles. Their disappearance indicates that by this time the alliance between working women and writers which Woolf was in the habit of invoking had in fact become unsustainable.

3
Professing Literature

Working Women and Women Writers

The ambivalence towards the commodification of literature and literary journalism that is evident in 'Reviewing' sits uneasily with the celebration of women's access to the profession of literature for which Woolf is best known. Throughout her career, from her beginnings as a reviewer to her most famous feminist essays, writing for money always represented for Woolf the mark of professionalisation, a legitimation of women's 'scribbling' into an acceptable and socially recognised occupation. This legitimation was so important for Woolf that it led her to curtail the history of women's writing to the disadvantage of the aristocratic women whom she saw as *amatrices* rather than professionals. When placed against Woolf's definition of the common reader, though, this celebration of professional women of letters reveals a deep-seated contradiction in her perception of the history of literature. On the one hand, there is her awareness of the importance of the professionalisation of women's writing as an instrument of emancipation. On the other, there is her suspicion, as a writer and a reader, of the institutionalisation of literature and of the professional critic as a figure that symbolises a restriction rather than a widening of access and, consequently, a weakening of literature's universal appeal.

This ambivalence is also apparent in *A Room* (1929), where Woolf's insistence upon the connection between financial independence and the ability to write leads her to a mystification of the distinction between earned and inherited income. Within the argument of *A Room* the same sum of money, 'five hundred pounds a year', is used first to indicate the legacy received by the narrator upon the death of her paternal aunt (*RO*, 48) and then the income which a woman writer might be able to earn following the ground-breaking example of Aphra Behn (85). Like the room of one's own of the title, the sum of five hundred a year is used as a symbol to indicate the very strong link between financial independence and psychological autonomy that forms the main contention of the essay. But as this symbol also works to erase the distinction between private and earned income, the argument of the essay itself is caught in a vicious circle whereby the five hundred pounds a year become both the precondition of a woman's writing (since she 'must have money and a room of her own'(4) in order to write fiction) and its final outcome (as 'money dignifies what is frivolous if unpaid for' (84)).

This circularity in the argument put forth by *A Room* has its origins in the need to lend authority and credibility to its narrator by shielding her from accusations of partisanship and sex antagonism. As the narrator confesses, the receipt of her legacy of five hundred pounds has worked to free her from the burden of anger, subservience and bitterness which she identifies equally in the writings of Professor X and in *Jane Eyre*. Instead of working 'like a slave, flattering and fawning' with 'rust eating away the bloom of the spring, destroying the tree at its heart' (*RO*, 48), the narrator suddenly finds herself endowed with a private income which releases her from the need to please men or employers, so that she is free to express her opinions without fear to offend. This means that her own analysis of men's attitudes towards women's emancipation can be presented as a balanced, unprejudiced and disinterested account that is not influenced either by recriminations or by the need to please: 'I need not hate any man; he cannot hurt me. I need not flatter any man; he has nothing to give me' (49).

Working as a shield against the sway of patriarchal power, the legacy of five hundred pounds represents the financial and material basis which is required for the androgynous attitude to take hold. As the third pole mediating between women's embittered resentment and men's aggressive defensiveness, the narrator also offers the representation of an alternative lifestyle that is neither as lavish as the one she experienced in the men's college nor as meagre as that of the women's. In the section that precedes the revision of the history of women's writing in favour of the middle-class, income-generating woman, the scene of writing moves from Oxbridge to Bloomsbury, where the narrator stops to have her first meal as a paying customer rather than as a guest. Neither sumptuous nor inadequate, this meal functions as a third term, a balanced but nutritious fare that stands in sharp contrast with the extremities she experienced in Oxbridge. It is paid for with a ten-shilling note whose presence in her purse is greeted by the narrator as a miraculous appearance: 'it is a fact that still takes my breath away – the power of my purse to breed ten-shilling notes automatically. I open it and there they are' (47).

As Elizabeth Abel has remarked in *Virginia Woolf and the Fictions of Psychoanalysis* (1989), the image of parthenogenesis offered by the narrator's purse links together the issues of money, feeding and mothering that are so prominent in the text. Abel argues that the insistence on the five hundred pounds legacy that runs through *A Room* masks the ambivalence towards mothering that is inscribed in the play between the different narrative voices making up the argument of the essay. In characterising money as the result of parthenogenesis, that is of reproduction without intercourse between the sexes, the narrator effects for Abel a decisive split of the biological meaning of mothering from its nurturing aspect. On the one hand, there is Mrs Seton, the biological mother who has exhausted herself by giving birth to thirteen children and has as a consequence been unable to provide her daughters with the 'wine and partridges and servants carrying tin dishes on their heads' (*RO*, 26) that the text insists are necessary for nourishing the mind as well as the body. At the opposite pole from Mrs Seton is the paternal aunt, Mary Beton, who left the narrator the enabling legacy 'for no other reason than that I share her name' (47).[1]

The shift from Mrs Seton to Mary Beton, from 'the mother who bears [the narrator], and therefore cannot feed her' to 'the one who feeds her, but does not give birth',[2] works for Abel to diffuse the anger provoked by inadequate nurturing which is debarred from the economy of the text. As she puts it, 'Although the declared value of the legacy is freedom from corrosive work and thus from anger and bitterness toward men, its dramatized value is freedom from hunger and thus anger and bitterness toward women.'[3] By linking together motherhood, the legacy and the anger that the text tries so hard to expel, Abel's reading of *A Room* also opens the way for questioning the insistence on inheritance – both financial and literary – that characterises the text. Although Abel concedes that the ostensible aim of *A Room* lies in the identification of a matrilineal heritage in response to 'a defensively misogynist construction and conflation of gender and textuality',[4] she also insists that the project is undermined by the other, negative side of this idealisation, which blames the mothers for the lot of the daughters.

This ambivalence towards mothering also inflects the question of the value of women's work, whether paid or unpaid, professional or not. A notoriously ventriloquist text, *A Room* speaks with different voices and to different audiences at one and the same time, arguing for the importance of women's earning power to the audience of female Cambridge undergraduates, while whispering under its breath that paid employment often fosters in women 'fear, anger and bitterness'. As it has often been noted, *A Room* is constituted from the beginning as an ongoing argument which opens, as it were, *in media res*: 'But, you may say, we asked you to speak about women and fiction – what has that got to do with a room of one's own?' (*RO*, 3). The link between the ostensible topic of the talk and its title is represented as a digression from the proscribed aim which is also a movement backwards both to the origins of the talk and to the roots of women's exclusion from culture as agents or subjects rather than as objects.

But in re-examining the historical and material circumstances that have led to that exclusion, Woolf is implicitly answering another question, coming this time not from her Cambridge audience, but from the likes of Professor X who insist on the 'mental, moral, and physical inferiority of the female sex' (*RO*, 39). Although the question is never explicitly articulated in *A Room*, its origins can be traced back to a real-life, rather than fictional, encounter between Woolf and some proponents of the inferiority of women. About ten years before the publication of *A Room* Woolf had been involved in a polemic with 'Affable Hawk' (the pseudonym of Desmond MacCarthy, a member of Bloomsbury and therefore a friend) in the *New Statesman* on 'The Intellectual Status of Women' (1920; *WE*, 30–9). The polemic had originated with MacCarthy's review of a collection of essays by Arnold Bennett, *Our Women: Chapters on the Sex-Discord*, which supported Bennett's conclusion 'that women are inferior to men in intellectual power' and that, quoting Bennett, ' "no amount of education and liberty of action will sensibly alter" ' their inferiority (31).

In characteristic fashion, Woolf's reply was made up by a two-throng attack. Fist of all she disputed MacCarthy's facts by calling in Sappho as the example of a woman poet whose achievements were undoubtedly fostered by the exceptional amount of education and liberty enjoyed by women in Lesbos at the time. Then she set out to undo the terms of the discussion by reversing MacCarthy's and Bennett's claims about women's mediocrity when compared with men's achievements. The point was, Woolf argued, that genius does not arise in opposition to mediocrity, but as the fulfilment of a long tradition of practice. Articulating for the first time the argument that will later form the backbone of *A Room*, Woolf stated that 'the conditions which make it possible for Shakespeare to exist are that he shall have had predecessors in his art, shall make one of a group where art is freely discussed and practised, and shall himself have the utmost freedom of action and experience' (37).

By the time Woolf came to write *A Room* the background of this discussion was erased and what remained was a primary digression or diversion from the question of women and fiction to that of the material and historical conditions that are necessary if women are to produce their own equivalent of Shakespeare. Within the logic of *A Room*, this insistence on the production of a female Shakespeare comes into constant clash with the need to redefine the very notion of artistic and cultural value that would put Shakespeare at the pinnacle of national achievement. So although Woolf insists on casting Shakespeare as the supreme embodiment of the androgynous ideal, warning that 'it is fatal for anyone who writes to think of their sex' (*RO*, 136), she also speculates that 'the book has somehow to be adapted to the body' and that 'women's books should be shorter, more concentrated, than those of men' (101).

This clash between different systems of values is precariously resolved within *A Room* by drawing in the audience of women undergraduates from Cambridge as the anonymous predecessors that will pave the way for the emergence of a female equivalent of Shakespeare. Having shed the various fictional identities she had assumed throughout *A Room*, in the last few pages of the essay the narrator takes up the voice and position of a conventional public speaker and concludes with what she acknowledges is a classical and dutiful peroration. Building on her claim that 'masterpieces are not single and solitary births' but require 'many years of thinking in common, of thinking by the body of the people' (85), she addresses her original audience of young women studying at Cambridge by asking them to devote their 'very laborious and highly obscure career[s]' (148) to the constitution of a collective body from which Shakespeare's fictional sister will be reborn, 'drawing her life from the lives of the unknown who were her forerunners, as her brother did before her' (149).

To fulfil the promise embodied by Judith's myth, the professional young women of Woolf's time are invited to 'live another century or so . . . and have five hundred a year each', to learn 'the habit of freedom' and to 'escape a little from the common sitting room' (148–9), so that they might produce for their successors the conditions which the poor Mrs Seton was unable to provide for her daughters. Those conditions will form the inheritance, both financial and spiritual, that will enable their own future daughters to become the (androgynous) women writers of tomorrow. As with Mrs Seton, then, the position of the audience of

Cambridge undergraduates within the text is essentially a sacrificial one, which sees them not as the inheritors of Shakespeare's mantle, but as the providers for daughters who, like Woolf herself, will be absolved from the need to earn their own living and free to produce art unencumbered by fear, bitterness and anger.

Implied rather than directly represented in *A Room*, this kind of relationship between professional women and women writers shares many of its defining traits with those appearing in other texts by Woolf, whether fictional or discursive. Throughout Woolf's writings the representation of working women and women's work is always complicated by a certain ambivalence towards professionalisation, which often becomes apparent in the contraposition between two characters. In *Night and Day* (1919), for instance, Katharine Hilbery's pursuit of mathematics is presented as a mark of the heroine's difference from the family's expectations and demands. It also distinguishes her from her counterpart, Mary Datchet, whose involvement with the cause of women's suffrage and political activism stand in sharp contrast with Katharine's intensely solitary and private pursuit of the abstract, non-human world of mathematical relations. In *Mrs Dalloway* (1925), Elizabeth Dalloway is shown to be torn between her own biological mother, who is identified throughout the text by her lack of professional employment and her role as a society hostess, and her governess, Miss Kilman, whose envy, bitterness and rage mark her as Woolf's own re-interpretation of a Jane Eyre-like figure.[5]

In the essays, this unease towards the idea of women's paid employment is often inscribed not in the interplay between different characters, but in the relationship between writer/narrator and her audience. Whenever Woolf found herself addressing an audience of working women, both actual and future, her identification with them and the sharing of common experiences were always troubled by a series of distancing gestures that set her own experience as a woman writer apart from that of other professional women. In 'Professions for Women' (1931; *CD*, 101–6), which Woolf saw as a continuation of *A Room*, writing is presented much like in *A Room* as exemplary of a professional activity, and yet exceptional among the professions in its openness to women. But where *A Room* was concerned with the history and even the pre-history of women's professional involvement with writing, 'Professions for Women' starts at a point in time when writing has become a perfectly legitimate occupation, in fact the least threatening of the aspirations and ambitions that can be entertained by a young woman. '[W]hen I came to write,' the narrator explains, 'there were very few material obstacles in my way. Writing was a reputable and harmless occupation.... No demand was made upon the family purse. For ten and sixpence one can buy paper enough to write all the plays of Shakespeare – if one has a mind that way' (101). Here Woolf appears to take up the position of those who insist that the absence of a female Shakespeare is not due to material obstacles, since the requirements for the actual writing are minimal, but rather to the lack of a mind comparable to his.

This fictionalised account of Woolf's own professional experiences reverses the argument put forth in *A Room* through the tragic figure of Judith Shakespeare. Rather than presenting writing as a dangerous voca-tion that might lead those who pursue it to self-annihilation, it produces the image of writing as an activity that does not involve any struggle for recognition or emancipation. Historically more accessible to women than all the other professions, writing is portrayed by Woolf as a spon-taneous and effortless occupation whose natural course inevitably includes publication (and, therefore, monetary rewards) but does not necessarily involve professionalisation. Claiming ignorance of 'the struggles and difficulties' that characterise the lives of professional women, Woolf admits spending her first pay cheque on 'a cat – a beautiful cat, a Persian cat' rather than 'upon bread and butter, rent, shoes and stockings, or butcher's bills.' (102).

This contrast between writing as a frivolous occupation and the basic and quite drab realities of other kinds of women's work institutes a gap or gulf of positions between the narrator and her audience. Like many of the characters in Woolf's fiction who are represented as outsiders to the world of working and/or professional women, the narrator of this talk stresses her status as an *amatrice* who has not had to undergo the kind of material battles that characterise the working lives of her audience. The only point of contact or identification with her public is given by the slaying of the Victorian figure of the Angel in the House, the idealised version of the selfless, sacrificing and unnurturing mother represented by Mrs Seton in *A Room*. The killing of the Angel is given as the only professional battle that engaged the narrator in her pursuit of writing, 'the one act for which' she is prepared to 'take some credit'. Yet, once again as in *A Room*, this act which figures as the right of passage from *amatrice* to professional is immediately traced back to 'some excellent ancestor of mine who left me a certain sum of money – shall we say five hundred pounds a year? – so that it was not necessary for me to depend solely on charm for my living' (103).

In the version of 'Professions for Women' that was posthumously published by Leonard Woolf in *The Death of the Moth* (1942), the killing of the Angel is presented as the first of Woolf's professional experience. The second consists in the much more arduous task of 'telling the truth about my experiences as a body' (105) without incurring the censure of her own reason, which the essay presents as the internalisation of men's control over women's sexuality. In the longer version published by Mitchell A. Leaska in his 1978 edition of *The Pargiters*, Woolf's depiction of the conflict between the woman writer's imagination and her reason is followed by a peroration to the audience of young professional women addressed by the talk. Aware that their progress will be impeded by the lack of female predecessors in the career of their choice, Woolf exhorts her audience to avoid 'add[ing] to your burdens a very heavy and unnecessary burden, the burden of bitterness' by deploying the novelist's tool, the imagination, 'as a specific against bitterness'.[6]

To help her audience achieve this equanimity, the narrator then suggests that they should try and identify with the men they are battling against, the dispossessed *paterfamilias*, who find their privileged spaces suddenly occupied by what they are used to consider as household servants:

> Let us imagine how it appears to him. He has been out all day in the city earning his living, and he comes home at night expecting repose and comfort to find that his servants – the women servants – have taken possession of the house. He goes into the library... and finds the kitchen maid curled up in the arm chair reading Plato. He goes into the kitchen and there is the cook engaged in writing a Mass in B flat. He goes into the billiard room and finds the parlour maid knocking up a fine break at the table. He goes into the bed room and there is the housemaid working out a mathematical problem. What is he to do?[7]

With its ironic slant, this scene remains poised between two conflicting interpretations. On the one hand, the relocation of the fight for women's emancipation within the confines of the upper middle-class household works to professionalise the women servants by drawing a parallel between them and the audience of young professionals to whom the talk is addressed. In this sense, this fictional, ironic account of their professional battles aims to bring to light the connection between the domestic space from which the young professionals might be seen to escape and the public arena where their struggles for emancipation and recognition become visible. It is an anticipation of the argument Woolf will later develop in *Three Guineas* (1938) about the invisible thread that connects the 'servilities' of the private home to those of the public sphere (*TG*, 364). Unlike *Three Guineas*, though, which restricts its focus and its audience to that of a specific section of the body politic,[8] this scene suggests instead that the experience of professionalisation and the struggles and difficulties that attend to it cut across distinctions of class, linking the young women who are beginning to practise as 'barristers, architects, decorators, solicitors'[9] to women 'in service' as their unrecognised predecessors.

But this more positive interpretation of the analogy between professionals and servants is made problematic by the narrator's own positioning *vis-à-vis* her audience. In exhorting her audience: 'Imagine what it is like to be a man. Put yourselves into his shoes for a moment',[10] Woolf is herself taking up the voice and role of the Victorian Angel, with her calls to empathic identification with others at the cost of her own selfhood. Just like the Angel had enjoined the young journalist to ' "Be sympathetic; be tender; flatter; deceive" ' (*CD*, 101), so the narrator in her turn uses this imaginative reconstruction of the *paterfamilias*'s plight as the basis of her final peroration: 'Do not therefore be angry; be patient; be amused.'[11] The censuring of anger recalls the indictment of Charlotte Brontë's *Jane Eyre* in *A Room* which is here revealed as part of a class-bound ideal of femininity requiring that anger be substituted by 'patience' and 'amusement', a position of slight detachment rather than full-blown involvement.

This deployment of literature as a tool for the dissemination and practising of a certain ideal of femininity indicates the existence of a slippage between that ideal and the aesthetic norm of androgyny that barred the expression of anger and resentment from the literary field in *A Room*. This slippage, which is not visible in *A Room*, becomes, though, more prominent whenever Woolf finds herself engaged in the representation of working-class women and, in particular, in 'Memories of a Working Women's Guild' (1931; *WE*, 133–47). Woolf wrote the essay in response to Margaret Llewellyn Davies's invitation to write an introduction to *Life as We Have Known It*, a collection of autobiographical fragments by working-class women. The essay is divided into two parts. In the first one Woolf recollects her impressions of attending a Congress of Co-operative Women in Newcastle in 1913 and her subsequent meeting with Llewellyn Davies in London. In the other she relates her impression and evaluation of the material collected in the book in relation to her memories of the Congress. Thus, the structure of the essay exploits the ambiguity that is first introduced by the title, indicating that the memories here in question are both the working women's personal recollections of their own lives and Woolf's own memories of her first, direct encounter with those women.

At the same time, though, this doubling up of the narrative point of view dramatises within the essay the tensions and ambivalences which we saw structured the relationship of narrator/speaker to audience in *A Room* and 'Professions for Women'. 'Memories' differs from those two essays in that here the narrator herself is initially placed as a spectator/audience to the 1913 Congress of Co-operative Women and then as the reader/recipient of the autobiographical recollections of those same women. In the first part of the essay, Woolf's reflections upon the differences that divide her from the women speaking at the Congress are prompted by her experience of attending the Congress in the capacity of observer and member of the audience rather than delegate. Finding herself alienated by and uninterested in the demands for social improvements put forth by the speakers, Woolf both explains and enacts her detachment by describing the differences in material conditions between her own life and those of the delegates.

In charting the distance between herself and the women she is there to observe, Woolf employs a series of bodily metaphors which translate that gap into a split between mind and body. The demands for improved material conditions put forth by the Co-operative women are consequently assimilated by Woolf to the workings of a giant mind encompassing the whole country, to which she opposes her own embodied condition, stressing the importance of a bodily reaction of sympathy when opposed to a merely imagined identification. In a way that reverses the invitation to sympathise with men's plight she had proffered to the young professional women of the London/National Society for Women's Service, Woolf admits that '[a]ll these questions... which matter so intensely to the people here, questions of sanitation and education and wages, this demand for an extra shilling, for another year at school, for eight hours instead of nine behind a counter or in a mill leave me, in my own blood and bones, untouched' (135).

First introduced by Woolf in this context, the question of embodiment becomes one of the central themes around which the whole essay is organised and articulates some of the difficulties that had already been implied by the discussion of women's sexuality and its relationship to writing in *A Room* and 'Professions for Women'. Here bodies and aesthetic values are not essentially compatible. Instead of the woman fishing along the banks of the imagination for the deepest truths about women's sexuality, 'Memories' proposes the image of a collective body of women delegates as a metaphor for the rigidity and lifelessness of a military operation. Woolf's recollections of the Congress stress that 'there was something military in the regularity' with which one delegate followed another, as '[a] bell struck; a figure rose; mounted the platform; spoke for precisely five minutes; she descended'. Characterised by an unbending division of time and functions, the operation has the women delegates respond to its signals as if they were automatons. Comparing the delegates to 'marksmen' who 'sometimes...missed' and 'sometimes...hit', Woolf conveys both the sense of threat associated with 'the carefulness of the aim' and, at the same time, her reservations about the nature of those ends (134).

Coming as it does in connection with practical requests for improved material conditions and reforms of current laws, this comparison between the Guild women and the military implicitly links the Congress to the activities of Emily Pankhurst and her support for violent action both in relation to the question of women's suffrage and to England's participation in the First World War. In sharp contrast to the world of conscientious objectors and pacifists inhabited by Woolf herself, these analogies between an organised women's movement and military organisation all contribute to enlarge the distance that separates Woolf from the working women by quite literally unsexing them and making femininity a privilege linked to class position: 'They touched nothing lightly. They gripped papers and pencils as if they were brooms. Their faces were firm and heavily folded and lined with deep lines' (137).

References to the divergence of working women's bodies from a class-bound ideal of womanliness abound throughout the essay and are ascribed by Woolf herself to the difference in working and living conditions. The difference between signing a cheque to pay one's own bills and doing one's own washing in a tub filled with hot water is translated by Woolf into different physical traits, so that the conference delegates are depicted as strong and capable muscular bodies which evoke, by implication, the frail elegance and refinement of the body of their observer. Thus the bodies of working women are seen by Woolf as entirely and completely defined by their position in the social division of labour:

> They plunged their arms in hot water and scrubbed the clothes themselves. In consequence their bodies were thick-set and muscular, their hands were large, and they had the slow emphatic gestures of people who are often stiff and fall tired in a heap on hard-backed chairs.... It seemed as if their muscles were always taut and on the stretch. Their eyes looked as if they were always set on something

actual...Their lips never expressed the lighter and more detached emotions that come into play when the mind is perfectly at ease about the present. No, they were not in the least detached and cosmopolitan.

(137)

Reading the working women's bodies as if they were books, Woolf can only find in their lines and characters the signs of a homogeneous living experience that has left no space for individual variations of build or complexion. In the essay, the living conditions experienced by the Guild women are translated into the image of a physically powerful but inelegant collective body which is contrasted with a type of femininity defined as the aesthetic cultivation of delicacies and refinements of expression and behaviour.

This gulf that separates the working women from their ladylike observer signifies not just Woolf's class allegiances and her inability to sympathise with the conditions of working-class women, but also a serious disturbance in the allocation of gendered identities and positions within the essay. If the delegates at the conference are, as we saw, initially represented in military terms (always, for Woolf, the mark of mindless masculinity), their subsequent association with the domestic spaces of washing and cooking produces in its turn an ironic realisation of the ideal of physical rather than mental androgyny.[12] In this sense, they can be seen to function as the other side of the search for a female equivalent of Shakespeare that redefines androgyny not as the transcendence of historical and sexual limitations but as their embodiment. In the situation portrayed in 'Memories of a Working Women's Guild', androgyny stops functioning as a means of liberation from history and/or unification of opposing tendencies, and takes on the full weight of the contradictions experienced by Woolf in her position as the observer and then reporter of a gathering of working-class women.

In a movement that recalls the relief from conflicting pulls experienced by the narrator of *A Room* at the sight of a couple getting into a taxi together, the problems posed by the working women find a sudden resolution as the essay turns from Woolf's own recollections of the Congress to the memories and personal testimonies offered by the working women themselves. Suddenly illuminated by the light of personal testimony, the faces which Woolf had previously read as an uninterrupted expanse of hot-water tubs and cooking-pots stop being chained to their material conditions and take on something of the imaginative strength of fictional characters. The women that emerge from their autobiographical recollections are 'no longer addressing a large meeting in Newcastle from a platform, dressed in their best clothes' in an environment that had unsexed them in the eyes of their upper middle-class spectator. They are rather relocated within a private space, 'into the four-roomed houses of miners, into the homes of small shopkeepers and agricultural labourers', and in the working practices and conditions of a bygone era, 'into the fields and factories of fifty and sixty years ago' (*WE*, 142).

Turned into a route of access to the social history of the country, the autobiographical papers in Davies's book are reworked by Woolf into a larger narrative celebrating the survival of the human spirit in the harshest of conditions.[13] As Woolf herself sets out to supply a common theme linking the autobiographical fragments together, the working women undergo a slow transformation from automatons to human beings whose defining characteristic is the ability to experience beauty. In place of the narrowly utilitarian and materialistic terms set out at the Congress, Davies's book outlines the existence of an alternative dimension where the aesthetic experience becomes the repository of the human spirit: 'Put girls into a factory... when they are fourteen and their eyes will turn to the window and they will be happy because, as the workroom is six storeys high, the sun can be seen breaking over the hills' (143).

This celebration of the reparatory power of art opens up a point of tension within Woolf's aesthetic. On the one hand, the autobiographical impulse of the Guild women is presented as a means of liberating them from the material and physical restrictions of their conditions as working women. On the other, there is the notion of the androgynous mind set out in *A Room*, with its emphasis on the transcendence of personal experience as the necessary precondition for the creation of art. This tension is at the source of Woolf's hesitations and equivocations in the essay, which reproduces in the shifts of temporal perspective and authorial position the ambivalence at play in her historical situation as a spectator at the 1913 Congress. It will come increasingly under pressure during the decade that followed the writing of the essay, when Woolf will find herself the object of attacks as the representative of an excessively refined sensibility with no understanding or concern for the material conditions of life.

Woolf's response to these attacks will be to attempt to forge an alliance between women writers and the working classes as equally excluded from the realms of privilege inhabited by the young male writers of the 1930s. As she points out in 'The Leaning Tower' (1940;

WE, 159–78), while speaking in favour of the disposessed, the poets of the 1930s still continued to enjoy the privileges of an education and life style which inevitably skewed their angle of vision and their perspective. And yet this strategic alliance between women writers and working classes as 'commoners, outsiders' (178) is based itself on the transformation of the notion of the common reader, which is invoked by Woolf in this essay, into that of the outsider as defined in *Three Guineas*. Although Woolf presents them as synonyms, the two terms are in fact both semantically and in terms of her own definitions closer to antitheses, one underscoring the universality and the shared character of the experience of reading literature as a private individual, the other marking a clear separation between society as such and its margins. It is this conflict between commonality of experience and unbridgeable difference which Woolf voices in *Three Guineas*, the essay which marks the collapse of the strategies of mediation and reconciliation symbolised by the androgynous mind and thus opens up the search for alternative ways of articulating communal identities that will occupy Woolf in the last years of her life.

Art and Feminist Propaganda: *Three Guineas*

Although clearly related in content and setting, Woolf's two booklength essays are very different kinds of writing from the point of view both of form and of tone. Where *A Room* is playful and ironic, *Three Guineas* is dead serious and sarcastic at best; while the latter insists upon the truth of facts and photographs, the former relies on fiction and charm; where *A Room* is rich in images and narrative skill, *Three Guineas* presents the same argument three times over, in a progressively tighter and tighter circle that risks to strangle its readers in the monotony of its tone. Perhaps more significantly or in addition to all these discrepancies, there is in *Three Guineas* no equivalent of the hopeful message of reconciliation and resolution of conflict which *A Room* provides with the androgynous ideal and the image of the couple getting into a taxi together: *Three Guineas* seems, indeed, to signal the end of Woolf's reliance on marriage and heterosexual union as a prototype for the resolution of conflicts and splits.[14] Overtly an argument against war and conflict, *Three Guineas* explicitly rejects any attempt at healing rifts and mending splits but rather insists on a strict separation of spheres between educated men and their daughters and sisters.

Written in defence of pacifism, *Three Guineas* is the most combative and most partisan of Woolf's works, spoken from a position which

Woolf herself narrowly and very precisely defines as that of the daughter of an educated man (*TG*, 155). Unlike *A Room*, *Three Guineas* has never occupied a place of particular prominence in the canon of Woolf's work and was in fact received at publication as an eccentric and rather anachronistic pamphlet both by members of her family and by declared enemies.[15] In more recent years, though, *Three Guineas* has undergone a sort of critical re-evaluation that has linked it to *A Room* in its preoccupation with issues of sexual politics and their relation to the structures of power in British society. Reversing the charge of anachronism levelled at it in the 1930s, recent feminist readings of *Three Guineas* have tended to celebrate Woolf's foresight in her analysis of the connections that link patriarchy to Fascism as cultural and political systems that rest upon and promote a strict division of roles between the sexes.[16] In the case both of the initial reactions and of later reappraisals, however, the focus of discussion has always been the argument Woolf puts forth in this essay, implicitly making the question of the form the argument takes irrelevant or, at the very least, secondary to the meaning of *Three Guineas*.

In some respects, this very clear-cut separation of the politics of *Three Guineas* from its form reflects the political and historical climate of Britain in the 1930s, when a younger generation of poets and critics started to question the strong interest in form that had characterised the writing of the 1920s. While in the previous decade Woolf had criticised Bennett, Wells and Galsworthy for their drab materialism, in the 1930s she became herself the target of Marxist and socialist attacks which questioned the relevance of her experiments in artistic form to the political issues of the time. Accused of an excessive reliance upon a nebulous sensibility rather than hard fact, for many Woolf came to embody the refined taste and supreme delicacy of a dying ruling class whose beliefs and principles appeared to be totally ineffectual in the fight against Fascist brutality and violence. As Quentin Bell testifies, in the context of the Spanish Civil War and the rise of Nazism pacifism took on quite a different meaning from the one it had had during the First World War.

Although conceived in the early 1930s as a sequel to *A Room*, *Three Guineas* was late in coming and, by the late 1930s, had become part of Woolf's response to the urgency of the political situation in Europe and her quarrel with the generation of young writers whose involvement with literature was qualified by their political allegiances. Where *A Room* is explicitly directed to a female audience of young students (and, in Jane Marcus's terms, potential lovers),[17] *Three Guineas* symbolically addresses itself to the kind of male audience represented by Woolf's nephew, Julian Bell. Bell had been brought up in the midst of a group of conscientious objectors to the First World War, but had developed throughout his life a critical attitude towards the pacifist ethics of Bloomsbury which became reinforced by the spread of Nazism and Fascism in Europe during the 1930s.[18] In 1937 he came back from China, where he held a lectureship in English, to go to Spain as an ambulance driver, where he was killed in the battle of Brunete in July of the same year.

Unable to understand the motivations that had led Bell to join the fighting, Woolf carried on her argument with him after his death through *Three Guineas*. A few weeks after Bell's death Woolf wrote to her sister that she was 'completely stuck on [her] war pamphlet' as she was 'always wanting to argue it with Julian' (*L* 6, 159). In September 1937 she recorded in her diary thinking about *Three Guineas* in connection with one of Bell's last essays, 'War and Peace: A Letter to E. M. Forster'[19] (*D* 5, 111); almost a year after his death she admitted she had 'always been thinking about Julian' while writing the essay (*D* 5, 148). This sense of an ongoing dialogue with Bell is preserved by the epistolary form of *Three Guineas*, while the connection with the Spanish Civil War returns in the pictures of horror that are invoked by the essay like a refrain.

As a defence of pacifism written in this changed context, *Three Guineas* treats the relationship between art and politics as one of the constituent problems it attempts to address not just explicitly but also, and more significantly, implicitly, at the level of form and in terms of its strategies of argumentation. Like 'Memories of a Working Women's Guild', it is written as a long letter prompted by a request for co-operation coming, this time, not from Margaret Llewellyn Davies, but from a male representative of a society dedicated to the prevention of war. This main letter in its turn contains two other sets of letters that have been solicited by similar requests for financial and material support – from the treasurers of a women's college in Oxford or Cambridge and of a society of professional women, respectively. The relation between the main letter and the two subsidiary letters is both logical and chronological, in that the narrator introduces their requests as a follow-up to the line of argument she is pursuing, but actually claims to have received them *before* the letter that deals with the prevention of war. Having thus separated the logic of the argument from the logic of the story, Woolf can then give her discussion the classical structure of a dialectic exchange where each of the statements made by either the narrator or the female correspondents is met by an objection which is in its turn taken apart and disproved bit by bit.

But unlike the syllogism whose structure it imitates, the argument in *Three Guineas* does not proceed in a linear, progressive fashion, but rather unwinds in a series of concentric circles which resemble the movement of a snake strangling its prey. With all its appearance of stringent logic, *Three Guineas* does not so much demonstrate the existence of a link between patriarchy and Fascism as state it as a matter of fact, needing as little logical proof as the pictures of dead bodies from Spain which work as the subtext of the essay. Woolf introduces these pictures very early on, at the beginning of the first section, where she is trying to establish the truth about the ethical value of war, whether it is as contemptible and horrifying as Wilfred Owen described it or as commendable as the Bishop of London finds it. Having surveyed various sources as to the merits and faults of war, she concludes that the scholarly or scientific approach does not leave one any more enlightened as to the ethical value of war, since '[i]t seems plain that we think differently according as we are born differently'. Yet, it is precisely this bewildering multiplication of points of view, the distance that separates Grenfell, advocate of militarism, and Wilfred Owen, victim of the war's senseless horror, that pushes the narrator to look for a shared value system, an 'absolute point of view... a moral judgement which we must all, whatever our differences, accept' (163).

Required to bridge the gaps between 'an educated man's daughter' and her correspondent lying at the other side of a deep gulf of silence, the intersubjective and incontrovertible truth that is invoked by the text is primarily to be found in the shared emotions of 'horror and disgust' (165) elicited by the pictures of dead bodies and destroyed houses published by the Spanish government which are described, but not reproduced, in the text. Woolf argues that as images these pictures need no argumentation to convince of their objective truth, 'they are simply statements of fact addressed to the eye' (164). Stripped of the veil of rhetoric, these photographs of war achieve in a flash that unity of mind and purpose which intellectual analysis and argument cannot bring about:

> When we look at those photographs some fusion takes place within us; however different the education, the traditions behind us, our sensations are the same; and they are violent. You, Sir, call them 'horror and disgust'. We also call them horror and disgust. And the same words rise to our lips.... For now at last we are looking at the

same picture; we are seeing with you the same dead bodies, the same ruined houses.

(165)

Healing the rift within that had been fostered by the analytical and scholarly approach to the problem, the strong emotions elicited by the pictures of the Spanish Civil War also effect a sort of sociolinguistic unification whereby male and female members of the same class come to speak the same language and therefore to share the same values. By imposing the recognition of a class homogeneity that is often denied, these photographs of dead bodies and victims of war act within the economy of the text as a bridging device that allows the narrator to address her correspondent through the gulf of both time and space which divides them and which Woolf characterises as the split between the private world of the Victorian home and the public sphere of national and international politics. As this connection or link, they work therefore as the visual equivalent of *Three Guineas*, turning its argument for the origin of Fascism in the male psyche from an hypothesis to be proven to a statement of facts.[20]

From this perspective, the narrow focus on the educated classes for which Woolf has so often been criticised has more than just a biographical significance, since it allows her to examine the connection between knowledge and power, education and class which is at the root of British society. In a repetition of the classical dilemma of feminist politics, *Three Guineas* swings between separatism and integration, envisaging the complete demolition of British civilisation as a utopian dream that must be renounced in the face of reality.[21] While inciting the women's college treasurer to burn the college to the ground in a celebration of women's resistance to assimilation by male society and its abhorrent values, the narrator is, nevertheless, caught out by her allegiance to the cause of pacifism which has curbing effects upon her radicalism. The women's college is reluctantly allowed to stand because without formal education women 'could not obtain appointments' and would therefore be 'again dependent upon their fathers and brothers' leading them to 'be consciously and unconsciously in favour of war' (*TG*, 203).

Led to withdraw her conditions by this reluctant recognition of the need for traditional education and degrees for women, the narrator still insists on imposing much more stringent and binding restrictions for the society of professional women. Practising a profession is not, Woolf argues, valuable in and of itself but only as a means to the end of preventing war. To realise this end, professional women must resist the temptation of turning themselves into mirror images of their male counterparts and practice their professions in accordance with their own values rather than those of their fathers, husbands and brothers. Turning her society for professional women into a sort of monastic order, Woolf demands of professional women that they should carry with them into public life the values that have traditionally been associated with women for as long as they inhabited the narrow confines of the private home: 'the four great teachers of the daughters of educated men – poverty, chastity, derision and freedom from unreal loyalties' (269).

Providing women's emancipation with a sense of continuity with their past, these four guiding principles are founded both in the private experience of human relationships which individual women have developed as part of their traditional role, and in the public equivalent of that experience which is to be found in great works of art. In an argument that clearly recalls Hegel's description of the master/slave dialectic, Woolf claims that having historically been the victims rather than the perpetrators of wrongdoing, women of her class have developed a higher kind of individual moral conscience than that of their male counterpart, who have used their power to indulge rather than curb their worst instincts. Taking Sophocles's *Antigone* as a sort of blueprint for the relations between the sexes in her class, Woolf draws here a parallel between Creon's abuse of power, albeit sanctioned by human law, and Antigone's transgression of that same law in the name of the higher moral authority invoked by her own sense of right or wrong. Opposing private and public morality, outward appearances and inward substance, Sophocles's *Antigone* presents a conflict of extremities that can only end in tragedy. In the Britain of the 1930s, Woolf is brought to the realisation that tragedy can only be avoided by bridging the gulf that separates Antigone's personal world from the public world of institutions and government.

As the role played by Sophocles's tragedy indicates, great art is privileged in Woolf's argument as a site for the exercise not of refined sensibility but of moral judgement. Located in public buildings and accessible to all, art provides the mediating element that links the private experience of submission and oppression to something located outside itself and rooted in history. Stressing the importance of preserving this art as available to all, Woolf also implicitly underlines the recognition of its value by a society that normally refuses such recognition to women's insights:

Go to the public galleries and look at pictures; turn on the wireless
and rake down music from the air; enter any of the public libraries
which are now free to all. There you will be able to consult the
findings of the public psychometer for yourself. To take one example,
since we are pressed for time. The *Antigone* of Sophocles...Consider
the character of Creon. There you have a most profound analysis by a
poet, who is a psychologist in action, of the effect of power and
wealth upon the soul... You want to know which are the unreal
loyalties which we must despise, which are the real loyalties which
we must honour? Consider Antigone's distinction between the laws
and the Law. That is a far more profound statement of the duties of
the individual to society than any our sociologists can offer us.

(272)

Far from expounding a doctrine of aesthetic purity, Woolf's deployment
of the *Antigone* effectively returns to an Arnoldian understanding of the
relationship between art and morality which is surrounded by danger in
the climate of the 1930s. As Woolf herself acknowledges in a footnote
appended to the passage quoted above, her understanding of literature
as the embodiment of ethics may at times appear to come very close to
using literature as a form of political propaganda itself, starring Creon as
the Fascist dictator and Antigone as either Mrs Pankhurst or Frau Pom-
mer. But Woolf insists that this kind of reductive reading would be
forced to leave out precisely those qualities that make art what it is,
thus reducing it to the function of a mere vehicle for a political message:
'If we use art to propagate political opinions, we must force the artist to
clip and cabin his gift to do us a cheap and passing service. Literature
will suffer the same mutilation that the mule has suffered; and there will
be no more horses' (395).

   In the context of the argument against male values put forth in *Three
Guineas*, Woolf's condemnation of propaganda as a form of castration
appears incongruous or at least puzzling, a sudden equation of virility
with fertility that seems to go against the grain of her intense dislike for
the valorisation of virility and manliness in British and European culture
in general. This disconcerting choice of words has been analysed by Jane
Marcus as the locus of an intersection between literature, politics and
the taxonomy of class which in the end supports rather than undermines Woolf's insistence upon a link between capitalist and patriarchal
forms of oppression. Marcus argues that Woolf was herself quite happy
to play the mule in support of the feminist cause and thus to align
herself as a woman with those who remained excluded from the

privileges of class and education enjoyed by her male counterparts. Redressing Q. D. Leavis's criticism of *Three Guineas* as too elitist and class-bound, Marcus insists instead on celebrating Woolf as 'a feminist, a socialist, artist and worker' without perceiving any conflict or tension between those identities.[22]

But while Marcus may be at ease with the image of Woolf as a socialist feminist, the one political stance she finds difficult to account for is precisely Woolf's pacifism, which she admits considering 'an ethical luxury, a self-indulgence at some historical moments'.[23] Difficult to reconcile with her interpretation of Woolf's politics as revolutionary, the opposition and resistance to war which is so fundamental to the argument of *Three Guineas* is for Marcus simply a leftover of the abolitionist and Quaker traditions that were part of Woolf's paternal heritage. In keeping with her own revolutionary socialism, Marcus condemns the rejection of violence 'as the strongest of the liberal bourgeois illusions because it pretends that violence is an ethical rather than a political problem, and thus allows the pacifist to avoid the idea of the revolutionary attack on private property'.[24] For Marcus, while pacifism is in itself a doomed stance, it was nevertheless turned by Woolf into a weapon of resistance against the enforced uniformity of the political opinions upheld by the male members of her family or by her friends.

By seeing pacifism on the one hand as a liberal illusion and on the other as a tool of feminist strategy, Marcus effectively reproduces the problem of conflicting and contradicting interests she worked so hard to eliminate from Woolf's political stance in *Three Guineas*.[25] If it is true, as Marcus remarks, that the pacifism of the essay remains incomprehensible to modern readers, it is also true that the resistance to war and violence is absolutely fundamental to the economy of the text and cannot simply be ruled out as a sort of excess that is marginal to the main thrust of the argument. In fact, and as we have seen, the need to prevent war acts as a corrective to the sort of radically revolutionary politics Marcus advocates, leading Woolf to renounce the complete overhaul of British institutions in the service of a higher cause. This is not to say, though, that Woolf's pacifism easily imposes itself as the ultimate good to strive for in a final resolution of the conflicting tendencies embodied and represented in the text. Woolf's insistence on the links between patriarchy and Fascism in fact represents an attempt to resolve a conflict of loyalties between the universal ethics of pacifism and the claims of the members of her own sex and class.

Far from representing *the* feminist position, *Three Guineas* plays out a confrontation between, on the one hand, a liberal understanding of feminism which would restrict it to the suffrage movement and the search for economic emancipation and, on the other, a more radical, separatist agenda bent upon building from scratch a completely alternative society promoting feminine rather than masculine values. The tendency towards separatism is fuelled by the white heat of legitimate anger and comes therefore in continuous contrast with the demands of pacifism, which not only bars the use of violence, but actually forces a realisation of the interdependence of the private and the public sphere upon upper- and middle-class women. As a symbol of this connection between private and public worlds, Woolf appropriates the classical literary topos of Westminster bridge, which has worked as a locus for thinking about modern life in poetry from Wordsworth to T. S. Eliot. The bridge founds her narrative authority and yet represents also the connection that has made it possible for what Woolf calls, in psychoanalytic terms, 'an infantile fixation' to grow into the international threat of Fascism (*TG*, 341). While the narrator is portrayed suspended on the bridge in the attitude of an observer, uncertain as to whether she should cross and join the other side or not, the procession of patriarchs marches on towards the inevitability of war.

Translating the march of progress into a tragic drive towards self-destruction, Woolf's image of the patriarchal procession also questions the value of women's progress towards financial emancipation which, while freeing them of the patriarchs' power, still subjects them to the less personal and yet all-pervasive dominance of the market-place. In the last section of the essay, Woolf finally marks a clear-cut departure from her attempts to reconcile the professional and artistic sides of writing by restricting even further her audience and constituency. If the daughters of educated men have the duty of learning a profession to emancipate themselves from their fathers, they are, however, firmly excluded by Woolf from practising those values that distinguish them from the dictators themselves. Drawing out a comparison that had remained implicit throughout her argument, Woolf points out that professional women are often forced to prostitute themselves in order to earn their living and therefore cannot be trusted with the protection of 'intellectual liberty and our inheritance of culture' (281):

> So to ask the daughters of educated men who have to earn their livings by reading and writing to sign your manifesto would be of no value to the cause of disinterested culture and intellectual liberty, because directly they had signed it they must be at the desk writing

those books, lectures and articles by which culture is prostituted and intellectual liberty is sold into slavery.

(288)

Matching the clear-cut distinction between art and propaganda she proposed earlier, this separation of professional women from those who enjoy an independent income is the founding moment of Woolf's alternative form of society, a sort of underground cell which would work from within to resist the spread of violence. As the true inheritors of Antigone's moral authority, the non-professional daughters of educated men need not join the procession or cross the bridge that brings the private home in communication with the public world; they are therefore protected from contagion by either infantile fixations or the lure of money. Their financial independence from both patriarchs and marketplaces singles them out as the repositories of critical judgement and discernment, making them capable of distinguishing truth from falsehood, fact from propaganda, good art from bad. Self-contained and self-assured, the daughters of educated men in receipt of legacies and private incomes cannot, like the college treasurer or the professional woman, be bribed and cajoled into supporting the prevention of war; they must be convinced, as the narrator herself and her male correspondent have been, by the plain truth of the photographs from Spain. If the connection between 'the photographs of dead bodies and ruined houses' on the one hand and 'prostituted culture and intellectual slavery' on the other is made clear enough, then, Woolf claims, 'the daughters of educated men will prefer to refuse money and fame, and to be the objects of scorn and ridicule rather than suffer themselves, or allow others to suffer, the penalties' graphically represented in the Spanish pictures (292).

Functioning as an alternative to the Westminster bridge of the professional march, these pictures thus join the daughters of educated men who have five hundred a year and a room of their own to their brothers in a recognition of common humanity and universal abhorrence of the consequences of war. Running over and above their differences, this recognition is constantly threatened by the violent emotions produced by the battle for women's emancipation, which here, unlike in *A Room*, are located in both sexes. Clearly sided and sexed, the narrator of *Three Guineas* is allowed to indulge in the partiality of strong emotions that had been debarred from *A Room* as possible threats to the authority of its speaking position(s). To the dizzying and seductive multiplication of narrative identities typical of *A Room*, *Three Guineas* opposes then a progressive narrowing down of its political constituency to such limited

dimensions that it risks becoming a soliloquy rather than an exhorta-
tion addressed to a social group. As the cumbersome diction indicates,
the identity of 'daughter of an educated men who does not need to earn
her living' offers only a temporary and very precarious reconciliation to
the tug of conflicting loyalties and divergent interests.

4
Sketching the Past, or the Fictions of Autobiography

Literature and the Scene of Memory

The restriction of Woolf's audience to the daughters of educated men in *Three Guineas* signals the end of her strategies of fashioning readerships joined together by the shared experience of private reading. Although *Three Guineas* tries to bridge the gulf that separates the daughters of educated men from their brothers, it also resists any attempt at assimilating its intended readership to the wider body of societies and international campaigns set up to prevent yet another European conflict. These two opposing tendencies are exemplified by the multiple and contradictory functions which the text ascribes to the Spanish photographs of civilian war casualties. Presented as the unifying testimony of the horrors of war that should bring together brothers and sisters in a unanimous condemnation, the photographs also work to inscribe a deep gap between language and vision, words and images.

As the gulf between text and photographs is also the gulf that separates the narrator of *Three Guineas* from her male correspondent, the essay reveals the extent to which Woolf's construction of the common reader and of other, related types of audience rests upon a coincidence of text and image. *Three Guineas* has in fact no equivalent of the metaphorical figures that in other essays function to embody their argument in one single image, like the trespassing narrator of *A Room* or the killing of the Angel in the House in 'Professions for Women'.[1] The images it does deploy, like the march of the professions or the casualties of the Spanish conflict, are divided into two sets representing the two sides of the argument: the horrors of war and the patriarchal institutions that still structure public life in Britain. These two sets of images are joined together not by a third one but rather by the argument of the essay, which is to say that the causal link that joins them is crafted through language. Although *Three Guineas* offers an explicit reflection of the ways in which words and images interact, it is the one text by Woolf where they remain separate and do not manage to coincide.

This coincidence, and the ability of words and images to converge and erase the distinction between writing and vision, is at the centre of 'A Sketch of the Past', the memoirs Woolf wrote during 1939–40. Started at the time when Woolf was working on *Roger Fry* (1940) and then continued while she was writing *Between the Acts* (1941), these autobiographical notes were meant to provide a rough outline of her recollections to be reworked later into a more finished product. But if the idea of the sketch that is coterminous with these notes suggests the sense of an unfinished and provisional formation, it also indicates a coming together of verbal and visual forms of representation which is central to Woolf's thinking about the relationship between writing and memory. In this sense, 'A Sketch of the Past' offers Woolf's most extensive reflection on the ways in which the creation of images both depends upon memory and structures its contents.

As a hybrid form, the sketch returns time and time again in Woolf's writings, cutting across boundaries of genre that usually keep fiction and novels separate from essays and criticism, and essay and criticism separate from biography and autobiography. The sketch appears in Woolf's writing under many guises, but is generally found to function as the visual equivalent of the text it occurs in, a sort of mirror reflection that concentrates narrative into an image. It can be Lily Briscoe's painting in *To the Lighthouse* (1927), the period tableaux of *Orlando* (1928), the pictures of horror from the Spanish Civil War in *Three Guineas* or the scenes from the pageant of *Between the Acts*. But the sketch is also the method of apprehending and communicating history deployed by Woolf in her *Common Reader* articles and her essays on literary figures. Omnipresent and all-pervasive, the sketch achieves for Woolf that coincidence of method and style that marks such diverse and heterogeneous works as integral parts of an *oeuvre*.

For a writer who usually displays an intense awareness of the technical and formal aspects of her work, Woolf has left surprisingly few comments on the idea of the sketch as one of her most pervasive and, perhaps, also most instinctive ways of writing.[2] While providing a wealth of information about each and every stage of her artistic development, diary and letters remain by and large silent on the topic of the sketch, even as they show Woolf drawing a quick characterisation or relating a scene observed in the streets. Against this inconspicuous background, 'A Sketch of the Past' stands out as the only text where Woolf turns back to reflect upon the meaning of the sketch to her life and work. As in most of her other works, the memoirs of 1939–40 look at the sketch in relation to portraits and characterisations on the one hand, and to larger scenes or tableaux on the other. But whether it is involved in the representation of people or of landscapes, the sketch always remains for Woolf the distinctive way in which the past is remembered and recorded.[3]

As we shall see, this intersection of writing, remembering and vision raised for Woolf a series of troublesome questions relating to the distinction between art and life. These tensions are also mirrored in the publication history of 'A Sketch of the Past', which was first published posthumously in 1976 as part of a collection of autobiographical writings by Woolf edited by Jeanne Schulkind with the title of *Moments of Being*. The collection included a series of manuscripts from the British Library and the Monks House Papers, all at various stages of revision. The manuscripts were identified as five separate texts spanning the breadth of Woolf's own literary career from its very beginning to the end of her life. The first of them, 'Reminiscences', was written between 1907 and 1908 to celebrate the birth of Julian Bell, Woolf's first nephew. Addressed to the still unborn child, 'Reminiscences' tells the story of Vanessa's and Virginia's interconnected lives from their first encounter in the nursery to the death of their half-sister, Stella Duckworth. A later group of three texts forms the Memoir Club contributions, papers written respectively in 1920–21, 1922 and 1936 and read out at meetings of the original members of the Bloomsbury group over the years. Of these, '22 Hyde Park Gate' follows on from where Woolf left off in 'Reminiscences', giving an account of how she and Vanessa lived under the influence of George Duckworth in the years that preceded the death of their father in 1904. 'Old Bloomsbury' traces the beginning of the group that took its name from the London district the Stephens moved to in the same year, while 'Am I A Snob?' turns its focus upon the present of writing by substituting introspection for recollection.

'A Sketch of the Past' is the last in order of composition but its subject matter covers the same ground already mapped out by Woolf in 'Reminiscences'. Because of their self-reflective character, the memoirs occupy a very central position in Schulkind's collection, which is underscored by the way in which the material has been organised. Rather than following the chronology of composition, which would have placed 'A Sketch' at the end of the collection, Schulkind decided on an order based on the chronology of the events narrated, attempting in this way to re-create out of these fragments a coherent autobiographical narrative of Woolf's life.

This editorial decision exemplifies the kind of dilemma that has surrounded the first publication of various biographical and autobiographical writings on and by Woolf in the 1970s. On the one hand, the autobiographical material is presented as a scholarly aid to the understanding of Woolf's artistic production; on the other, the very publication of writings that are generally considered as 'private' can be seen to stimulate the kind of voyeuristic interest that is not normally associated with scholarly enterprises. In Schulkind's case, the decision to publish these far from finished memoirs and recollections is justified by the appeal to Woolf's status as a 'profoundly individual' writer whose work therefore calls for a better understanding of her life; at the same time, however, *Moments of Being* does not come with the full scholarly apparatus of notes, footnotes and corrections, 'since to do so would have greatly impaired the enjoyment of most readers' (*MB*, 7).

This assumed tension between the scholarly and the popular, the serious and the pleasurable repeats at another level a distinction between different forms of writing that Woolf attempted to preserve throughout her life. Separating what she considered to be her major works (her novels) from the rest of her literary activities, this hierarchical disposition of genres is perceived by Woolf both as a necessity and as a problem. It is a necessity in so far as it keeps her fiction separate from more partisan and also more personal kinds of writing that do not correspond to the androgynous ideal of impersonality she expounds in *A Room*. This hierarchy of genres becomes a problem, however, when measured against the dissatisfaction Woolf felt for the form of the novel and her continuous search for new forms of discourse that would question its boundaries. As we shall see, Woolf's insistence upon the need for a hierarchical disposition of genres raises special difficulties for the writing of autobiography and memoirs, whose generic status is complicated rather than simplified by relentless attempts at securing the boundaries that separate the life from the letters, facts from fictions, reality from invention.

In this panorama of distinctions which collapse as soon as they are asserted, the notion of the sketch emerges as the formal solution that allows Woolf to hold in a precarious balance the diverging pulls of a series of binary oppositions. From the beginning, 'A Sketch of the Past' presents itself as an informal piece, jotted down in a hurry and located in the space between other, more important kinds of writing. Taking up the tone and form of the diary or journal, Woolf opens her memoirs with a piece of family gossip that has the function of belittling their importance and, at the same time, laying the responsibility for her undertaking upon the shoulders of her elder sister, Vanessa Bell. The origins of the memoirs are traced back to a specific point in time, '[t]wo days ago – Sunday 16th April 1939 to be precise', and to a remark by 'Nessa' inciting her younger sister to start writing her memoirs before she gets 'too old' to remember it all. Woolf gives in to her sister's suggestion mainly because she is 'sick of writing Roger's life' and hopes that the 'two or three mornings' spent 'making a sketch' might act as a refreshing digression from her 'proper' work (*MB*, 64).

But having thus created a domestic space to confine her memoirs in, Woolf is suddenly reminded of her own dangerous tendency to make of any kind of writing a professional and well-turned piece of work. To keep the memoirs in their place, she must exercise a stern kind of discipline which rules out pauses for reflection and demands instead immediate action. 'As a great memoirs reader,' she adds, 'I know of many different ways [in which memoirs can be written]'. This professional expertise, though, is seen as a potential threat to the very status of the memoirs as a provisional, unfinished piece of writing that functions as a digression from work. Stressing once more that the time to be devoted to the memoirs is strictly limited, 'I cannot take more than two or three [mornings] at most', Woolf thus gets rid of the professional considerations about form and plunges straight in: 'So without stopping to choose my way... I begin: the first memory' (*MB*, 64).

The implied contrast between the informality of the memoirs and the careful consideration of structure and form that characterises Woolf's other writings could not be greater. On one side, there is the suffering and the commitment required by Roger Fry's biography, which automatically and by implication place it in the realm of 'proper' art; on the other, the spontaneous and immediate kind of writing which liberates Woolf from the constraints of professional literature but whose very informality prevents her from considering it as 'work'. From this contrast between opposing kinds of writing, Woolf thus manages to shape her memoirs in the form of the sketch, a rough and yet true-to-life account of her own past.

But the strict and uncomplicated separation of life and letters that Woolf thus brings about becomes problematic almost as soon as it is asserted. On the next page, and right after she has finished giving a summary description of her first two memories, the question of the form – and, therefore, of the 'literariness' – of memoirs returns as an interjection and interruption to her recollections. Lamenting the inadequacy of the description she has just given when compared to the feelings aroused by her recollections, Woolf insists that the gap between immediate experience and its written re-creation can only be bridged by making the subject of that experience a part of the memoirs itself. Rather than presenting the past as a sequence of events disconnected from the moment of writing, the memoirs should for Woolf blend together narrative sequence and pure description, recollection and introspection. Thus, the form of the diary entry that initially signified the absence of literary ambitions has already, a few weeks later, become an informed choice defined by something more than a purely negative contrast with 'proper' literature: '2nd May ... I write the date, because I think that I have discovered a possible form for these notes. That is, to make them include the present – at least enough of the present to serve as a platform to stand upon' (75).

This understanding of the memoirs as the form that links the past to the present focuses for Woolf upon the issue of characterisation and description of the figures that peopled her childhood. Woolf insists that while a mere chronological account of events does not necessarily convey the essence of personality, personality in its turn is revealed throughout the course of one's life rather than presented as whole and complete at any particular point in time. This dialectic of extension and concentration is resolved for Woolf only with death, which acts like the ending of a book or a novel, putting a full stop to any further developments and thus fixing character once and for all. As a consequence, some of the peripheral figures that peopled her childhood and have died since are remembered by Woolf exactly as she saw them then, 'they have never been altered'. Their clear-cut outlines are compared with 'characters in Dickens', 'caricatures' which, while 'immensely alive', still do not present a great artistic challenge and 'could be made with three strokes of the pen' (73).[4] Quick and summarily executed, the portraits Woolf offers of these characters encompass their personalities in a few, overriding traits that admit of no complexity or subtlety. Like a Dickensian narrative, they stick in one's memory not because of their unpredictability, but rather as a consequence of their representative or exemplary character: they are types rather than individuals.

This contrast between the lasting power of generalisations on the one hand and the ephemeral nature of uniqueness on the other informs Woolf's very different treatments of the maternal and the paternal figures in her memoirs. As Woolf herself admits, the figure of her mother represents a sort of bedrock against which her theory of characterisation appears to break down. Having died when Woolf was only thirteen, Julia

Stephen should have left in her daughter's memory an impression as strong as that of any other peripheral character she encountered in her childhood. Rather than remaining fixed at some point in her daughter's past, however, Julia's invisible presence accompanied Woolf well into her adult life, until she was exorcised by the writing of *To the Lighthouse* (1927):

> I suppose that I did for myself what psycho-analysts do for their patients. I expressed some very long felt and deeply felt emotion. And in expressing it I explained it and laid it to rest. But what is the meaning of "explained" it? Why, because I described her and my feeling for her in that book, should my vision of her and my feeling for her become so much dimmer and weaker? Perhaps one of these days I shall hit on the reason; and if so, I will give it, but at the moment I will go on, describing what I can remember, for it may be true that what I remember of her now will weaken still further.
>
> (*MB*, 81)

In Woolf's account, three different moments in time find their final resolution through the process of writing her memoirs. Julia's death, the writing of *To the Lighthouse* and 'A Sketch of the Past' are all placed on a continuum where the act of writing first works to lay to rest the trauma of Woolf's early loss, and is then used to read *To the Lighthouse* as a (psychoanalytic) 'cure' for that trauma. In this sequence, the writing of *To the Lighthouse* comes to work as a sort of repetition of Julia's death, which leaves Woolf with increasingly dimmer and weaker memories of her mother. As Mrs Ramsay takes her place, the figure of Julia is returned for Woolf to the mythical haze that her untimely death threw back upon her.

In 'A Sketch of the Past', this blurring of features and the threat of oblivion that accompanies it attaches itself mainly to the maternal figures in Woolf's life, to the point where it becomes impossible to separate this sense of oblivion and erosion from Woolf's description of their character and personality. Both Julia and Stella represent for Woolf the essence of an ineffable femininity, a secret, unspoken and silent quality which makes them particularly unsuitable to a Dickensian treatment of character. Men, on the other hand, are often described by Woolf as 'types' embodying a set of traits or features that make them instantly recognisable as members of a certain group or family tree. From Julia's first husband, Herbert Duckworth, to Stella's widower, Jack Hills, to

Leslie Stephen himself, the portrayal of men as characters poses no great artistic problems to Woolf, who seems always to find the right pigeon-hole to slot them into. Herbert Duckworth, for instance, is described as 'the perfect type of public school boy and English gentleman' (90), insipid but inoffensive; Jack Hills 'stands in [Woolf's] mind's picture gallery for a type – and a desirable type; the English country gentleman type' (101), while Leslie Stephen takes on, quite predictably, the robes of the Cambridge intellectual, sharp and rigorous but 'lack[ing] pictur-esqueness, oddity, romance' (109).

This susceptibility of the male characters to utter and exhaustive description, to a final, conclusive verdict that admits of no further appeal is matched by the form Woolf gives to the memories of her father in particular. While her recollections of Julia are quite diffuse and never crystallise into any specific detail or event, the figure of Leslie Stephen is enclosed for Woolf by a series of scenes or episodes whose frames are incredibly precise and definite. Stephen's actions are not only always firmly located within the bounds of a specific room of the family home, but, to a certain extent, his very person is identified by Woolf with the gloom and doom of Victorian upholstery and furniture. Although Woolf makes some attempts at enlarging his character beyond the narrow limits of the Cambridge intellectual, her father remains for her the figure most directly associated with the years of imprisonment and frustration that followed Stella Duckworth's death in 1897. Impul-sive and temperamental, Leslie Stephen became then fixed for Woolf in the figure of the Victorian patriarch which clashed against and partly overran her more loving memories of him.

If Julia obsessed her daughter through her very elusiveness, Leslie Stephen left an indelible mark on her through the force of his tempera-mental outbursts. Both legitimised and encouraged by the Victorian worship of the man of genius, these emotional tempests are presented by Woolf at one and the same time as the sign of his humanity, of that surplus that made him more than just a 'type', but also as the mark left by a specific historical time and place upon his character. Thus, the trait which is eccentric to the 'Cambridge intellectual' tag comes itself to dominate Woolf's memories of her father as it crystallises in her descrip-tion of the terrible 'scenes' awaiting her and Vanessa each Wednesday. This was the day when, right after lunch, Vanessa presented her father with the weekly accounts for housekeeping. 'The danger mark,' Woolf recounts, was around 'eleven pounds' and, when exceeded, it provoked Stephen into 'an extraordinary dramatisation of self pity, horror, anger', which was directed at Vanessa, but to which Woolf herself was a spectator in a position that filled her with 'pity' for Vanessa and 'rage and frustration' towards her father (*MB*, 144).

Deprived of the sympathy and nurturing Julia first and then Stella offered him, Stephen found himself confronted with an undemonstrative and unresponsive Vanessa, whose very impenetrability exacerbated his demands even further. These 'scenes' became, then, symbolic of a cross-generational battle over the definition of womanhood and femininity, where Woolf's father, mother and half-sister stood for the Victorian ideal of the 'Angel in the House', while she and Vanessa fought incessantly to preserve their autonomy as artists as well as women. Although the Wednesday episode functions very much as the primordial example of this battle, 'scenes' always tend to occur in Woolf's memoirs in connection with the issue of sexuality and appropriate behaviour. As with the episode of Vanessa's affair with Stella's widower, 'scenes' always carry for Woolf the connotation of an excessively emotional reaction which is not so much genuine as inspired by a sense of propriety and decorum, a sense of outrage that is faked rather than felt. While they are in the literal sense faithful reproductions of real family dramas, these 'scenes' also circumscribe a somewhat artificial space where 'life' takes on the semblance of (bad) 'literature'.

Because of its operatic and histrionic character, the Victorian reaction to issues of sexuality in general and femininity in particular is seen by Woolf as a potential threat to the integrity of her autobiographical writings, casting a strong doubt upon the authenticity and genuine character of such a picturesque environment. Organised in a succession of symbolic or representative episodes, Woolf's memoirs show an ever-increasing convergence between her life-history and her fictional stories which can only be explained by recourse to 'irrational' (Woolf's own word) or magical beliefs:

> These scenes, by the way, are not altogether a literary device – a means of summing up and making a knot out of innumerable little threads. . . . I find that scene making is my natural way of marking the past. A scene always comes to the top; arranged; representative. This confirms me in my instinctive notion – it is irrational; it will not stand argument – that we are sealed vessels afloat upon what it is convenient to call reality; at some moments, without a reason, without an effort, the sealing matter cracks; in floods reality; that is a scene – for they would not survive entire so many ruinous years unless they were made of something permanent; that is a proof of

their 'reality'. Is this liability of mine to scene receiving the origin of my writing impulse?

(142)

This description of the intersection between scenes, memory and writing is the crucial point of 'A Sketch' and not only because it brings to the surface the anxieties about the erosion of the distinction between life and literature that run through much of the memoirs. Like the sketches of Dickensian characters 'made with three strokes of the pen', the scenes from Woolf's past are then both memorable and definite, fixed in time as well as in meaning. But what we have here also is a classical statement of the mimetic relation which insists that writing only imitates something that is already there in reality and which the artist receives as if she were a passive receptacle (a 'vessel'). Underneath all this and just about emerging through it, there is also, though, a certain intimation of violence, of 'irrational' forces at play which suddenly 'flood' this floating vessel with a sea of memories that threatens to submerge it.

It is at this point that a strong parallel between Woolf's understanding of the workings of memory and Freud's notion of the 'primal scene' suggests itself. In his 1918 study of the Wolf Man case, Freud argued that his analytical work had uncovered a particular traumatic scene at the origin of his patient's neurotic illness, which Freud, unlike Woolf, explicitly identifies with a description of parental intercourse. The scene, Freud was quick to point out, had not been spontaneously recollected as a *memory* by his patient but had rather been constructed through the course of the analysis. It emerged through the examination of the latent content of the crucial dream about white wolves which initiated the animal phobia from which the patient takes his pseudonym in Freud's account. The status of this scene as 'the product of construction'[5] raised, as Freud admitted, unanswerable questions as to whether the infant child had really observed an actual event or had in fact *a posteriori* projected his own sexual fantasies upon an innocent image of his parents. Freud himself wavered between asserting its reality and casting it as a fantasy; in the end, he inconclusively concluded that the question 'of the reality of the primal scene' was a *'non liquet'*[6], a legal phrase which indicates a suspension of judgement when faced with unclear evidence either way.[7]

In his seminal analysis of Freud's Wolf Man case, Peter Brooks has argued that this refusal to conclude represents 'one of the most daring moments of Freud's thought, and one of his most heroic gestures as a writer',[8] highlighting an awareness of the fictional character of all narrative constructs that is akin to that of major modernist writers such as Proust, Mann and, yes, Woolf herself. As the most famous and exemplary of Freud's case histories, the story of the Wolf Man registers for Brooks precisely the provisional, unresolved character of all types of biography in so far as they are dependent on narrative as their main structure of explanation. Rather than constituting a failure of Freud's methods, the openness of the question of the reality of the primal scene, and the attending issues of the temporality of recollection and reconstruction which it raises, represent then for Brooks its culmination, the major contribution made by psychoanalysis to the modernist interrogation of the significance of narrative to civilisation.

But Woolf's explorations of the form of the scene in her memoirs reveals that, at least in her case, the interrogation of narrative structures which undermined the distinction of fact from fiction represented as much of a threat as an opportunity. Her attempts to explain away the convergence of fact and fiction, life and letters illustrated by the memoirs initiate in fact a chain of infinite regression that only returns Woolf to her initial assertion of their distinction. Rather than describing the kind of open-ended '*non liquet*' invoked by Freud, Woolf's memoirs close off into a tight circle that cannot let the question of origins rest and keeps on shifting the level of discourse from art to personal history and back again.

Her belief in the existence of a form of reality organised and structured like a work of art is itself traced back to a cluster of three memories or scenes located in the St Ives of her childhood. These three memories are presented as instances of 'moments of being', that is, of sudden revelations that break up the fabric of everyday life to reveal the true nature of reality. While two of them are of a violent, extreme character, the third and central one represents for Woolf a revelation of the network of relations that shape life into an integral whole. She recalls looking at a 'flower bed by the front door' and realising that 'the flower itself was a part of the earth; that a ring enclosed what was the flower; and that was the real flower; part earth; part flower. It was a thought I put away as likely to be very useful to me later' (71). Through this memory, the child's first aesthetic experience is made to give birth both to her consciousness of living in time *and* to the mimetic philosophy of art espoused by Woolf in her memoirs. In clear contrast with the brutality and horror of her other two memories, the perception of beauty as a perfect integration of parts and whole showed to Woolf the way towards making sense of the traumas that besieged and marred her own childhood. Julia's, Stella's and Thoby's deaths can thus all be absorbed into a pattern which, albeit stark and relentless in its pursuit of the young Virginia, nevertheless gives some kind of meaning to the repeated losses.

Effectively indistinguishable from the act of writing itself, Woolf's insistent search for the meaning of life endows her subsequent choice of career with a strong sense of mission that almost turns it into a mystical or religious activity. Linked to the scenic character of memory, writing is often seen by Woolf both as an antidote to and a substitute for the act of remembering itself. As an antidote, its role is to bind together into a meaningful structure those disconnected episodes and fragments which are perceived as threatening when experienced or remembered in isolation. As Woolf makes clear in her comments on *To the Lighthouse*, writing has in this case a therapeutic function that is both a liberation and a relief. It is 'the shock-receiving capacity', Woolf insists, that 'makes me a writer' since 'a shock is at once in my case followed by the desire to explain it'. Writing turns traumatic events from 'a blow from an enemy hidden behind the cotton wool of daily life' into 'a token of some real thing behind appearances' (72). But this making (up) of scenes to stave off the assault of traumatic events also has the effect of eroding the distinction between memories of past events and their fictional re-elaboration, turning writing into a substitute for the act of remembering itself. If it is true that scenes survive the onslaught of time because they are real, it is also true that for Woolf 'reality' is an attribute that belongs more properly to art than to life.[9]

Given these premises, it is perhaps not surprising that what Woolf describes as preparatory notes were never re-worked into a definitive autobiography. Never conceived as an autonomous entity, a 'thing in itself', life acquires reality for Woolf only in so far as it is sanctioned by writing. Through this relationship of dependence, her autobiographical narrative takes the shape of a progression towards the moment of writing, a present that symbolises the culmination of a promise that was already there in the beginning of her life. As the text that performs and enacts this circular trajectory, 'A Sketch of the Past' works not so much as a prelude to future books, but as the preface to Woolf's whole writing career. In the world described by Woolf's memoirs, the sketch does not come before the finished picture, but is rather the seal that completes it.

Orlando: Literary History as Family Romance

If Woolf's memoirs never stood a chance of developing beyond the stage of the preparatory sketch, *Orlando* is the book that comes closest to giving an extended autobiography encompassing the whole panorama of her adult life. Ostensibly a tribute to her friend and lover Vita Sackville-West, *Orlando* exploits the collapse of differences between art and life at work in 'A Sketch of the Past' with the aim of reinventing Woolf's own genealogical tree as a fantastic reinterpretation of the history of English literature. In doing this, it translates history into a two-dimensional landscape painting that acts as a scenographic background for Orlando's adventures. And yet, precisely because those adventures remain characterised almost exclusively by their relationship to history, the background also becomes the only thing that matters in *Orlando*, thus producing the exchange between different levels of meaning and interpretation that give it its unique flavour.

As the central narrative event of the book, Orlando's sex-change from male to female functions as the motor for the book's unsettling shifts between foreground and background, appearance and reality. In this sense, the androgynous character of Orlando works both as the origin and as the reflection of the uncertain generic identity of a book which claims to be a biography but flaunts all the conventions of realism and narrative verisimilitude. As a disturbance of established categories and entrenched oppositions, *Orlando* also works to rewrite the meaning of androgyny in Woolf's work. It transforms her relationship to Sackville-West into a form of lesbianism that is not the antithesis of heterosexuality but rather an 'escapade' that remains tightly contained and circumscribed by the legal and institutional framework of marriage.

This coexistence of possibilities that are usually considered to be mutually exclusive is both cause and effect of *Orlando*'s delight in the collapse of rigid distinctions, be they epistemological, historical or sexual. Poised between two of Woolf's most experimental works (*To the Lighthouse* (1927) and *The Waves* (1931)), *Orlando* shares with the near-contemporary *A Room* (1929) a veritable relish in the seductive power of humour, which it seems, however, to celebrate for its own sake, without any further aims in mind. While *A Room* states its central message unambiguously already in the title cover, *Orlando* offers its readers no sure foothold, no steady ground for its own interpretation. As Rachel Bowlby has shown in her introduction to the World's Classics edition of the text, the history of *Orlando*'s critical reception testifies to the distance that separates its world of infinite possibilities from that of closed classificatory systems and fixed oppositions (*O*, xii-xlvii). Incapable of accommodating and accounting for the fluctuations that characterise *Orlando*, literary criticism has traditionally insisted upon a structure of absolute exclusions, whereby Woolf's fantastic biography comes to be considered as either a mere *divertissement* or a serious work of criticism, but never the two together.

One the mirror-image of the other, these kinds of absolute and clear-cut critical judgements return *Orlando* precisely to the world of fixed and immutable distinctions from which it so successfully escapes. And yet, as Bowlby points out, the impossibility of settling once and for all these opposing claims about *Orlando's* value indicates itself the irreducibility of the text's character as neither mere joke nor pure criticism. Just like its protagonist, who emerges triumphant and untouched by the ravishing of time, *Orlando* the book placidly refuses to be forged into either subservience or antagonism but retains throughout the character of a highly eccentric version of literary history.[10]

The first and most evident instance of *Orlando's* indecisive and fluctuating attitude is represented by the confusion that surrounds its generic status. Subtitled by Woolf *A Biography*, the book presented from the very start a series of classificatory problems, not the least of which was the marketing difficulty of selling an alleged biography as a work of fiction. Irritated at the booksellers' refusal to shelve *Orlando* as a novel, Woolf predicted a gloomy future for such a confusing article. 'But the news of Orlando is black,' she wrote in her diary, as shops insisted that '[n]o one wants biography' and were not swayed by the Hogarth Press's assurance that it was a novel: 'it is called a biography on the title page ... It will have to go to the Biography shelf' (*D* 3, 198).

Mimicking the back and forth movement of the either/or dialectic, Woolf's report of the exchange between publishers and booksellers ends up by looking like a parody of the system of logical exclusions from which *Orlando* tries to escape. Trapped in a world not of its choosing, *Orlando* itself undergoes in Woolf's eyes a sort of devaluation, as the difficulty of selling this strange ware is deemed 'a high price to pay for the fun of calling it a biography' (198), dismissing the pleasure and enjoyment she derived from its writing as a mere prank. Yet, even as a prank, *Orlando* still manages to scramble and upset those well-established oppositions that would make of its light-hearted and easy-going character a guarantee of popularity and success ('And I was so sure it was going to be the one popular book!', Woolf laments (198)).

Although *Orlando* subsequently went on to beat Woolf's record sales for *To the Lighthouse*, this link between the question of its generic status and the issue of its value (both monetary and artistic) reflects one of the central preoccupations of the book itself. Like the real-life Vita Sackville-

West it is modelled upon, the book's central character, Orlando, is an aristocrat and remains such throughout the many changes of fortune and circumstances s/he undergoes. More persistent than his/her biological sex, Orlando's social status is never really put into question, even when it appears to be challenged by the lawsuits that would attempt to deprive Orlando as a woman of her rightful inheritance. Having left England as a man in the seventeenth century, the female Orlando returns in the eighteenth only to be greeted by the law's inability to grapple with her changed circumstances. Her existence, and her right to ownership of the ancestral estate, are put into question as the courts attempt to establish whether Orlando is dead, or a woman 'which amounts to much the same thing', or, finally, 'an English duke who had married one Rosina Pepita, a dancer; and had had by her three sons, which sons now declaring that their father was deceased, claimed that all his property descended to them' (*O*, 161).

Suspended by the law 'in a highly ambiguous condition', Orlando becomes the embodiment of the kind of disjunction between reality and its legitimation that is at the centre of the concerns addressed by the book. Within the fictional world of *Orlando*, the rules of logic and dialectic upheld by the law appear totally incapable of accounting for an exception to the norm, leading the law itself to formulate a series of mutually exclusive and contradictory hypotheses. Prepared to incur ridicule in order to assert itself as the ultimate authority in the facts of life, the law is compelled in the end to admit the momentary defeat of the binary logic it worships as Orlando is permitted to return to 'her country seat' where she is 'to reside in a state of incognito or incognita, as the case might turn out to be' (161).

In a move that is typical of the strategy deployed by Woolf in *Orlando*, the absurdity of the lawsuits is contrasted with the total and assured recognition Orlando as a woman receives from both animal and human members of staff upon her return to the ancestral home:

> No one showed an instant's suspicion that Orlando was not the Orlando they had known. If any doubt there was in the human mind the action of the deer and the dogs would have been enough to dispel it, for the dumb creatures, as is well known, are far better judges both of identity and character than we are. Moreover, said Mrs Grimsditch, over her dish of china tea, to Mr Dupper that night, if her Lord was a Lady now, she had never seen a lovelier one, nor was there a penny piece to choose between them....
>
> (163)

The passage echoes with innumerable ironies. At first, and as usual, Orlando's biographer is given the task of voicing the banality of a simple reversal of the nature/nurture opposition, whereby the 'dumb creatures' are presented as paragons of intuition and understanding when compared to the imbecility of the law. In the face of Orlando's recent change of sex, though, this blind faith in the reliability of natural as opposed to human distinctions cannot be sustained and is indeed ridiculed as soon as it is asserted. Brushing aside the question of Orlando's sexual identity with a *non sequitur*, Mrs Grimsditch shows that absurdity is not the prerogative of the law and of more sophisticated kinds of discourse but affects any attempt at establishing a ground for authoritative judgement, be it that of nature or that of nurture.

This refusal to settle for the claims of either biology or history also means that neither of the two genres *Orlando* purports to be – novel and/or biography[11] – offers an adequate description of its status. The book opens not with the recounting of genealogy required by the conventions of biography, but *in media res*, with the kind of plunge into action that is more typical of fiction than of historical narratives. 'He – for there could be no doubt of his sex, though the fashion of the time did something to disguise it – was in the act of slicing at the head of a Moor which swung from the rafters.' (*O*, 13) But the boldness of this immediate start is counteracted by the aside the biographer addresses to his/her readers. Interposed between subject and verb, the aside functions as an interruption of the narrative flow which raises simultaneously both the question of Orlando's sexual identity and that of the problematic status of his/her biographer. It introduces the voice of the biographer as a break in the convention of the omniscient narrator which thus works to undermine rather than support the truth claims made by traditional biography. And yet, because the omniscient narrator here speaks not as a biographer but as a storyteller, the aside also disturbs any easy identification of *Orlando* with the genre of the novel and, more in general, with the conventions of fictional (as opposed to historical) accounts.

Having established in its first sentence an equivalence between the problem of the book's genre (biography and/or novel) and that of its hero/ine's sex (male and/or female), *Orlando* then spends the next two chapters in preparing the ground for the full deployment of its impact. In the early stages of Orlando's life, the disturbance of sexual identity and the confusion of generic status are presented more as a future potential than as an actuality. Orlando's fated love-story with Sasha and his subsequent retreat to the countryside are told in a manner that by and large respects the demand for verisimilitude required of realistic fiction, with only a few interventions from the biographer which, although puzzling, do not really disturb the progression of the story. While the biographer may occasionally speculate on the meaning of Orlando's physiognomy or comment upon Elizabethan moral standards, s/he generally enjoys in these chapters the kind of complete and total access to Orlando's consciousness that is normally denied to biographers. Like the river Thames in the months of the Great Frost, Orlando as a youth is characterised by a total transparency that flattens out even the most brooding depths of his psychology into the charming picture of the nobleman as an adolescent. Following Orlando as surely in the midst of King James's court as along the corridors of his ancestral home, both biographer and readers are lulled into the illusion of inhabiting the imaginary world he belongs to.

But the illusion of immediacy and presence created by the conventions of realist fiction is suddenly shattered as soon as the story approaches the climactic point. Orlando's removal to the Middle East coincides with the narrative revelation of his/her darkest secret, that sex-change which the biographer does his/her best to advertise as loudly as possible. Making the notion of *dénouement* quite literal, the scene of Orlando's sex-change represents the fulfilment of the expectations for a scandalous revelation that had been set up by the biographer's asides in the preceding chapters. At the same time, by transferring the notion of *dénouement* from the structure of the plot to its contents *Orlando* also exposes the highly artificial and implausible character of a life modelled upon literary clichés. Thus, Orlando's lack of surprise or astonishment at the sight of her new body highlights by contrast the absurdity and the excess of the biographer's fight with moral conventions. It also embodies Orlando's double status both as a genuine, albeit quite naïve, character in a story and as a vehicle for Woolf's snipes at both literary and social conventions.

This change in Orlando's status is preceded and, as it were, ushered in by another change in the status of the book. After the straightforward narrative of the first two chapters, chapter three of Orlando's life opens with a long proviso or note of caution from the biographer, who laments the inadequacy of historical documentation to aid the reconstruction of this most crucial period in the life of his/her subject. 'The revolution which broke out during [Orlando's] period in office, and the fire which followed' are conveniently blamed for the destruction of 'all those papers from which any trustworthy record could be drawn'. As a result of the political upheavals, Orlando's career 'in the public life of his country' has had to be pieced together 'from the charred fragments that remain', making it necessary for his/her biographer 'to speculate, to surmise, and even to use the imagination' (115).

Introducing for the first time the question of historical documentation, the biographer's cautionary remarks break up the kind of novelistic illusion that had enveloped the book and its readers in the preceding chapters. In a gesture that both prefigures and mirrors Orlando's throwing aside of the blankets to reveal a woman's body, the biographer here exposes for all to see that gap between events and their narration that had been covered over by his/her previous incarnation as the omniscient narrator of Orlando's life. Professing ignorance and a kind of (fake) humility, the biographer is now compelled to renounce the smooth development of a well-joined narrative for the bitty and incomplete accounts offered by the diaries and letters of first-hand witnesses.

Paradoxically, and with a move that is typical of the way *Orlando* works, this opening of the gap between events and narration does not so much undermine the legitimacy of the story being told as it establishes the only conditions under which this enterprise could take place. Neither biography nor fiction, Orlando's implausible life can only exist in a world that has been removed from the demands for both historical accuracy and verisimilitude. As the condition that makes possible the suspension of disbelief characteristic of fiction, the demand for verisimilitude indicates the extent to which even the construction of imaginary worlds is dependent upon a principle of resemblance to historical reality. By playing the conventions of the two genres one against the other, *Orlando* effectively manages to take fiction away from that constriction in order to define a space where quite literally anything goes – even the outlandish idea of a sex-change accompanied by a life that comes very close to being eternal.[12]

Although *Orlando* presents itself most openly and most obviously as a cutting critique of biographical writing, this critique is nevertheless accompanied by a deft excavation of the conventions that regulate the writing and reading of fiction in general, and of traditional novels in particular. As Woolf remarks in a diary entry that is often quoted in connection with *Orlando*, the book was initially conceived as her own personal reinterpretation of 'a Defoe narrative' that should have brought together and given expression to 'all those innumerable little ideas & tiny stories which flash into my mind at all seasons'. Provisionally entitled 'The Jessamy Brides', the book was to figure 'two women, poor, solitary at the top of a house', with the suggestion of a lesbian relationship between them. In stark opposition to the careful consideration Woolf used to give her other novels, this was to be written in a quite instinctual and immediate way, 'as I write letters at the top of my speed...My own lyric vein is to be satirised. Everything mocked. And it is to end with three dots...so' (*D* 3, 131).

While *Orlando* will turn out to be quite faithful to the spirit (if not the letter) of its initial conception, its final transformation from 'The Jessamy Brides' into the mock-biography of Vita Sackville-West stands in need of explanation. Woolf's choice of her friend and lover Sackville-West as the pretext for her literary escapade has unanimously been seen as a tribute to the latter and a celebration of the erotic relationship they enjoyed. In this view, the allusion to marriage contained in Woolf's initial title represents simply a satirical stab at an institution that could not accommodate and/or contain either Sackville-West's or Woolf's own sexuality. Quite appropriately, it was Sackville-West herself who first suggested this interpretation of Orlando's Victorian marriage in a letter which, with unwitting irony, she addressed to her husband. Intimating Harold Nicolson to 'keep this *entirely* to yourself', Sackville-West complained that 'Shelmerdine does not really contribute anything either to Orlando's character or to the problems of the story (except as a good joke at the expense of the Victorian passion for marriage)' and that 'marriage and motherhood' are not really compatible with the integrity of Orlando's character: they 'would either modify or destroy Orlando ...they do neither'.[13]

Sackville-West's criticism of Orlando's consistency echoes to a certain extent Arnold Bennett's reservations about Woolf's ability to create conventionally convincing characters in *Jacob's Room* (1922). Although she might not have been aware of it, her criticism measured *Orlando*'s artistic success against the rather well-known and long-established norms of internal consistency and resolution of the plot that properly belong to the tradition of the nineteenth-century European novel and of the *Bildungsroman* in particular.[14] While in that tradition marriage generally functions as both the motor and the resolution of the plot, in *Orlando* it appears to Sackville-West as an accessory that has been appended to a story that has no room for it. Neither of the story nor extraneous to it, marriage thus intervenes to disturb the exchange of tributes and compliments between Sackville-West and Woolf that had surrounded the publication of the book.

The criticism Sackville-West shares with her husband but not with Woolf reveals then a certain discrepancy between her own and Woolf's understanding of *Orlando* both as a book and as a character. On the one hand, there is Sackville-West's desire to preserve the integrity of her fictional alter-ego as a spirit who is free to roam the ages as well as the streets of London at night-time, unattached both in terms of personal relationships and with reference to historical reality. On the other, there is Woolf's need to place her relationship to Sackville-West within the frame of her lifelong engagement and involvement with writing and the history of literature. In the light of *Orlando's* continuous fluctuations between genres and genders, Sackville-West's insistence upon the integrity of both character and plot takes on the connotation of a naive reading or, at the very least, a misreading of the book that is in sharp contrast with the sophistication and literary knowledge displayed by Woolf in her writing.

Far from constituting just a cheap joke at the expense of the Victorians, marriage then works in *Orlando* as a complex literary *topos* through which Woolf negotiates both her position in the history of English literature *and* the terms of her relationship to Sackville-West. It occurs at two crucial points in the narrative of Orlando's life. In the first one, Orlando's marriage to Rosina Pepita faithfully reproduces the romantic and exotic background of Sackville-West's own family history and ushers in Orlando's change of sex. In the second instance (the one to which Sackville-West had objected so strongly), the rebellion and anti-conformism that had characterised Orlando's first marriage are reversed, as her wedding to Marmaduke Bonthrop Shelmerdine, Esquire initiates her descent into respectability. Having acquiesced at last to the demands of 'the spirit of the age' Orlando finds that her second marriage has effected a welcomed transformation: '[s]he was certainly feeling more herself. Her finger had not tingled once, or nothing to count, since that night on the moor' (*O*, 252).

The irony that is the distinguishing feature of *Orlando* reinforces rather than undermines the seriousness of the function performed by marriage in the life of the female Orlando. While at one level marriage can be seen as a form of compliance with and submission to the Victorian ideal of femininity, at another it effects a liberation of Orlando's individual spirit for the occupation she prefers. Unencumbered by the embarrassing sentimentality that had snatched her pen when she was single, Orlando finds that her new status inaugurates for her a season of happy and undisturbed productivity: 'Now, therefore, she could write, and write she did. She wrote. She wrote. She wrote' (254). Depicted by Woolf as a liberation from the demands of her historical circumstances, Orlando's second marriage is thus made to function as a comment and a revision upon his first, romantic elopement with Rosina Pepita.

Whereas Orlando's secret marriage had initiated the period of wild fluctuations that characterised her *interim* existence, her wedding to

Shelmerdine coincides with the settlement of the lawsuits and the final resolution of the question of Orlando's sex and status. The marriage to Pepita is annulled, the 'children pronounced illegitimate' and finally, but most importantly, Orlando's *interim* existence is brought to a close as her sex 'is pronounced indisputably, and beyond the shadow of a doubt...female' (243). Nullifying quite literally the effects and consequences of the first marriage, the resolution of the lawsuits clears the way for the reconciliation with historical existence symbolised by her second, Victorian marriage. Closing off the gap between narrative and events that had been opened wide by Orlando's change of sex, matrimony releases the female Orlando into modernity, where the present of writing and that of the events narrated seamlessly coincide.

As her biographer remarks, what is experienced by Orlando the character as a liberation from the strictures of historical existence amounts to a sort of death-sentence for *Orlando* the book. Eliminating at the root the conditions that make narrative possible, the blissful coincidence of writing and living that follows Orlando's wedding does away with the need for biography and introduces the section of the book that deals with the present of writing. In a clear imitation of Woolf's own fictional treatment of the modern subject, the last section of the book abandons the narrative reconstruction of Orlando's life in favour of a series of disjointed episodes that describe her experience of modern living. Jolted from the sparkling lights of Edwardian London on to the sensorial assault of the department store and finally back to an elegiac recollection of his/her long life, Orlando retraces the steps of Woolf's own artistic development from the more conventional realism of *Night and Day* (1919) through to the formal experiments of *Mrs Dalloway* (1925) and *To the Lighthouse* (1927). Displacing the expected culmination of Orlando's story in the award of a literary prize, this exercise in self-mimicry ostensibly works as a critique of the conventions of traditional biography, but also manages to push aside Sackville-West's literary achievements and substitute for them Woolf's own dazzling performance.

In the context of this unspoken rivalry with the object of her apparent admiration, *Orlando* can be seen to appropriate for Woolf's own literary activities the claims to legitimacy and rightful inheritance that are embodied in Sackville-West's aristocratic lineage. Once again, and as in 'A Sketch of the Past', Woolf's narrative of the Sackville-Wests' family history maps the same kind of psychological ground as Freud's theories of the child's fantastic re-elaboration of its origins. First published in Otto Rank's *Myth of the Birth of the Hero* (1909), Freud's short paper on

'Family Romances' stressed at the outset that the child's tendency to construct for itself an alternative set of parents partakes of 'the nature of myths' in its function as 'the fulfilment of wishes and as a correction of actual life'.[15] Originated by the child's feelings of neglect and rivalry with their siblings, these alternative lines of descent represented for Freud a means of avenging the slights suffered by the child while maintaining intact the exalted, idealised perception of the parents that characterised its early years.

As with all the other literary conventions deployed in *Orlando*, the family romance is both invoked and parodied by Woolf's fantastic reworking of the Sackville-Wests' lineage into an off-beat, eccentric version of the history of English literature. As it has often been remarked, 'Orlando' is a name that resounds with the echoes of literary allusions, from the French medieval epic of the eleventh-century *Chanson de Roland* through to the Italian romance *Orlando Furioso* (1502–32). Although Woolf's letters, diaries and reading notebooks carry no indication that she was consciously thinking of this literary ancestry in connection with *Orlando*, the book itself offers one cryptic clue that points in the direction of the Italian tradition of Renaissance romances. In the plates that accompanied the first edition of the book, Woolf chose her niece Angelica Bell to stand in as Sasha, the fake Russian princess Orlando falls madly in love with and is then abandoned by in his youth.[16] Angelica Bell is then given a special mention 'for a service which none but she could have rendered' (O, 6) in the mock preface to the book. In Ariosto's poem, Angelica is also the name of the archetypal *femme fatale,* who bewitches the loyal and chaste Orlando, ultimately causing his descent into madness and his undoing.[17]

Buried beneath the rubble of fake acknowledgements, Woolf's oblique reference to *Orlando*'s literary lineage shares the same paradoxical status that characterises the book as a whole. Working both as a joke at the expense of the scholarly reader and as an indication of the seriousness of her literary ambitions, the cryptic clue that connects Woolf's *Orlando* to its literary ancestry defines the implied readership of her 'joke' as a restricted circle of people 'in the know' that comes very close to resembling the Bloomsbury group. As Woolf herself indicates in the diary entry that first mentions the name Orlando, the book represents a point of transition between the focus on individual consciousness that had characterised her earlier novels and the interest in larger groups or communities that is evident in *The Waves* (1931), *The Years* (1937) and *Between the Acts* (1941):

One of these days, though, I shall sketch here, like a grand historical picture, the outlines of all my friends. . . . It might be a way of writing the memoirs of one's own times during people lifetimes. The question is how to do it. Vita should be Orlando, a young nobleman. There should be Lytton. & it should be truthful; but fantastic. Roger. Duncan. Clive. Adrian. Their lives should be related.

(D 3, 157)

Joining *Orlando* to the diary and both to the memoirs she will be writing more than ten years later, the *tableau vivant* envisaged here reveals the firm and inescapable connection that existed for Woolf between her artistic and her social ambitions. Staging her closest friends and relatives as the protagonists of contemporary history, Woolf's projected book mirrors the transformation of what was originally the informal gathering of a group of friends into the self-elected aristocracy of English culture in the 1920s. Like *Orlando*'s substitution of literary for social lineages, Bloomsbury's shift from the nobility of blood to that of the mind represents neither a radical upturn of the English class system nor a completely uncritical endorsement of it. As the site of transaction between personal and national history, Bloomsbury, like *Orlando*, does not choose either side of the dialectic but simply oscillates between homage and critique.

5
Images of History

Feminist Histories

As an attempt to write social history under the guise of fiction, *Orlando* forms a close couple with *A Room* (1929), Woolf's other main historio- graphic text. The two books share a consistent preoccupation with the question of writing English literary history from a position that is inflected by sexual difference. This preoccupation is articulated in both texts through the notion of androgyny, even though *Orlando* and *A Room* differ significantly in their interpretation of it. While in *Orlando* androgyny allows Woolf to occupy two different positions at the same time by presenting traditional historical narratives concurrently with her jocular critique of them, *A Room* deploys androgyny to reinforce a more conventional version of literary history that recognises Shake- speare as the pinnacle of national achievement. This divergence in the reading of androgyny offered by the two texts is also reflected in the different ways in which they articulate the relationship between history and fiction that is central to Woolf's representation of the androgyne. As a text that straddles distinctions, *Orlando* offers a vision where history and fiction happily coexist and tend to exchange places, but where neither one is privileged as more truthful than the other. In *A Room* fiction is established from the outset as the only form of writing capable of articulating the truth of women's relationship to, and place in, lit- erary history.

Originally entitled 'Women and Fiction', *A Room* grew out of two talks Woolf delivered at Cambridge on 20 and 27 October, 1928. No manu- script of the talks has survived, but from contemporary accounts and a later article derived from these lectures and published in *Forum* about six months later these appear to have been stylistically quite different from the final version of *A Room*.[1] They contained no fictional frame or scenes and, judging from the evidence provided by the published article, they were limited to arguing for women's financial independence by backing it up with an overview of the history of great women novelists such as Jane Austen, the Brontës and George Eliot. As the editor of the manuscript versions of *A Room* comments, in 'Women and Fiction' 'the situation of women at Oxbridge is unmentioned, and the anger of men unnoticed. There is no reference to the androgynous state of mind that, according to Woolf, a good writer needs . . . And there is nothing fictional in the article – no narrator or novelist named Mary, nothing about Shakespeare's sister.'[2]

The missing features that are so characteristic of *A Room* were added to the text of the Cambridge lectures through an extensive rewriting which occupied Woolf for over a month between March and April 1929. In reworking her lectures for publication as a separate book, Woolf integrated within their argument a fictional account of the experiences she had had while staying at Cambridge. The famous comparison between the fare of men's and women's colleges, for instance, was based on Woolf's first-hand experience of dinner at Newnham and lunch at King's College, although the recollections of those who participated at both denied either the extreme poverty of the one or the lavish abundance of the other real occasion. At the time Woolf was also engaged in the drafting of an article on the 'Phases of Fiction' which she had started when revising *Orlando* and which was intended as a reply to E. M. Forster's *Aspects of the Novel* (which also originated in a series of Cambridge lectures). The title for *A Room* came to Woolf while she was at work on the earlier article, whose publication was shelved to give precedence to that of *A Room* in the autumn of 1929.[3]

Born of her twin preoccupation with women and fiction, *A Room* presents a vision of history that stresses its role in the suppression and erasure of women's voices. Asking herself 'why no woman wrote of a word' of Elizabethan literature 'when every other man, it seemed was capable of song or sonnet' (*RO*, 53), the narrator answers by highlighting the discrepancy between fictional or dramatic representations of women, and the picture of women's daily lives offered by history. Quoting from Trevelyan, she remarks that while fictional portraits of women emphasised their power and splendour, in real life Elizabethan women found themselves subjected to routine beating, confinement, physical and psychological brutality. From her survey, she concludes, 'a very queer, composite being thus emerges. Imaginatively she is of the highest importance; practically she is completely insignificant' (56).

Aiming to bring together the fictional and the historical versions of the life of Elizabethan women, *A Room* then proposes the myth of Judith Shakespeare as its own fictional re-creation of Trevelyan's account. The narrator speculates that 'if a woman in Shakespeare's day had had Shakespeare's genius' (62) she would have been denied access to the education and freedom of action that is necessary to the development of its potential. Kept at home and forced to attend to her alloted domestic duties, Judith would have 'scribbled some pages up in an apple loft on the sly' which she 'was careful to hide' (61). Even if she had managed to escape the strictures of the patriarchal home, she would have had to face a world that had no place for Shakespeare's 'extraordinarily gifted sister' (60) and would have 'gone crazed, shot herself or ended her days . . . half-witch, half-wizard, feared and mocked at' (64).

As a mythological creation which embodies the nature of the relationship between women and history, Judith's story supplants the historical and archival research which the narrator invites 'some brilliant student at Newnham or Girton' to undertake by collecting the mass of information about the details of the lives of Elizabethan women lying 'in parish registers and account books' (*RO*, 58). In a movement that is typical of the strategy of indirection deployed by Woolf in *A Room*, the importance of this alternative line of research is apparently disavowed and belittled with a gesture that simultaneously asserts it as a radical critique of traditional historiography. Thus, the life of the average Elizabethan woman, Woolf suggests tongue-in-cheek, should be called 'by some inconspicuous name so that women might figure there without impropriety' (58).

As the ghost book that Woolf never authored, this projected history of the life of the Elizabethan woman reintroduces into the argument of the essay the questions about historiography and its relation to fictional narratives that are enacted and yet obscured by the textual strategies of *A Room*. Prompted by the apparent absence of female dramatists and poets in Elizabethan literature, Woolf's inquiry into the living conditions of sixteenth-century women indicts history as such with the repression and suppression of women's talents while casting fiction and the products of the imagination as their saviours. Thwarted and frustrated by the lack of historical information in her search for an answer to her original question, Woolf is thus compelled to resort to her myth-making abilities to fill in the gaps of historical documentation with the figure of Shakespeare's putative sister.

This substitution of an imagined historical book with a myth, this filling in of the gaps of history through the power of fiction and of the imagination is a movement that is typical of *A Room* and could in fact be said to be what the essay is all about. It occurs once again later on in the text, where the narrator realises that her prescriptions for a specifically feminine aesthetic to be modelled on Jane Austen's and Emily Brontë's achievements runs against the obstacle of the lack of knowledge about women's psychological make-up: 'And yet, I continued, approaching the book-case again, where shall I find that elaborate study of the psychology of women by a woman? If through their incapacity to play football women are not going to be allowed to practise medicine —' (102).

As in the case of the substitution of the myth of Judith Shakespeare for the history of Elizabethan women, this other, scientific study of the psychology of women is replaced in Woolf's narrative by Mary Carmichael's *Life's Adventure*, an invented work of fiction that is made to represent the contemporary moment in the history of women's writing. As one of the three Marys who are proposed as fictional alter egos of the narrator at the start of *A Room*, Mary Carmichael occupies in the text a position midway between that of Mary Seton, who appears towards the beginning of the essay, and Mary Beton, who closes off its fictional part. At first, Woolf's account of *Life's Adventure* appears to concentrate more on the formal characteristics of the novel than on its psychological contents. It is introduced as a possible point on a developmental curve that takes the history of women's writing from personal concerns and the need for self-expression to the impersonality and objectivity traditionally associated with a work of art. As such, *Life's Adventure* is made to function as a sort of test case for the future of women's writing.

Woolf admits, though, that when compared to the smooth and flowing sentences of Austen's style or to the even progression of her stories, Carmichael's novel appears clumsy and abrupt, full of jerks and jolts as well as sudden departures from the expected line of development. 'Mary is tampering with the expected sequence,' the narrator as reader observes; 'First she broke the sentence; now she has broken the sequence.' Although feeling as if 'on a switchback railway when the car, instead of sinking, as one has been led to expect, swerves up again', she is nevertheless prepared to give her author the benefit of the doubt, waiting for the 'situation' that would confirm whether these deviations from traditional expectations are being carried out 'not for the sake of breaking, but for the sake of creating' (105–6).[4]

Just like the swerve in the railway carriage, this passage signals also a change of criteria in the evaluation of Carmichael's fictitious novel. The formalism that had characterised the initial approach is abandoned in favour of a more functional type of criticism, where literary value is determined not through reference to a 'gold standard' but rather as a reciprocal relationship between form and content. All suspicions and misgivings relative to Carmichael's somewhat innovative style are dispelled as Woolf encounters the 'situation' she had been waiting for:

> And, determined to do my duty by her as reader if she would do her duty by me as writer, I turned the page and read . . . I am sorry to break off so abruptly. Are there no men present? Do you promise me that behind that red curtain over there the figure of Sir Chartres Biron is not concealed? We are all women you assure me? Then I may tell you that the very next words I read were these – 'Chloe liked Olivia . . .' Do not start. Do not blush. Let us admit in the privacy of our own society that these things sometimes happen. Sometimes women do like women.
>
> (*RO*, 106; ellipses in original)

Breaking up her account of Carmichael's novel to make sure that her audience is the intended one, Woolf here moulds her own argument in the shape of the imaginary novel she had been reading. Like *Life's Adventure*, *A Room* is full of interrupted sequences and elliptical sentences which thwart the expectations bred in its readers by familiarity with the history of literature and with the rules of genre. Here, the interruption signals a sudden shift from the objectivity and detachment that had characterised Woolf's initial response to Carmichael's novel to a jocular intimacy that presumes the existence of a long intercourse and common knowledge between the speaker and her audience. As in *Orlando*, the blanket of literary conventions is thrown aside to reveal, this time, the collective body of a secret society of women writers and readers.[5]

While Woolf intimates that this secret society has been in existence for far longer than it is commonly acknowledged, the public revelation of its existence is closely tied up with women's entrance into the professions. This passage from the confinement of the private home to the freedom of the public sphere has affected the relationship between women and fiction on two levels. As far as literature is concerned, women's access to the professions has meant a move from a male-dominated view of women's relationships and characters to a woman-centred perspective upon women's lives, with an attendant enlargement of the situations and events being represented in fiction. At the level of actual human relationships, the development of professional interests in women's lives has, Woolf argues, made possible a less claustrophobic and more wide-ranging interaction between women, one that is not dominated or deflected by their relationships with men. The dramatic revelation that 'Chloe likes Olivia' is accompanied by the less moment-ous and more prosaic observation that 'they share a laboratory', and, with it, an identity that is located outside the boundaries of the family home and which will, Woolf speculates, 'make their friendship more varied and more lasting because it will be less personal' (109).

Postulating a direct correspondence between fictional representation and historical reality, Woolf claims then that the change in women's conditions represented by their free access to the professions will also produce a change in the kind of representations of women offered by literature, as women themselves begin to write of women as colleagues and friends rather than as the objects of men's passions. Bridging the gap between fiction and history that Woolf had highlighted in her discussion of Elizabethan women, Carmichael's novel heralds a brave new world where the obscurity of women's lives will finally be dispelled as 'Olivia – this organism that has been under the shadow of the rock these million years – feels the light fall on it and sees coming her way a piece of strange food – knowledge, adventure, art' (110).

Aided by the unlimited freedom bestowed by fiction upon the imagi-nation, the narrator of *A Room* charts, then, a course for the history of women's writing which overturns the model implied in Woolf's account of the story of Judith Shakespeare. In Judith's case, the historical situa-tion was presented as the obstacle to the full expression of her ability to create fictions and thus give full expression to the imagination. But within the history of women's writing traced by the narrator of *A Room*, Judith's story represents in fact the symbol of women's unrealised potential which finally finds its full expression in the revelations and innovations introduced by Mary Carmichael's imaginary novel. Both conceived as embodiments of the oblivion and repression that charac-terise women's relationship to traditional historiography, these two tales propose fiction as the only discourse that can give voice and expression to what has been left out of history. As such, they both work as *a poster-iori* justifications of the initial, strategic substitution of the fictional for the dialectical mode, bearing out Woolf's contention that, when it comes to the question of women and writing, 'fiction ... is likely to contain more truth than fact' (5). Although cast in a tone that charac-teristically manages to combine self-deprecation and irony, this identi-fication of the truth of women's lives with the truth of fiction is the centrepiece of Woolf's attitude towards traditional historiography and is the source of the incessant search for an alternative way of writing women's history that runs throughout her career as an essayist and a literary critic.

This abiding interest in the writing of women's lives finds its clearest expression in Woolf's continual fascination with the marginal and half-forgotten figures which people the history of English literature. Captioned by Woolf herself as 'the obscure', these marginal figures form the linchpin of her historiographic enterprise, as both its object and the method which shapes it. Woolf's most explicit reflections upon the connection between 'the lives of the obscure' and the writing of literary history occur in the essay of the same name which was published in the first *Common Reader* in 1925 (*E* 4, 118–45). Composed by a group of three pieces which were originally published in separate form, the essay offers Woolf's own reinterpretation of the lives of minor literary families ('Taylors and Edgeworths'), of a fallen woman ('Laetitia Pilkington') and of a brilliant entomologist ('Miss Ormerod'). Uneasily suspended between fact and fiction, Woolf's re-visitations of these half-forgotten lives represent, as Andrew McNeillie points out, an attempt to confront and rectify the legacy of both patriarchal and personal history represented for Woolf by her father's involvement with the *Dictionary of National Biography*.[6]

In the version Woolf revised for publication in the *Common Reader*, 'Lives of the Obscure' is prefaced by a short introductory paragraph which sets the whole essay in the context of a visit to a dusty and decrepit country library. As a receptacle for discarded and unwanted books, the library is characterised by an atmosphere of slumber and old age that equally envelops both its visitors and its books. As 'the elderly, the marooned, the bored, drift from newspaper to newspaper', the neglect suffered by the books which line the library shelves is translated into an image of physical degradation, where the books act as a sort of mirror to the condition of the visitors to the library, and thus reveal the existence of an inescapable link between the state of literature and the interests of its readers. Rather than supporting the view that books are forgotten or die because of their intrinsic lack of artistic value, Woolf's image of the country library and its patrons manages to shift the burden of responsibility for their death onto the shoulders of posterity. 'Why disturb their sleep? Why reopen those peaceful graves, the librarian seems to ask, peering over his spectacles, and resenting the duty, which indeed has become laborious, of retrieving from among those nameless tombstones Nos 1763, 1080, and 606' (*E* 4, 118).

Their anonymity underlined by their identification by number rather than by name, the books which Woolf manages to recover from the rubble-heap of history are revitalised to the point of taking up a life of their own by their contact with an interested reader. Answering the question she imagined the resentful librarian should have asked her, Woolf adds:

> For one likes romantically to feel oneself a deliverer advancing with lights across the waste of years to the rescue of some stranded ghost...waiting, appealing, forgotten, in the growing gloom. Possibly they hear one coming. They shuffle, they preen, they bridle. Old secrets well up to their lips. The divine relief of communication will soon be theirs. The dust shifts and Mrs Gilbert – but the contact with life is instantly salutary. Whatever Mrs Gilbert may be doing, she is not thinking about us.
>
> (119)

Through this image of the dead who await communication and contact with the living, Woolf here maps her historiographic enterprise upon one of the classical topoi of Homer's *Odyssey*, where Ulysses is directed by Circe to visit Hades before he heads back for Ithaca.[7] Just as in the *Odyssey* the dead can only speak after they have drunk of the sacrificial blood offered by Ulysses, so in Woolf's reinterpretation of this classical literary theme the obscure who have lain dormant throughout the centuries are reawakened by the infusion of life brought about by the reader's renewed interest.

But in Woolf's reworking of this classical episode the effect of a successful resuscitation of the dead is to interrupt and check the tendency to imagine the lives of the obscure along the patterns long enshrined in the literary tradition. The reader's interest in the lives of the obscure is presented as a breath of fresh air which releases Mrs Gilbert and the rest of the 'young Taylors' from the stultifying grip of classicism and back into life in Colchester 'about the year 1800' (*E* 4, 119). Thus, while Woolf might imagine herself as a romantic deliverer of these literary ghosts, the ghosts themselves appear to oppose to such flights of fancy the reality of an everyday life that has remained untouched by the suggestions of literary models. As Woolf observes, the shape of these forgotten biographies resembles more 'the clouds of a balmy evening...thick with the star dust of innumerable lives' (121) than the clear-cut and well-defined forms of classical literature.

Even in the lives of the obscure, however, this kind of hazy and diffused representation is at times suddenly pierced by the appearance of a scene or a character whose contours stand out sharply from the background of anonymity and everyday life. The first part of the essay, which is dedicated to the history of the Taylors and the Edgeworths, is thus shaped by Woolf in the image of the pattern she discerns in the lives of the obscure, with the perfect anonymity and tranquillity of Ann Taylor's family functioning as a sort of backdrop to the biographical sketch of Richard Edgeworth. As a symbol of exaggerated and disproportionate egotism, Edgeworth represents for Woolf the other pole of the literature of obscurity, which she saw as inhabited by figures 'all taut and pale in their determination never to be forgotten' (121).

As the father of Maria Edgeworth, Richard works as the pivot that allows Woolf to effect an ironic reversal of the father/daughter relationship inscribed in traditional history. He introduces the pathetic motif of the failed patriarch, whose incessant attempts at leaving a mark upon history only served to highlight the exceptional character of the lives of those who surrounded him:

> Imperturbable, indefatigable, daily increasing in sturdy self-assurance, he has the gift of the egoist. He brings out, as he bustles and bangs on his way, the diffident, shrinking figures who would otherwise be drowned in darkness.... We see him through their eyes; we see him as he does not dream of being seen. What a tyrant he was to his first wife! How intolerably she suffered! But she never utters a word. It is Dick Edgeworth who tells her story in complete ignorance that he is doing anything of the kind.
>
> (123)

Effectively amounting to a manifesto of Woolf's historiographic method, this reading of Edgeworth's memoirs in spite of authorial intentions and in the light of her own personal experience of patriarchal institutions represents an *avant la lettre* example of the poetics and the politics of 'reading against the grain' which has been favoured and championed by feminist critics in more recent times. While Woolf herself does not name this kind of reading method as a feminist or even a gender-inflected one,[8] the advocacy of forgotten and anonymous lives in the history of English literature turns out here to have an agenda and a mission which goes well beyond that of an innocuous, antiquarian interest in the past.

In its original version published in the *London Mercury* in January 1924, 'Lives of the Obscure' comprised only the essay on the Taylors and the Edgeworths and was introduced by a couple of paragraphs where the relationship between these anonymous lives and the mainstream of English literature was made more explicit. There Woolf argued for the existence of an inextricable link between the mass of half-forgotten books which are too close to life to attain transcendence and the few exceptional masterpieces scattered throughout the history of Western literature. Seemingly subscribing to the classicist identification of aesthetic value with permanence, Woolf nevertheless insists that the survival of the great classics themselves depends upon the existence and availability of more impermanent and more transient forms of writing: 'For imagine a literature composed entirely of good books; imagine having nothing to read but the plays of Shakespeare, the poems of Milton, the essays of Bacon...Starvation would soon ensue. No one would read at all' (140). In Woolf's formulation, then, the very notion of aesthetic value enshrined in the classicist paradigm is radically reworked, as the permanent character of isolated achievements is shown to be inseparable from the transient and the impermanent quality of masses of anonymous books.

In her analysis of particular autobiographical writings, this interdependence between the memorable and the forgettable is translated by Woolf into the play between background and foreground which we have already seen in place in 'Taylors and Edgeworths'. While clearly motivated by a desire to rescue innumerable forgotten women from the sway of patriarchal history, the reading by contrast which aims to reverse the relationship between major and minor historical figures nevertheless represents for Woolf both an irresistible temptation and a problematic solution to the issue of women's historical obscurity. As she herself remarks in her commentary on Richard Edgeworth's memoirs, the reversal of the hierarchical relation between the author and his subjects transforms the narrative of his life into a series of unrelated and isolated sketches with no linking thread to unite them. Having to supply the links through the use of her imagination, the reader who goes against the grain is thus tempted to stray from the trace of proven historical facts and make up a fictional account of the past. Though highly suggestive, these improvised and unfinished sketches point to a region beyond the documented, where history disappears together with the foreground and the mythical or the archetypal takes over: 'But here we encounter one of the pitfalls of this nocturnal rambling among forgotten worthies. It is so difficult to keep, as we must with highly authenticated people, strictly to the facts. It is so difficult to refrain from making scenes which, if the past could be recalled, might perhaps be found lacking in accuracy' (123–4).

While 'Taylors and Edgeworths' manages to contain the temptation of fiction within a broadly historical frame of facts, in the last of the essays of 'Lives of the Obscure' the relationship of history to fiction stops being one of containment and becomes instead one of complete reinvention and recreation. As Andrew McNeillie points out in his notes to 'Miss Ormerod', Woolf's account of the life of the nineteenth-century entomologist is only loosely based upon biographical and documentary sources and is for the most part a product of her own extremely fertile imagination. Describing Woolf's ostensible quotations as 'seldom verbatim' and as 'inventions only indirectly derived from Ormerod [the original source]' (144, n. 1), McNeillie highlights the relative autonomy from the tyranny of documentary accuracy and faithfulness enjoyed by Woolf in the outlining of this particular half-forgotten life. At the same time, this knowledge of the fictional character of 'Miss Ormerod' helps to explain the strong similarities in both atmosphere and structure that can be found between this essay and Woolf's autobiographical and fictional writings.

From the start, 'Miss Ormerod' is distinguished from the other two essays of this group by a rather direct introduction into the narrative which signals a shift of genres from the essayistic and discursive to the fictional and narrative: 'The trees stood massively in all their summer foliage spotted and grouped upon a meadow which sloped gently down from the big white house' (131). Similarly, in place of the formulaic introductions typical of traditional biographical accounts, we are given a scene from Eleanor Ormerod's childhood which sums up the whole course of her life. The essay opens with a vision of Eleanor as a young girl left alone in the house with just a glass tumbler containing some insects to entertain herself with. Instead of 'shak[ing] the tumbler, upset[ting] the grubs, and scrambl[ing] down from her chair', the young Eleanor 'set perfectly still', her eyes 'reflective, even critical' and yet 'sh[ining] with increasing excitement' as she observed that '[o]ne of the grubs had ceased to float' and 'the rest, descending, proceeded to tear him to pieces' (132).

This first view of Miss Ormerod's entomological passion closely resembles in its violence other primeval scenes that figure prominently both in Woolf's fiction and in her memoirs, and, like those other scenes, also functions as a sort of compressed version of the narrative which is to follow.[9] As the child's captivated fascination with the grubs anticipates her career as a brilliant entomologist, so her father's brutal dismissal of her observations comes to stand as just the first instance of patriarchal domination and suppression, reinforced in this case by Miss Ormerod's own mother.

In underlining this fight between the forces of repression and those of affirmation in the life of Eleanor Ormerod, Woolf is once again making use of a way of reading which goes beyond the grain of authorial intentions to get at the meaning buried beneath the conventions of filial devotions. Following one of the very few genuine quotations from Ormerod's memoirs, Woolf expostulates:

> 'We deeply felt the happiness of ministering to his welfare,' Miss Ormerod wrote, 'for he would not hear of our leaving him for even twenty-four hours and he objected to visits from my brothers excepting occasionally for a short time. They, not being used to the gentle ways necessary for an aged invalid, worried him... the Thursday following, the 9th October 1873, he passed gently away at the mature age of eighty-seven years.' Oh, graves in country churchyards – respectable burials – mature old gentlemen – D.C.L., L.L.D., F.R.S., F.S.A. – lots of letters come after your names, but lots of women are buried with you!
>
> (135–6)

Playing Charlotte Brontë to her Jane Eyre, Woolf here interrupts her fictional re-construction of Eleanor Ormerod's life to draw attention to the discrepancies between the facts as deposited in the historical record and the truths of women's lives. Here, Woolf's embittered exclamation reveals that the marks of distinction acquired by the fathers presuppose the theft and murder of their daughters' creative potential. In this way, it turns upon its head the kind of father/daughter relationship that is enshrined in cultural institutions such as the *DNB*, where Eleanor Ormerod is summarily described as a 'distinguished entomologist' without an entry of her own, but subsumed under her father's life.

But if Woolf's attempt to recover women's lives from obscurity is motivated by the search for a lost inheritance, the means by which she sets out to effect this recovery of lost treasures are, by her own admission, fraught with perils and difficulties. In 'Lives of the Obscure' as much as in *A Room*, fiction functions as the repository of the truth about women's lives that has been repressed and suppressed by the historical record. Charged with the task of converting the fragmentary traces of women's existence into a story without gaps, fiction is used by Woolf as a sort of alternative version of the historical truth which is rooted in the imagination rather than in facts. This use of fiction as an alternative to traditional historiography is motivated by a twofold aim, whose different components are not always compatible. On the one hand, because fiction is not factual, it can be used to fill in the gaps of the historical record in relation to women by inventing stories (as in the case of Judith Shakespeare and Mary Carmichael's fictitious novel) or freely elaborating upon the details of existing lives (as with Eleanor Ormerod). At the same time, however, this use of fiction as a supplement to and a corrective of the existing historical record also implicitly challenges received notions about the nature and definition of historical facts and narratives.[10]

Whether aiming at the integration of women's lives into history or challenging the foundations of traditional historiography as such, the role played by fiction in Woolf's critical essays is nevertheless always predicated on its opposition to factual or historical narratives which confines Woolf's recreations or inventions to a region that is neither history nor pure imagination. As her sketches of obscure figures never coalesce into an example of an alternative form of historiography but remain mere traces of a lost possibility, so the failure of Woolf's historiographic project highlights both the opportunities and the limits of the essay as a genre which could offer an alternative to traditional historical narratives. Seeing in its extreme pliability and flexibility a source of artistic liberation, Woolf had found in the essay the only form which could accommodate the mix of fiction and facts which she thought necessary for the recovery of women's lives from the oblivion of patriarchal history. Unlike the novel, which shares with the essay a certain formlessness but a very clear epistemological status, the essay represented for Woolf an opportunity to explore a border area between dialectics and fiction where truth-claims did not need to be substantiated by facts and facts themselves could be turned into suggestive or evocative elements in forgotten narratives.

The Imagination as a Golden Cage

As Woolf's experiments with the form of the essay tended to underline their closeness to fiction rather than to argument, in her critical writings the epistemological ambiguity intrinsic to the essay was often stretched to the point where her most ambitious pieces in the genre became effectively indistinguishable from the form of the short story. This closeness and the ambiguous character of a number of her shorter pieces has been remarked upon by Susan Dick, the editor of Woolf's shorter fiction. Faced with a number of pieces of dubious status which she generically calls 'sketches', Dick claims to have adopted a combination of epistemological and formal criteria to judge which pieces should be included and which excluded from her collection. She insists that essays such as 'Miss Ormerod' which, while highly imaginative, still preserve some kind of grounding in historical reality cannot be clearly classified as fiction. Conversely, those among Woolf's pieces which, although previously published among her essays, appear to Dick as 'works in which the characters, scenes, and actions are more imaginary than they are factual, and in which the narrator's voice is not necessarily identical with the author's' have instead been reprinted as part of her short stories (*SF*, 2). As one of these highly ambiguous pieces, 'Three Pictures' represents perhaps the ideal ground for a test of Dick's criteria of classification.

Originally published by Leonard Woolf in *The Death of the Moth* (1942) and then reprinted in the *Collected Essays*, 'Three Pictures' (*CE* 4, 151–4; *SF*, 228–31) was apparently written in June 1929 and based on a real event Woolf had witnessed and reported in her diary about two years earlier, in September 1927. Although its very close connection to a real event should have disqualified the piece from inclusion in Dick's collection, Woolf's account of the original event is cast in such a form as to put in question the stability of any criterion of distinction between the factual and the imaginary, the real and the fictional. Set apart from the rest of the diary entry and endowed with a title, this description of the burial of a young sailor from Rodmell is shaped from its very beginning more like a work of art than like the written record of a genuine occurrence. The contrast between the tragedy of the young death and the gaiety of the gravedigger's family thus comes to look to Woolf 'more like a picture, by Millais, or some other Victorian, of life & death, youth & the grave, then any real sight. It was quite unconscious; yet the most deliberate picture making; hence, unreal, sentimental, overdone' (*D* 3, 154).

By the time this sketch of 'a graveyard scene' was turned by Woolf into 'Three Pictures', the ambiguities which are only hinted at but cannot be fully explored in the diary entry had become the organising principle of the piece. Divided, as its title indicates, into three separate scenes, 'Three Pictures' both analyses and dramatises the problem of representation as the contrast between a formulaic and conventional interpretation of reality and the shocking truth that lies behind it. Setting the young sailor's death as the final revelation of that truth, the piece supplements the scene inspired by the real event with a narrative antecedent in the form of two other scenes or sketches. In the first of these pictures, the young sailor is seen returning home to an equally young wife amid the celebrations of the entire village. Whole and complete in itself, this picture is then juxtaposed to the second image, where the sunny character of the sailor's homecoming is offset by the dark note of an inhuman cry waking the narrator in the middle of the night. These two discordant and apparently unrelated pictures are then brought together in the third scene, where a visit to the local graveyard reveals that the inhuman cry had been uttered by the young sailor's wife upon discovery of her husband's sudden death.

Through its recourse to a classical dialectical movement, the progression of the narrative in 'Three Pictures' thus offers a neat resolution of the split between the fiction of happiness represented by the first scene and the reality of death inscribed in the second. But the same cannot be said for the level of discourse, where the narrative impulse itself is presented as the origin of a deep separation between the narrator and the events she observes. From the beginning, the narrator is positioned as a total outsider to the scene of collective rejoicing at the sailor's return, while the narrative act itself is construed as the indulgence of a voyeur:

> So now at the turn of the road I saw one of these pictures. It might have been called 'The Sailor's Homecoming' or some such title. A fine young sailor carrying a bundle; a girl with her hand on his arm; neighbours gathering round; a cottage garden ablaze with flowers; as one passed one read at the bottom of that picture that the sailor was back from China, and there was a fine spread waiting for him in the parlour... Everything was right and good as it should be, one felt about that picture. There was something wholesome and satisfactory in the sight of such happiness; life seemed sweeter and more enviable than before.
>
> (*SF*, 228)

Here the narrative activity comes to be presented as a (poor) substitute for the intimacy and knowledge denied to the outsider, so that it is forced into a series of splittings and disavowals which produce a rather complex effect. As detached from the storytelling as she is from the events she is observing, the narrator of this first original scene inhabits effectively two registers and two genres at the same time. On the one hand, she is the voice which relates the events and, as such, is identical with the process of narrating them. But in the passage above, the activity of narrating is prefaced by a gesture that frames the observed scene within the confines of a generic or stereotypical representation ('The Sailor's Homecoming') and, in so doing, effectively distances the narrator from both the activity of narrating and the contents of the story. In this way, the narrative act itself is split into its constituent parts in a movement that mirrors the dialectics of the story.

But while this split will eventually be resolved in the tragic and shocking outcome of the story, its initial presence signals a discomfort with the activity of narrating which will not go away. In the opening paragraph of the piece, Woolf traces the origin of this ambivalence back to the very conditions that make the narrating both possible and necessary:

> It is impossible that one should not see pictures; because if my father was a blacksmith and yours was a peer of the realm, we must needs be pictures to each other. We cannot possibly break out of the frame of the picture by speaking natural words. You see me leaning against the door of the smithy with a horseshoe in my hand and you think as you go by: 'How picturesque!' I, seeing you sitting so much at your ease in the car, almost as if you were going to bow to the populace, think what a picture of old luxurious aristocratical England! We are both quite wrong in our judgements no doubts, but that is inevitable.
>
> (228)

Exchanging her position in real life for her fictional incarnation as the daughter of a manual labourer, Woolf here locates the original split not so much in the narrative activity itself but rather in the relationship between narrative persona and its addressee. The space between writer and reader where the narrative activity takes place is also, Woolf claims, the space which prevents them from acquiring full knowledge of and intimacy with each other. Confined to their well-defined roles, each side of the relationship appears to the other as a fixed and rigid representation of a conventional kind which reflects rather than challenges established prejudices and expectations. Crucially, the distance that separates narrator and addressee and the character of the representations it fosters are ascribed here directly to the existence of class divisions which work to confine each of the participants in the narrative act within worn-out and well-established stereotypes.

Situated at the other extreme from the use Woolf makes of fiction in 'Lives of the Obscure', 'Three Pictures' reveals the existence of a very strong complicity between literary and social conventions in the representation of both real and fictional events. Usually diagnosed by Woolf as the tendency and/or temptation to make up pictures or scenes, this complicity is most explicitly analysed in her writings on the visual arts, where it often takes the form of an insistent comparison between writing and painting as art forms. Surrounded by painters in an atmosphere that was deeply imbued with the spirit and the practices of the artistic avant-garde, Woolf struggled throughout her life to define the differences between writing and painting in terms of their relation to the social body and its expectations. With the example of her sister Vanessa Bell always firmly before her eyes, she often used Post-Impressionist painting as the representative of a purely formalistic understanding of art, to which she opposed her own need for what she saw as a more communal and, to a certain extent, more 'human' art form. Inevitably, perhaps, given the circumstances of her personal life, this conflict between social and aesthetic values became for Woolf indivisible from the relationship of mirroring and rivalry she enjoyed with her sister.[11]

One of the early essays written by Woolf on the subject, 'The Royal Academy' (1919; *CD*, 13–18), focuses on an exhibition of well-established British painters to underline the connection between bad art and social conformity. Woolf opens the essay with a description of the approach to the exhibition through a courtyard which features both a statue of King Albert and a group of very expensive cars. In a parody of the English tendency to read pictures and images as symbols of something else, Woolf describes the reaction of the average spectator to this incongruous grouping of statue and cars as one of servile celebration of the British Empire:

> "The motor-cars of Empire – the bodyguard of Europe – the stainless knight of Belgium" – such is our English romance that nine out of ten of those passing from the indiscriminate variety of Piccadilly to the courtyard of Burlington House do homage to the embattled tyres and the kingly presence of Albert on his high-minded charger with some nonsense of this sort.
>
> (13)

Pointing out that the cars simply belong to the rich and have no relation to the statue itself, Woolf reveals a fundamental disjunction between the heightened patriotic sentiments expressed in the hackneyed phrases and the reality of the social milieu, where cars and art exist side by side without necessarily providing a justification for each other's existence.[12]

Having established this connection between the translation of images into clichés and the conventions of British society, Woolf proceeds then to exploit the possibilities for satire and ironies thus opened up by presenting the Royal Academy exhibition in the guise of a dinner party. Taking to task the exaggerated realism of the pictures exposed at the show, Woolf pretends to fall prey to their illusion as she goes from room to room greeting the pictures of Dukes and ladies in evening dress as if they were guests at the party. The illusion is of very short duration, though, as she discovers that the guests resemble characters from fictional stories more closely than actually living persons: 'But scenes from Rudyard Kipling must take place with an astonishing frequency at these parties in order that the English maidens and gallant officers may have occasion to insist upon their chastity on the one hand and protect it on the other, without which, so far as one can see, there would be no reason for their existence' (14).

The already quite implausible character of the representations offered at the exhibition is compounded for Woolf by its one-sided concentration upon the most positive and most commendable of human traits at the expense of the more disagreeable facts of life. Just as the picture of chaste maidens and valiant gentlemen is not completed by the necessary figure of the anti-hero,[13] so the few pictures of working-class life included in the show are turned simply into occasions for sentimentality and easy commotion. From the painting of the impoverished family of a dead fisherman to that of the cocaine addict, all the pictures exposed at the Academy are modelled upon well-rehearsed and quite worn out narrative patterns:

> The point of a good Academy picture is that you can search the canvas for ten minutes or so and still be doubtful whether you have extracted the whole meaning. There is, for example, no. 248, *Cocaine*. A young man in evening dress lies, drugged, with his head upon the pink satin of a woman's knee. The ornamental clock assures us that it is exactly eleven minutes to five. The burning lamp proves that it is dawn. He, then, has come home to find her waiting? She has interrupted his debauch? For my part, I prefer to imagine what in painters' language (a tongue well worth separate study) would be called 'a dreary vigil.'
>
> (15)

Reading pictures as if they were inscriptions in a foreign tongue, Woolf here mocks the long-standing tradition of thinking about the sister arts which tends to see painting in a parasitic relation to literature. She insists that the realism of the Academy paintings makes them far from complete representations, in constant need of a verbal supplement to their suggestions. These pictures do not work exclusively or primarily at the visual level, but rather force upon their audience a collective emotional response that is rooted in their recognition of the social and political myths inscribed in their images: 'It is indeed a very powerful atmosphere; so charged with manliness and womanliness, pathos and purity, sunsets and Union Jacks, that the shabbiest and most suburban catch a reflection of the rosy glow. "This is England! these are the English!" one might exclaim if a foreigner were at hand' (17).

In 'The Royal Academy' social convention and artistic formulae are seen to go hand in hand and to reinforce each other in the definition of a British imperialist identity that is clearly set off from its 'other', the foreigner. In a later essay devoted to the paintings of Walter Sickert, though, Woolf examines the interaction between the two in antagonistic rather than collaborative terms ('Walter Sickert', 1934; *CE* 2, 233–44). Extending the metaphor of the dinner party she had already deployed in 'The Royal Academy', she places her discussion of Sickert's work within the frame of a fictional conversation among the guests of the party. In this context, the analysis of his paintings is preceded by the exchange of pleasantries and small talk which creates a common ground or space among the guests. From the difficulties of transport encountered by the guests in reaching their destination, the talk then veers to the recently introduced system of traffic lights and to its effects upon the visual perceptions of modern men and women. Observing that '[c]olours are used so much as signals now that they will very soon suggest action merely' one of the guests hyperbolically prophesies that '[w]e shall soon lose our sense of colour' as a direct consequence of 'living in a highly organised community' (233).

Lamenting the passage from an aesthetic to a functionalist appreciation of colour and images, the conversation among the guests at the party exposes the other side of the process of communication. While the talk about the traffic lights is used itself to break the ice and create a common space, the establishment of a new code for the reading of colour is apocalyptically deplored as the first step in the transformation of human activity into mere automatism. Far from being a simple chance remark on the way to more important subjects, the example of the traffic lights introduces into the fictional conversation of the party guests the conflict between the world of art and the world of social intercourse that is at the heart of the whole essay. While Woolf had parodied and mocked the perfect coincidence of the language of social conventions and of painting in 'The Royal Academy', here she finds herself confronted with a total disjunction between the language of pure form advocated by the avant-garde and the language of everyday communication that joins all the guests together. Led by the first mention of the problem of colour in the opening remarks, the conversation of the party guests comes to rest upon the work of Sickert and the interpretation of his art. As two of the guests attempt to translate Sickert's art in terms of its relation to different literary genres and modes, the rest of the party brushes aside their attempts to compare his paintings to biography, fiction or poetry and reverts instead to an analysis of pure formal relations that stresses the autonomy of painting from verbal expression: 'And they fetched a book of photographs from Sickert's paintings and began cutting off a hand or a head, and made them connect or separate, not as a hand or a head but as if they had some quite different relationship' (235–6).

The appearance of Sickert's paintings marks the end of the all-inclusive conversation and the beginning of a long rift between the formalists and the remaining two guests of the party. Isolated and silent in their magic circle of pure forms, painters and art critics become themselves inscrutable pictures in the eyes of those who do not understand their bodily language:

> Now they are going into the silent land; soon they will be out of reach of the human voice, two of the diners said, watching them. They are seeing things we cannot see, just as a dog bristles and whines in a dark lane when nothing is visible to human eyes. They are making passes with their hands, to express what they cannot say; what excites them in [the photographs from Sickert's paintings] is something so deeply sunk that they cannot put words to it. But we, like most English people, have been trained not to see but to talk.
>
> (236)

Through the comparison between the painters and the dog, the narrator here places the circle of the formalists in a realm outside culture and yet not quite as accessible as nature. Like 'savages' in their lack of an adequate language for the expression of their thoughts and ideas, the painters also indicate a fundamental failure in the long tradition of linguistic excellence fostered by the English. If the painters themselves are cut off from intercourse with the remaining guests, these in their turn do not have the means for gaining access to the painters' area of silence.

But if the setting of the piece in a dinner party conversation is used by Woolf to draw out the discrepancy and distance between the language of art and that of society, the choice of Walter Sickert as the painter under discussion here works as a resolution of the rift between form and content. Although stranded at the edges of the circle of *connoisseurs*, the two diners whose voices can still be heard in the essay refuse to leave Sickert's art completely in the hands of the formalists and claim Sickert himself as the authority who vindicates and validates their literary approach to painting. He is said to have always considered himself ' "a literary painter... like all decent painters" ', which leads the two estranged guests to speculate that Sickert might not belong to the kind of artists represented by the rest of the company, who 'bore deeper and deeper into the stuff of their own art'. He is rather 'among the hybrids' who 'are always making raids into the lands of others' and cannot be confined to either literature or art (243).

Begging the question about the validity of a biographical and psychological approach to art criticism raised by the formalists, this reflection upon the relationship between different art forms and their interaction represents a disguised plea for the validity of literature as an art form. If the art of painting suffers from the tendency to read each and every image as a sign or symbol, the art of literature has to contend with a similar debasement of words to simple vehicles for everyday communication. And yet, as the structure of Woolf's essay shows, this dependence on everyday language also endows literature with a far wider appeal than that enjoyed by the language of pure forms and relations which was for her associated with modernist painting.

Autobiographical in both setting and content, 'Walter Sickert' forms a close pair with another fundamental essay Woolf wrote in 1930 as a brief introduction to the catalogue of an exhibition of paintings by Vanessa Bell. Although the two sisters had by this time established a consistent pattern of collaboration, with Vanessa providing both the illustrations and the dust-jackets for her sister's books, the 'Foreword to *Recent Paintings by Vanessa Bell*' (CD, 97–100) is uncommon and exceptional in presenting a direct commentary by Woolf upon her sister's work. Reflecting its introductory character in its form, the essay charts the course of a viewer's progress towards Bell's art. It mimics the indecisions and uncertainties experienced by the average spectator when confronted with Bell's reputation as an avant-garde female artist by circling around the question of personality and autobiography in art which will then become the focus of Woolf's discussion. Trembling on the threshold of the gallery where Bell's paintings are exhibited, the viewer is moved to enter Bell's world not by any considerations of perfect form and balances between masses, but by the force of the artist's somewhat scandalous reputation: 'Were it not that Mrs Bell has a certain reputation and is sometimes the theme of argument at dinner-tables, many no doubt would stroll up Bond Street, past Messrs Colling's, thinking about morality or politics, about grandfathers or great aunts, about anything but pictures as is the way of the English' (97).

Although Woolf goes on to specify the nature of her sister's reputation in purely artistic terms, this hint at the unconventional character of Bell's own family set-up reinforces the opposition between the freedoms (both artistic and otherwise) enjoyed by the members of the avant-garde and the rigid conventions of British society. Thus, the image of the threshold between the gallery and the street comes to embody for Woolf the rift between the public dimension of the modern city and the private world of serenity and peacefulness created by Bell's work:

> But once inside and surrounded by canvases, this shillyshallying on the threshold seems superfluous. What is there here to intimidate or perplex? Are we not suffused, lit up, caught in a sunny glow? Does there not radiate from the walls a serene yet temperate warmth, comfortable in the extreme after the rigours of the street? Are we not surrounded by vineyards and olive trees, by naked girls couched on crimson cushions, by naked boys ankle deep in the pale green sea? Even the puritans of the nineteenth century might grant us a moment's respite from the February murk, a moment's liberty in this serene and ordered world.
>
> (98)

The image of the threshold between the street outside and the serenity of the exhibition gallery inside echoes vividly the division between the inner circle of painters and art critics and the two more literary-minded guests of the party in 'Walter Sickert'. But whereas in the previous essay, painting and writing were presented as alternative and competing forms of access to the secrets of Sickert's paintings, here Woolf's written introduction is meant to ease prospective viewers into the world of comfort and serenity created by her sister's canvases of sunny foreign lands.

Developing further the antithesis of inside and outside first suggested by the image of the threshold, Woolf thus assimilates the opposition of public to private to the contrast created by canvases of the Mediterranean with the cold and dark atmosphere of a London street in winter. If in a sense this contrast disturbs a too-easy association of Bell's paintings with the domestic subjects and treatments deemed to be suitable to women painters, on the other hand the allusion to foreign lands also underscores the remote and inaccessible character of Bell's inner world. 'No stories are told; no insinuations are made,' Woolf observes. The portraits themselves are described as 'pictures of flesh which happens from its texture or its modelling to be aesthetically on an equality with the China pot or the chrysanthemum' (98). As people and characters are objectified into the colours that compose their incarnate, so Bell's paintings rebuke any attempt at penetrating their contents in the way Woolf found so satisfactory and fulfilling in 'The Royal Academy' and 'Walter Sickert'. Objective and impersonal, the subjects painted by Bell are surrounded by an aura of anonymity which extends to the painter herself and thus both invokes and resists the initial titillation of biographical interest described by Woolf at the outset.

Moving from the contents of the paintings to their author, Woolf as the average viewer encounters even there the sense of exclusion and rejection elicited by the emergence of a different and altogether silent language. Immune to the various attempts to make her fit some preconceived ideas about women's and men's difference in interests and focus, Bell is seen by Woolf as a complete and total inhabitant of the inner circle, the *sancta sanctorum* of modern art which rejects the idea of personal expression in art in favour of formal relationships. As 'a painter's painter', Bell is described as revealing the 'full meaning' of her art 'only to those who can tunnel their way behind the canvas into masses and passages and relations and values of which we know nothing' (99). And yet it is precisely because '[h]er pictures do not betray her' the way in which 'twenty-seven volumes of fiction' would have betrayed 'a novelist' that, Woolf insists, 'they intrigue and draw us on.... claim us and make us stop. They give us an emotion. They offer a puzzle' (99).

Defying the formalist dictum that would have psychology and emotions expelled from the realm of art, Woolf here sets forth the claims of the common viewer to a share in the world created by Bell's canvases. In Woolf's interpretation and understanding of this world, silence itself, the absence of words does not function as the merely negative side of the dominance of the verbal she laments in British culture, but rather as an alternative space filled in with the eloquence of a point of view whose difference is neither protested nor defended but simply stated. Through her association with avant-garde painting and with its rejection of narrative or literary tropes, Bell comes then to represent the ideal of the woman artist as Woolf had expressed it in *A Room*. Relieved by the pressures brought to bear upon her art by psychology and a sexed body,

Bell can then turn the silence that has historically sprung from the oppression of women's voices and artistic gifts into a positive difference that sets her apart from preconceived ideas about the nature of women's art. Far from offering an androgynous combination of both male and female attributes, both literary and figurative languages, Bell belongs for Woolf to that independent tradition of women artists who charted the course of their own work without any reference to public expectations about the intrinsic nature of that work.

In this sense, Bell comprises both the image of the silent woman who has left no trace in the historical records and the extremely accomplished artist who, like a new Jane Austen, has managed to create an independent vision that bears no relationship to and is not influenced by the sway of public opinion. If such an achievement is commended by Woolf as comparable to Shakespeare's in *A Room*, her shorter essays often offer a more ambivalent and more qualified appreciation of both Austen's and Bell's work. Insisting that their success has always been achieved at the price of a radical restriction of their areas of influence and/or work, Woolf establishes a certain correspondence between the exclusive circle of painters which surrounds her sister and the narrow emotional and social range of Austen's novels. As she points out in 'Jane Austen' (1925; *E* 4, 146–57), the formal perfection of her work has its roots in the absolute discrimination Austen exercised in matters of both sensibility and class, which after her became indissolubly welded in a certain definition of literary taste: 'Spasms and rhapsodies, she seems to have said, pointing with her stick, end *there*; and the boundary line is perfectly distinct' (148).

In an earlier version of the same essay, the kind of taste which is exemplified by Austen's work is shown to be closely linked to the definition of an ideal of femininity that turns women's own bodies into aesthetic objects. Commenting upon the proliferation of editions of Austen's works and the favour she enjoys especially among male critics, Woolf suggests that her celebrity and fame might be due to something more than just the objective and absolute aesthetic value of her novels:

> It would be interesting, indeed, to inquire how much of her present celebrity Jane Austen owes to masculine sensibility; to the fact that her dress was becoming, her eyes bright, and her age the antithesis in all matters of female charm to our own. A companion inquiry might investigate the problem of George Eliot's nose; and decide how long it will be before the equine profile is once again in favour, and the

Clarendon Press celebrates the genius of the author of *Middlemarch* in an edition as splendid, as authoritative, and as exquisitely illustrated as this.

(155)

This joining of books and female bodies in the same aesthetic category enables Woolf to reverse the conjunction and reveal the sex-based bias operating in the construction of the literary canon. As Austen's formal triumphs become indistinguishable from her own personal appearance, so Eliot's relegation to a lesser status cannot be ascribed simply to her worth as an artist, but must as surely be related to her life-choices and her refusal to conform to social dictates about women's behaviour. Thus, while allegedly celebrating the universal value of Austen's work, the critics are effectively shown by Woolf to be directed by subtle discriminations between different life styles and ideals of womanhood, which she sarcastically reduces to differences between nose shapes, recalling Herbert Spencer's claim that, had it not been for Eliot's nose, he would have married her.[14]

Woolf's comments about Austen highlight the way in which a certain definition of literary taste as restraint and measure is closely bound up with the regulation of women's sexuality and behaviour. They also indicate, though, that her own identification of the perfect woman artist with the one that remains silent about her own personal life has as much to do with questions of gender and sexual difference as with the topography of class. This connection between the aesthetic ideal of impersonality and its class determinations is never explicitly analysed in her writings on Austen or Bell. What is clear, though, is that for Woolf the containment of women's sexuality within the tightly controlled boundaries of 'good taste' is structurally indivisible from the influence exercised by class in outlining the limits of English fiction. In 'The Niece of an Earl' (1932; *CD*, 92–6), a review of George Meredith's novels, Woolf argued that this influence represents the great unspeakable of English literature, even though it lends to that literature its particular national character: '[o]ne is supposed to pass over class distinctions in silence; one person is supposed to be as well born as another; and yet English fiction is so steeped in the ups and downs of social rank that without them it would be unrecognisable' (92). Both invisible and ubiquitous, class acts for Woolf as a sort of hygienic glass screen which prevents any intercourse between members of different classes which is not based on reciprocal ridiculing and caricature. Because English fiction owes its comic spirit to the existence of class divisions and social rankings,

Woolf complains that it has failed to challenge the assumptions that lie behind those divisions. Rather than bringing down the glass screens that separate the different classes and thus liberate its members for a fuller type of intercourse, in Woolf's eyes English fiction has limited itself to reflecting and reproducing 'a nest of glass boxes . . . each housing a group with special habits and qualities of its own' (93).

Having thus failed to bring down the barriers that cut across the body of society, English fiction finds itself in a condition of isolation that resembles very closely the one experienced by the lonely two diners of 'Walter Sickert' or by the viewer of Vanessa Bell's paintings. On the one hand, it cannot aspire to the status of pure art because of a close connection to precisely those biographical and psychological elements which the formalists deplore and condemn. On the other, it cannot even claim the realm of life as its absolute domain, as its ability to reflect and interpret objective reality is strongly hindered by its participation in the material conditions that shape that reality. Expelled from the realm of pure art, fiction cannot even shape itself into that reservoir of common language and shared experience Woolf is continually seeking for. Thus, for Woolf, the most painful consequence of class divisions is not the possibility of internecine conflict, but rather that of reciprocal indifference: 'There is no animosity, perhaps, but there is no communication. We are enclosed, and separate, and cut off' (92).

The image of the glass screen or box to indicate the connections between the limits of the imagination and the taxonomy of class is a recurrent one in Woolf's writing. It organises her discussion of many autobiographies by women ('The Memoirs of Sarah Bernhardt', 1908; *E* 1, 164–71, 'Ellen Terry', 1941; *CD*, 173–8), where their lives are represented as being enclosed into separate, isolated compartments that share with the 'glass boxes' of English fiction their firmly defined boundaries. In the case both of Terry and of Bernhardt the analogy between life-writing and glass boxes is of course suggested by their professions as actresses, where the stage and the different parts they played on it functions as a metaphor for the different aspects of personality that are inscribed in their autobiography. Bernahrdt's memoirs are described by Woolf as a collection of 'separate and brightly coloured beads' (*E* 1, 164) which 'scarcely connect', so that the life is shown in fact to have far less coherence than the succession of scenes that makes up a play. The dramatic sense, the eye for detail and for the expressive gesture is, Woolf insists, the same both in the theatre and in Bernhardt's re-interpretation of her own life. But this attempt to stage the life as if it was a play only succeeds for Woolf in reproducing the effect of 'coloured and animated photographs' rather than that of a coherent, dramatic narrative (166).

But if Bernahrdt's memoirs call into question any clear-cut distinction between the life and the art, the real person and the fictional character, Woolf's essay on Ellen Terry indicates on the other hand that a very neat separation between the two sides produces exactly the same result. Terry's life as it emerges from her autobiography and correspondence with Bernard Shaw is marked for Woolf by the same lack of continuity, by the same absence of vital links as that of Bernhardt's; it is not 'an Academy's portrait, glazed, framed, complete' but 'rather a bundle of loose leaves upon each of which she has dashed off a sketch for a portrait' (*CD*, 174). The visual metaphor for the act of memoirs-writing is, as we have seen, typical of Woolf's perception of the peculiar character of autobiography; in this case it is reinforced by Terry's association, through her marriage to Watts, to that circle of Pre-Raphaelite painters and artists with which Woolf's own family had strong connections.[15] It also suggests, though, an act of mirroring of one's self that, in Terry's case, remains incomplete as the sketch-book only furnishes parts and fragments of her personality, but obstinately refuses to provide a sense of how all those separate parts coalesce into a whole.

Terry is consequently portrayed as a child born to the theatre, then as the adolescent wife of Watts 'who sits mum in her corner while the famous elderly people talk over her head' (*CD*, 175), then, 'skipping a page or two', as a mother of young children who has escaped from her early marriage to retire to the countryside rolling pastry and scrubbing children, but was later compelled to return to the stage for financial necessity. These series of incongruent parts are reduced by Woolf to 'two sketches fac[ing] each other; Ellen Terry in blue cotton among the hens; Ellen Terry robed and crowned as Lady Macbeth on the stage of the Lyceum' (176). The two pictures offer no links to each other and, the essay concludes, precisely because of this absence of connecting threads of reason or narrative, they give us a sense of Terry's unique personality, of what in her exceeded the fixed roles and frames of theatrical life. And yet, precisely because of the mystery they refuse to reveal or resolve, they become emblematic not just of Terry herself but of the distance and difference that separates fictional representations of character and people in their uniqueness.

In suggesting that the essence of Terry as a person exceeds the conventional frames of her own representation of motherhood and acting, Woolf here returns once more to the issue of characterisation she broached in relation to mother- and father-figures in 'A Sketch of the

Past'. Just like with *Reading at Random*, which she started writing at around the same time as 'A Sketch' and which was meant to reply once and for all to the painters' accusations that literature could not aspire to the status of art, both 'A Sketch' and 'Ellen Terry' take form against a background of thinking about the relationship between modern painting and literature. In a polemic with Mark Gertler, who, as Woolf reports in 'A Sketch', had sustained that the autobiographical impulse made literature impure from an artistic point of view, Woolf retorted that 'if one could give a sense of my mother's personality one would have to be an artist. It would be as difficult to do that, as it should be done, as to paint a Cézanne' (*MB*, 85). While Terry's memoirs could not aspire to be the written equivalent of a Cézanne, Woolf insists that it is their very inconclusiveness, the suggestions of their gaps and unspoken links that gives them a meaning and a significance that is perhaps as substantial as that of great works of art. In this she reversed the aesthetic criteria upheld in Bloomsbury, which located the value of the work of art in the relation between forms rather than the suggestiveness of the unfinished and fragmentary, of the incomplete.

This insistence on the importance of the small, of the inconsequential rather than of the accomplished work of genius is repeated in her review of the autobiography of Queen Marie of Romania. Published in 1934 under the title of 'Royalty' (*WE*, 154–58), Woolf's review praises this royal autobiography as a momentous step in Western history which signals the end of a whole social order based on a rigid division between the private and the public sphere. Queen Marie's autobiography amounts for Woolf to the opening up of the 'beautiful brightly lit room' where members of the royal family have been 'worshipped, stared at, and kept shut up, as lions and tigers are kept . . . behind bars' (154). While an autobiography calls forth by necessity reflections upon the psychological rather than the political effects of this seclusion, Woolf insinuates in her review that the opening up of the psychological or personal reality of being a member of a royal family can nevertheless have unforeseen political and historical consequences. In this version of the 'personal is political', she brings out the fact that the mystique and the power enjoyed by royal families is dependent upon their forced and artificial differentiation from the rest of humanity, on their inhabiting a golden cage which, when removed, will bring out the commonality of the human experience and thus undermine the very foundations of political power in the British Empire.

Rising to the challenge offered by this royal autobiography, Woolf then proceeds to draw out a comparison between Queen Marie's personal recollections and Queen Victoria's official documents. Whereas Queen Marie's prose is praised by Woolf for its freshness and vivacity, Victoria's is condemned from an aesthetic and literary point of view for its pomposity and formal stiffness. But as Woolf had already remarked in relation to her sister's paintings, the absence of any trace of personal expression in Queen Victoria's public statements has worked to reinforce rather than undermine the Queen's hold upon the imagination of her subjects. Although Victoria's writing is compared to the sound of an 'old savage beating with a wooden spoon on a drum', it is precisely this lack of eloquence that is seen to lie at the basis of 'her prestige'. Woolf argues that 'her inability to express herself' led 'the majority of her subjects' to regard her as 'a woman immune from the usual frailties and passions of human nature' (155–6).

Turned by her writing into the disembodied voice of authority, Victoria is taken by Woolf as the paragon of a woman unsexed not so much by her participation to the political process as by her inability to express herself in writing. Written self-expression is thus implicitly construed by Woolf as the mark of full womanhood, while political power is turned into its negation, so that to be a woman and to be a queen are revealed as mutually exclusive propositions that cannot coexist. Against the background of the impenetrable figure of Victoria, Queen Marie's exposure of the personal and private component of royal life marks the end of a political system based upon the principle of disembodiment:

> When a gift for writing lodges in a family, it often persists and improves; and if Queen Marie's descendants improve upon her gift as much as she has improved upon Queen Victoria...what will be the effect upon their loyal subjects? Will Buckingham Palace look as solid then as it does now? Words are dangerous things let us remember. A republic might be brought into being by a poem.
>
> (158)

This insistence on the democratic, radical power of language both subtends Woolf's historiographic project of rescuing the obscure from oblivion and is at odds with the kind of formalist understanding of art that emerges from her better-known writings and from her discomfort with Mark Gertler's indictment of literature. On the one hand there is the need to give a voice to those whose voices have been muffled or silenced in the course of history. On the other there is a strong sense that those half-heard voices, those unspoken words offer in and of themselves a challenge that is both artistic and historical: they are the voices and words of Anon, of Woolf's own re-interpretation of the notion of impersonality in a sense that is meant to work as an alternative to the abstracted, cut off, elitist art of the painters in 'Walter Sickert'. Straddling the difference between these two impulses, the historiographic and the artistic, there is always for Woolf the question of the imagination as the faculty that allows her to fill in the gaps of the historical record but is itself continuously checked and limited by her own historical and social position, by that sharp division in classes that occludes the breadth of what she liked to call 'the poetic vision'.

Going for depth and detail rather than for range, Woolf hoped to transcend those limitations by uncovering the underlying continuity of human life, that 'submerged current' of semi-conscious and atavistic existence that stretched back to Mrs Swithin's dinosaurs and as far forward as Chloe and Olivia's half-lit cave. The contradiction she identified in her often quoted diary entry of 1929, 'Now is life very solid or very shifting? I am haunted by the two contradictions. This has gone on for ever: will last for ever... this moment I stand on. Also it is transitory, flying, diaphanous. I shall pass like a cloud on the waves.', (*D* 3, 218), continued to haunt her throughout her life and found characteristically no final solution or synthesis. In the end, 'writing essays about oneself' proved to be the only precarious response to the contradiction, the only form of synthesis available for *the* modernist woman writer who still remained, as T. S. Eliot remarked in her obituary, the last of the Victorians.[16]

Postscript: Angels and Harpies

This book opened up by making a case for aligning Woolf's work with that strand of European modernism that has come to be known as 'essayism'. Defined mainly in the writings of Lukács, Musil and Adorno, the notion of essayism has always carried with it a critique of modernity as the triumph of rationalisation and the culmination of a linear, progressive vision of history. When understood in this sense, essayism becomes effectively indistinguishable from the Marxist critique of the dialectic of the Enlightenment and might therefore suggest a certain compatibility of intents between that critique and Woolf's historiographic project. But the point of this inquiry has not been that of substituting one critical framework (Marxism) for the feminist approach that has dominated Woolf studies in the last three decades or so. Essayism was used here as a critical angle capable of articulating and addressing the question of Woolf's relationship to literary history, both in terms of the history she wrote and in terms of the history that has been written about her. In their turn, Woolf's writings on history, women and the essay were deployed to read critically and help to contextualise the idea of essayism that is linked to the Marxist critique of modernity.

In keeping with the double focus of this study, I would now like to conclude by concentrating on two moments of writing about history that chart both the similarities and the differences between Woolf's approach and that of writers and critics usually associated with the Marxist tradition. The first of these moments is Walter Benjamin's well-known statement of the catastrophic and elegiac image of history that he identified with Paul Klee's painting *Angelus Novus*. It occurs within the 'Theses on the Philosophy of History', which were completed in the Spring of 1940, at a historical moment when the apocalyptic erasure of modern civilisation seemed to have gone from prophecy to realised possibility. Benjamin's reading of Klee's painting reverberates with the echoes of that moment, describing Klee's messenger as 'the angel of history' intent on contemplating the destruction of humanity:

> His eyes are staring, his mouth is open, his wings are spread.... His face is turned towards the past. Where we perceive a chain of events, he sees one single catastrophe which keeps piling wreckage upon wreckage and hurls it in front of his feet. The angel would like to stay, awaken the dead, and make whole what has been smashed. But a storm is blowing from Paradise; it has got caught in his wings with such violence that the angel can no longer close them. This storm irresistibly propels him into the future to which his back is turned ... This storm is what we call progress.[1]

Caught in the wind of progress, Benjamin's angel demonstrates a suspicion towards the relentlessly linear temporality of modernity which can also be traced in Woolf's writings, from her satirical depiction of the 'march of the professions' in *Three Guineas* (1938) to her insistence on rescuing from the debris of history precisely the figures that the present has abandoned, of which no trace has remained in cultural history. In many ways it is Woolf herself, in her activity as the chronicler of the obscure and the nearly forgotten, who fulfils the role of healer and resuscitator of the past that Benjamin identifies as the angel's lost mission. But Benjamin's vision of the past as an apocalyptic collapse that 'keeps piling wreckage upon wreckage' at the angel's feet is emphatically not Woolf's own, since for her the past is more likely to mark a sense of continuity and the possibility of a different future than a chaotic heap of disasters.

This sense of the past as the repository of different stories offers an alternative to the twin vision of progress and catastrophe embodied in Benjamin's angel. It is evident in Woolf's lifelong attraction for the idea of writing a continuous history of English literature from the point of view of those who had been traditionally excluded from it: the eccentrics, the obscure, the anonymous writers and singers of pre-Renaissance literature. As Woolf made clear in *A Room* (1929), this re-writing of literary history was for her intrinsically linked to the possibility that her own work might be able to survive the onslaught of time. But this stress on continuity was also accompanied for Woolf by the need to rescind herself from those aspects of the past that risked fixing the future once and for all. Symbolised by the image of the Angel in the

House, the stranglehold which the past has on the present remained for Woolf always associated with the question of the cultural definition of femininity and of women's space and place, both in society and in time.

If Woolf, then, shares with Benjamin a focus on the figure of the angel as a privileged locus for articulating her relationship to history, her interpretation of that figure indicates that for her the shape and move- ment of history is always inflected by the intervention of sexual differ- ence. As a ghost emanating from the Victorian past, the Angel in the House is alternately seen as a threat and as an opportunity, depending on the position of the historian. When Woolf presents herself as aspiring to the status of female Shakespeare, as she does in 'Professions for Women' (1931), the angel appears as an obstacle to be overcome on the road to the development of an independent voice for the modern woman writer. But when Woolf is operating as the historian of the obscure, the Angel in the House becomes herself one of the anonymous and self-sacrificing figures whose presence in history needs to be recorded and whose memory must be preserved.

This stress on the positioning of the literary historian *vis-à-vis* a past that is never fixed into one single, determining image distinguishes Woolf's conception of history from later, contemporary versions of Benjamin's melancholic angel. Although Benjamin's rejection of pro- gress and apocalyptic vision of history have often been ascribed to the mystical side of his writing rather than to his Marxism,[2] the figure of the angel continues to guide attempts at defining a materialist approach to the history of literature. Franco Moretti's 1988 essay on the methods and practices of contemporary criticism is a case in point. Entitled 'The Soul and the Harpy', the essay takes its name from an image Moretti found carved on a tomb now preserved in the British Museum. The bas-relief, as Moretti describes it,

> shows a harpy – the upper half of its body a woman, the lower a bird of prey – carrying off a small human body...the soul of the deceased. Below the harpy is clutching the soul tight in its claws, but higher up her Greek arms are holding her in an attentive and tender embrace. The soul is doing nothing to get out of the harpy's clutch. It seems calm, relaxed even....But at the same time the soul must know that there is no escape from the grip of the claws. For this reason it does not lower its gaze, but rests its head trustingly on the harpy's arms. Precisely because there is no escape it prefers to delude itself about the affectionate,

almost maternal nature of the creature dragging it away with her in
flight.
  Can we blame it?³

Moretti offers this description as a last attempt to convince his readers
that literature works not so much as an agent of liberation from and,
even, of subversion of the status quo but rather as a unique tool for the
enforcement of political and ideological consensus. In his iconography,
the harpy comes to represent his vision of literature as the privileged
instrument for entrapping and ensnaring the human soul within the
cruel mechanics of a social system which is characterised by a deep
division between its predatory reality (the harpy's clutches) and its
comforting appearance (her Greek arms). In this classical interpretation
of ideology as a form of false consciousness, Benjamin's angel is transformed into a predatorial winged creature who does not 'awaken the
dead' but lulls them into the false security of a sleep that Moretti
suggests is not much better than death.
  The reading of the British Museum bas-relief suggested by Moretti is
then stark in its simplicity. The harpy's female body is seen to act as a
deceptive cover-up of its inhuman, rapacious truth as the agent of
spiritual death. In this reading, a Marxian interpretation of the relationship between base structure and superstructure is grafted upon Virgil's
representation of the Harpies in the *Aeneid*, where they appear as foul,
hungry creatures who threaten Aeneas and contaminate his food. But
Margaret Ann Doody has suggested that this Roman Imperial interpretation of the harpy offers a revision of an earlier, more positive reading
of this mythical figure that has its origins in Asia Minor, at the extreme
Eastern border of the classical world. Drawing on the same image analysed by Moretti in 'The Soul and the Harpy', Doody describes this
oriental harpy as having 'an angelic aspect' in its capacity as the carer
for the soul.⁴ For Doody the negative representation of the harpy offered
both by Virgil and by Moretti signifies the persistence of a fear of the
feminine and its sexuality that she claims is at the foundations of Greco-
Roman civilization but was not, crucially, shared by other cultures
where women flourished and occupied positions of power.
  This alternation between negative and positive readings of the figure
of the harpy on the British Museum tomb indicates perhaps that the
hybrid character of that representation cannot ultimately be erased and
re-traced back within the folds of one single and unitary image. Like the
Sphinx for Oedipus, the harpy remains an enigmatic figure, whose body
of half-woman and half-bird proves intractable to any attempt at

establishing once and for all the place and space where it properly belongs. As this riddle, she illustrates the dangers and attractions of 'talking in pictures', of a language that borrows its impact and power from the field of vision. Woolf, among others, was especially attuned to the difficulties that accompany the search for one image capable of encompassing her idea of history. In this sense, her choice of the andro-gynous Orlando comes to signify both the temptation of giving a body to her vision of history and her awareness of the problems that surround its fixation into a specific form. Like harpies and angels, the androgyne offers an image that is both truthful and deceptive, a resolution that poses the original problem all over again.

Notes

Introduction: Viriginia Woolf, European Essayist

1 Arnold Bennett,' Is the Novel Decaying?' (1923), p. 47.
2 Maria DiBattista has provided a similar interpretation of this diary entry which she claims indicates 'not so much that Woolf's center will not hold' but rather that it 'eludes...the spirit's grasp' (*The Fables of Anon* (1980), p. 24). As DiBattista concentrates exclusively on the novels, her reading of this entry does not examine the link between this sense of reaching out without being able to grasp the true 'reality' and the question of the essay, which I argue is essential to Woolf's own understanding of her artistic project.
3 Virginia Woolf, *To the Lighthouse* (1927), p. 28.
4 For examples of this conceptions of the essay see Orlo Williams, *The Essay* (n.d.) and Bonamy Dobrée, *English Essayists* (1946). In *The Rise and Fall of the Man of Letters* (1969), John Gross has offered a modified definition of this conjunction between the essay and the idea of the gentleman by identifying the *belletrist* with the unattached, freelance commentator on literary matters whose emergence and disappearance he traces from the early nineteenth century to the first half of the twentieth. In Gross's terms, the man of letter is defined by its opposition to the professional academic, much in the same way as the common reader stands in contrast to 'the critic and the scholar' for Woolf (see especially Gross's 1991 Afterword). For a discussion of the idea of the common reader in relation to Woolf's essayistic practice see below, Chapter 2.
5 For examples of these postwar readings see David Daiches, *Virginia Woolf* (1942); Dorothy Brewster, *Virginia Woolf* (1962).
6 Georg Lukács, 'On the Nature and Form of the Essay', p. 7.
7 Graham Good, *The Observing Self*, p. 8.
8 Gillian Rose, *The Melancholy Science*, pp. 11–26.
9 Theodor W. Adorno, 'The Essay as Form' (1958), p. 5.
10 John Snyder, *Prospects of Power*, p. 159.
11 This focus on the possibility of fashioning and refashioning the self characterises, according to Stephen Greenblatt, also the theatre of the Renaissance; see his *Renaissance Self-Fashioning* (1980).
12 Snyder, *Prospects*, p. 174.
13 Ibid., p. 178.
14 Ibid., p. 172.
15 Snyder's choice of Woolf and Rich as representative feminist essayists leaves out some crucial interventions made by feminists writing in the 1970s and 1980s, whose work might be seen to resemble more closely Montaigne's approach to subjectivity. See especially Hélène Cixous's 'The Laugh of the Medusa' (1975) and Rachel Blau DuPlessis's 'For the Etruscans' (1985). Snyder's arguments about the Baconian inheritance in feminist essayists are perhaps better reflected in more recent attempts to reclaim the essay as

an essentially feminine genre either on the basis of historical questions, such as the composition of the readership of essays in the eighteenth century, and of politico-ideological ones. For an example of the former see Beth Carole Rosenberg, *Virginia Woolf and Samuel Johnson* (1995) and Michael Kaufmann, 'A Modernism of One's Own' (1997); for the latter see the articles collected in Ruth-Ellen Boetcher Joeres and Elizabeth Mittman (eds), *The Politics of the Essay* (1993).

16   The reference to 'feminist pamphlets' is taken from Jean Guiguet's *Virginia Woolf and Her Works* (1965), where *A Room* and *Three Guineas* are listed under the heading 'Feminism and Pamphlets'. For Guiguet Woolf's feminist essays express that part of her character and personality that had been repressed in the novels in the pursuit of artistic purity. Woolf's constant interest in the feminist cause does not therefore reveal for Guiguet just 'a considerable degree of social consciousness' but also demands a revision of the interpretation of her work that would read into what has been seen as a self-centred concern with individual consciousness a way of breaking out of the strictures of neo-classicist aesthetics (p. 192). Guiguet's view of the repression of feminist concerns in Woolf's novels will be echoed over ten years later by Michèle Barrett in *Women and Writing*, but also in her more recent introduction to the Penguin edition of *A Room* and *Three Guineas* (1993).

17   Quentin Bell, *Virginia Woolf*; *The Letters of Virginia Woolf*, ed. Nigel Nicolson and Joanne Trautmann; *The Diary of Virginia Woolf*, ed. Anne Olivier Bell and Andrew McNeillie.

18   Michèle Barrett, Introduction, in *Women and Writing*, p. 1.

19   Among the suggestions for further reading listed by Barrett are Herbert Marder, *Feminism and Art* (1968); Nancy Topping Bazin, *Virginia Woolf and the Androgynous Vision* (1973); Carolyn Heilbrun, *Towards Androgyny*, 2nd edn (1973).

20   Elaine Showalter, *A Literature of Their Own*, pp. 263–97.

21   Toril Moi, *Sexual/Textual Politics*, p. 16.

22   For some of the stages of the debates initiated by Moi, see Janet Todd's *Feminist Literary History* (1988), which was explicitly conceived as a rebuttal of Moi's arguments; Naomi Schor, 'Introducing Feminism' (1986), and Diana Fuss, 'Getting Into History' (1989) both discuss the issues raised by Moi's version of the history of feminist criticism.

23   This increased popularisation of Woolf's essays is reflected by the fact that her work was represented within the Penguin 60s series not by her fiction but by a selection of essays, *Killing the Angel in the House* (1995), which included 'Professions for Women', 'The Feminine Note in Fiction', 'Women Novelists', 'The Intellectual Status of Women', 'Two Women', 'Memories of a Working Women's Guild', and 'Ellen Terry'.

24   See especially Brosnan, *Reading Virginia Woolf's Essays*, pp. 10–12, and Rosenberg, *Virginia Woolf and Samuel Johnson*, pp. xvi–xviii. The stress on the dialogic character of Woolf's relation to past authors had already been underlined by Gillian Beer, who set out to trace the lines of exchange between Woolf and literary history in *Arguing with the Past* (1989). As the title of her collection of essays indicates, though, Beer's notion of dialogue was more antagonistic than the one proposed by Brosnan or Rosenberg and was modelled on the parent/child relationship rather than on Bakhtin's theories.

25 For examples of comparative readings of Woolf's and Montaigne's essayistic practice see Juliette Dusinberre's *Virginia Woolf's Renaissance*, pp. 40–64; Catherine Sandbach-Dahlström, ' "Que scais-je?": Virginia Woolf and the Essay as Feminist Critique' (1997). See also the discussion of Woolf's reading of the *Essais* in Chapter 2 below.

26 Musil, *The Man Without Qualities*, book ii, chapter 62 (pp. 267–77). Musil's 'novel' appeared in German between 1930 and 1942, overlapping in some ways with Woolf's own work on *The Pargiters*, the project for writing a 'novel-essay' which she started in 1932 and then split off into *The Years* (1937) and *Three Guineas* (1938).

27 Claire de Obaldia's *The Essayistic Spirit* (1995) offers one of the clearest and most illuminating analyses of Continental Essayism, stressing the lines of continuity that link its earlier, modernist examples to its later revival in the works of prominent postmodernist and poststructuralist critics, from Barthes to Derrida. But because her interest lies in tracing those lines, de Obaldia is forced to effect a too clear-cut separation between 'Essayism' and the essay proper which closes off any possible exploration of the interaction between the issue of genre and that of gender.

28 Jane Marcus, 'Thinking Back Through Our Mothers' (1981), p. 7.

29 For one of the very few contemporary analyses of the issue of class in Woolf from a feminist perspective see Mary Childers, 'Virginia Woolf on the Outside Looking Down' (1992). Woolf's alleged blindness to class determinations was also at the centre of Q. D. Leavis's attack on *Three Guineas* in 'Caterpillars of the World Unite!', (1938). As I discuss in Chapter 3, though, the restriction of Woolf's audience to a certain class segment in *Three Guineas* is a direct consequence not so much of her own class position as of some of the rhetorical strategies of argumentation she chose for the essay.

1. Eccentric Histories

1 As most of Woolf's early articles were published anonymously, the beginnings of her career are surrounded by a high degree of uncertainty, and different editors have identified different essays as her first published piece of writing. In 1986 Andrew McNeillie opened the first volume of his edition of the essays with Woolf's review of William Dean Howells's *The Son of Royal Langbirth*, which appeared in the *Guardian* on 14 December 1904. Six years later Mitchell A. Leaska's notes to the early journals identified another article, 'Social England' (*Guardian*, 7 December 1904) as her first piece of published work (*PA*, n. 16, p. 219). This confirms the nebulous character of this period of Woolf's career, which offers the possibility of questioning the integrity of her *oeuvre* and thus destabilise her twin identity of modernist writer and feminist critic. As Michel Foucault argued in 'What is an Author' (1969), 'the word *work* and the unity it designates' (p. 104) are an integral part of the ideological function performed by the notion of authorship.

2 Throughout this section I will be using Woolf's maiden name whenever the reference is specifically to her early writings; in all other cases, she will be designated by her married name, as by convention. This alternation between maiden and married name is meant to underline the 'strangeness' or, as we

shall see, the 'eccentricity' of this period of her career to the identity of the
established figure we have come to recognise as 'Woolf'. In other words,
the Virginia Stephen of the pre-1912 period is not always necessarily the
same person, in critical terms, as Virginia Woolf the acclaimed novelist,
reviewer and feminist writer.

3   For a quantitative analysis of Woolf's development from writer of notices to
established critic see Jeanne Dubino, 'Virginia Woolf: From Book Reviewer to
Literary Critic' (1997).

4   In *Heidegger, Art and Politics* (1990) Phillipe Lacoue-Labarthe has proposed to
adopt the term *caesura* to designate the unique historical character of the Nazi
extermination of the Jews. As 'the moment at which the truth of the conflict
of representations appears as such' (p. 42), the *caesura* also works for Lacoue-
Labarthe to expose the logic of historicity: it is 'that which, within history,
interrupts history and opens up another possibility of history, or else closes off
all possibility of history' (p. 45). Although Lacoue- Labarthe claims that we
can only properly speak of a caesura in the history of the West in the case of
Auschwitz, my use of the term is meant in the wider sense of marking the
limits of a certain way of representing Woolf, her writing and the history of
her feminist reception. As Lacoue-Labarthe acknowledges, his identification
of Auschwitz with the caesura of Western history has a decidedly apocalyptic
and catastrophic flavour which underlines its similarity to Walter Benjamin's
depiction of the Angel of History (*Illuminations* (1955), p. 249). Woolf's own
vision of history was, as we shall see, rather different and tended to reject such
apocalyptic temptations even though she was not immune to their seduction,
as she shows in *Three Guineas*. For more on this, see below, Chapter 3. For a
discussion of Benjamin's view of history in relation to Woolf and feminist
criticism see below, Postscript.

5   Feminist critics have often been quite vocal in refusing Woolf's identification
with 'madness', which it is argued stemmed from her family environment and
from Bloomsbury as a way of dismissing Woolf's importance as a writer. For
examples of family accounts of Woolf's illness, see Quentin Bell, *Virginia Woolf*
(1972–73) and Leonard Woolf's autobiography (1960–69). In early feminist
studies of Woolf, androgyny was seen to act as a remedy or balance against the
deep psychological splits which occasioned Woolf's illness, see, for instance,
Nancy Topping Bazin, *Virginia Woolf and the Androgynous Vision* (1973). These
readings were then reversed in the late 1970s, with the publication of books
such as Roger Poole's *The Unknown Virginia Woolf* (1978), which argued that
the 'madness' that had normally been ascribed to Woolf had in fact belonged
more properly to the system that surrounded her, and especially to her doctors
and to Leonard. In more recent works, the focus of investigation has shifted
towards an interrogation of the frames of interpretation that have led to link
Woolf and madness so closely together. See, for instance, Hermione Lee,
Virginia Woolf (1996), esp. pp. 175–200, and, from a different angle, Daniel
Ferrer, *Virginia Woolf and the Madness of Language* (1990). For a critique of
Ferrer's approach and, more in general, of Woolf's identification with madness
see Jane Marcus, 'Pathographies' (1992).

6   Bowlby, *Feminist Destinations* (1997), p. 12

7   See especially Louise DeSalvo's *Virginia Woolf: the Impact of Childhood Sexual
Abuse* (1989). For a more detailed analysis of Woolf's autobiographical writings

and the questions of representation and memory they raise see below, Chapter 4.

8   See, for instance, 'Old Bloomsbury' (1921–22; *MB*, 179–201).

9   Brosnan, *Reading Virginia Woolf's Essays* (1997), p. 34.

10 See Jeanne Dubino and Beth Carole Rosenberg, Introduction, in *Virginia Woolf and the Essay* (1997), pp. 1–22, and Juliette Dusinberre, *Virginia Woolf's Renaissance* (1997), p. 3, where she states that 'Virginia Woolf's project was always twofold: the reading by women of literature written by men, and the discovery of women as writers and readers'.

11 Bowlby, *Feminist Destinations*, p. 14.

12 Although it was Toril Moi who initiated the debate for the appropriation of Woolf's work to what was then called 'French' feminism in *Sexual/Textual Politics* (1985), her arguments were in fact later reversed by Bette London's 1991 intervention in the debate. 'Guerrilla in Petticoats or Sans- Culotte?' argued for the deployment of 'French' feminism as a way of unsettling Woolf's canonisation rather than as the instrument that would have led, in Moi's claim, to her recognition as the 'greatest British woman writer of this century' (*Sexual/Textual Politics*, p. 8). The phrase 'mother of us all' is Jane Marcus's and is taken from 'Thinking Back Through Our Mothers' (1981), pp. 1–30.

13 Bette London, *The Appropriated Voice* (1990), p. 126.

14 Earlier studies of the essays were carried out in the late 1970s by Marc Goldman in *The Reader's Art* (1976) and Vijay Sharma in *Virginia Woolf as Literary Critic* (1977), both of whom concentrated on the theory of fiction developed by Woolf in her critical writing rather than on the intersection of feminism and history analysed in more recent works on the essays.

15 Brosnan, *Reading*, p. 63.

16 That Woolf at this time equated good writing with a fluent and seamless style is also testified by her own self- criticism. On reading the proofs for 'The Letters of Jane Carlyle' in 1905 (*E* 1, 54–8), she wrote to Violet Dickinson that the article was 'bad – such an ugly angular piece of writing, all jagged edges' (*L* 1, 202). Woolf tended to see the relationship between Carlyle and his wife as typical of the egotism of the Victorian man of genius, which she also saw reflected in her father's tyrannical demands upon her mother, half-sister and then Vanessa. The stylistic difficulties she feels she encountered with the article on Jane Carlyle's letters can be seen to reflect, then, her discomfort and unease at the kind of sexual politics inscribed in the Carlyles' marriage. For more on Woolf's portrayal of her father in later years see below, Chapter 4.

17 James Joyce's *Chamber Music* was published in 1907; *In a German Pension*, Katherine Mansfield's first collection of short stories, appeared in 1911; T. S. Eliot's *Prufrock* came out in 1917; Dorothy Richardson's *Pointed Roofs* was published in 1915, six months after Woolf's own *The Voyage Out*.

18 Hermione Lee, *Virginia Woolf*, p. 216.

19 For Woolf's descriptive pieces see for instance her 1903 journal (*PA*, 163–213); for her spoofs see 'Terrible Tragedy in a Duckpond' (*PA*, 150–2), which Brosnan analyses at length as a parody of journalistic conventions that shows the young Stephen to be already extremely aware of the ways in which sexual difference inflects the distinction between fact and fiction (*Reading Virginia Woolf's Essays*, pp. 30–4).

20 For examples of these crossovers see 'An Andalusian Inn' (1905; *E* 1, 49–52 and *L* 1, 187); 'A Priory Church' (1905; *E* 1, 53–4 and *PA*, 215); 'A Walk By Night' (1905; *E* 1, 80–2 and *PA*, 297–8).

21 As Émile Benveniste has shown, the 'I:you' relationship is constitutive of the realm of discourse, while the third person singular 'he or she' is the grammatical mark of narrative (*Problems in General Linguistics* (1966), pp. 205–22). Although Benveniste's distinctions refer specifically to French rather than to English, they have nevertheless been adopted by Hayden White as the basis for his analysis of the relationship between fiction and historiography (see *Tropics of Discourse* (1978) and *The Content of the Form* (1989)). White tends to see history as a camouflage or a mystification of the essentially interpersonal relation that structures language, so that in his writing history comes close to being a form of false consciousness. For an analysis of the relationship between history and fiction in terms not of radical opposition but rather of intersection see Paul Ricoeur, *Time and Narrative* (1984–88). For Woolf's own reflection on the process of writing history see below, 'Eccentrics, Obscure, Anons' and Chapter 5.

22 Woolf had in fact produced very early on her own semi- autobiographical and semi-fictional version of the Platonic dialogue in the short story set on Mount Pentelicus, which she had visited with her siblings in the autumn of 1906. The story is laid out as an argument between two elements of the British group of visitors to Greece. One of the tourists laments the fact that modern Greece and the Greeks represent a betrayal of their predecessors, while the other argues that the vision of Ancient Greece to which the modern country is compared is in fact the effect of a projection of an idealised version of the British ruling class upon the classics. The argument is resolved by the appearance of an epiphanic figure, a Greek monk who combines in his traits both the long beard and hair of his contemporaries and 'the nose and brow of a Greek statue' (*SF*, 67). For more on Woolf's reading of the Greeks in relation to the question of the essay see below, Chapter 2.

23 'Reading' offers perhaps one of the earliest indications of Woolf's sense of the connection between memory and vision, writing and painting, which she never fully articulated in any one single piece, but the traces of which can be followed through a variety of writings, from essays to short stories to memoirs. For a detailed analysis of this connection see below, Chapters 4 and 5.

24 For a study of the complex relationship existing between Woolf's work and her Victorian heritage see Perry Meisel's *The Absent Father* (1980) and Gillian Beer, *Arguing with the Past* (1989), pp. 138–58.

25 On this see 'How Should One Read a Book?' (1926; *E* 4, 388–400) and 'Hours in a Library' (1916; *E* 2, 55–61); for more on Woolf's sense of books as people see also the discussion of 'Lives of the Obscure' in Chapter 5 below.

26 On 'Byron and Mr Briggs' as well as Woolf's projected book of criticism see also Andrew McNeillie's Introduction (*E* 3, xvi–xvii).

27 The crossing over of fictional and historical boundaries is doubled here, as in the months immediately preceding the publication of the first *Common Reader* Woolf had been busy reading Thomas Otway's *Venice Preserved* (1682) to prepare for an article on Restoration theatre which was to include

Dryden as well, but which she never wrote (see Brenda Silver, *Virginia Woolf's Reading Notebooks* (1983), pp. 222–4).

28   For a critique of Woolf's historiographic approach to the women writing in the Renaissance see Margaret Ezell, *Writing Women's Literary History* (1993).

29   David Cannadine, *Aspects of Aristocracy* (1994), pp. 9–36.

30   This phrase was coined by the French historians who founded the journal *Annales* as a forum for the articulation of a slow-moving social history as opposed to the *histoire événementielle*, the faster history of events. Rachel Bowlby has pointed out affinities between Woolf's approach to history in *A Room* and the *Annales*, both published, as she stresses, in 1929; see *Feminist Destinations*, p. 32. As Franco Moretti has remarked, the understanding of the dynamic of history proposed by the *Annales* school has very strong elements of similarity with Darwin's evolutionary theory which is also articulated in terms of an underlying sense of duration (the 'links' in the evolution of the species) occasionally punctuated by sudden changes (genetic mutation); see *Signs Taken for Wonders* (1988), pp. 262–78. That Woolf's understanding of the permanence of history owes as much to Darwin as to her French contemporaries is made clear in *Between the Acts*, where Mrs Swithin envisages 'rhododendron forests in Piccadilly; when the entire continent, not then, she understood, divided by a channel, was all one; populated, she understood, by elephant-bodied, seal- necked, heaving, surging, slowly writhing, and, she supposed, barking monsters. . . from whom presumably, she thought, jerking the window open, we descend' (p. 8) – in the novel Mrs Swithin represents, of course, the type of the eccentric.

31   Lee, *Virginia Woolf* (1996), p. 90.

32   Louise DeSalvo has also stressed the sense of continuity that links ['The Journal of Mistress Joan Martyn'] to Woolf's later interest in marginalised figures. In her article 'Shakespeare's 'Other' Sister' (1981), DeSalvo argues that Joan Martyn represents another version of the myth of Judith Shakespeare that Woolf will outline in *A Room* more than twenty years later. Unlike Judith 'who died without writing a word', Joan Martyn 'kept her journal for more than a year' and is therefore 'the historian of her own times' (p. 79). In DeSalvo's reading she thus works as a more empowering model of women's relationship to history-making and functions as the predecessor of Woolf's own historiographic practices.

33   In this Woolf's understanding of the significance of family history for the nobility or the landed gentry resembles very closely Walter Benjamin's concept of the 'aura' that surrounds works of art as a condensation of their sacred history of devotion, see *Illuminations*, pp. 211–44.

34   For a reading of 'Miss Ormerod' see below, Chapter 5.

35   The two meanings of 'common' which are intertwined in Woolf's writings are also the ones which, according to Raymond Williams, have always constituted the semantic catch of the word, designating 'something shared or. . . something *ordinary*'; see *Keywords* (1976), p. 71.

36   On the historiographic concerns of *Between the Acts* see Gillian Beer, *Arguing with the Past* (1989), pp. 159–82; on the notion of community see her *The Common Ground* (1996), pp. 48–73, 149–78.

37   The texts of these essays as well as a few exploratory notes made by Woolf in preparation for this book were published as ' "Anon" and "The Reader" ' (1979).
38   Ibid., p. 373.
39   Ibid., p. 376.
40   Maria DiBattista has proposed a reading of the notion of anonymity in Woolf that links it to the androgynous ideal which 'releases and relieves the mind...from those censoring and legislating powers that ordain and govern the sphere of the appropriate both in fiction and in life' (*The Fables of Anon* (1980), p. 19). Poststructuralist readings of the issue of modernity and subjectivity in Woolf's work have all focused primarily on Woolf's novels and, as a consequence, they tend to underline Woolf's suspicion of and resistance against any attempt at forging a new synthesis or a new self out of the fragmentation of the modern subject. See Makiko Minow Pinkney, *Virginia Woolf and the Problem of the Subject* (1987), Daniel Ferrer, *Virginia Woolf and the Madness of Language* (1990). Yet, as Ferrer remarks at the end of his compelling book, such insistence on the deconstructive movement of Woolf's fiction always produces as its shadow an equally clear assertion of its constructive thrust (pp. 5–7; 148).
41   Silver, ' "Anon" and "The Reader" ', p. 380.
42   Ibid., p. 359–60.
43   Ibid., p. 369.

2. The Essay as Form

1   For an account of the relationship between Woolf and Montaigne see also the Introduction above.
2   Woolf shared her preference for De Quincey with her mother who, as Woolf recalls in 'A Sketch of the Past' (1939–40), kept a copy of *Confessions of an Opium-Eater* on her bedside table. John Barrell has argued that the significance of De Quincey's writings for the history of English literature and culture goes well beyond the interest in the exploration of an unbound subjectivity which characterises Woolf's reading of his work. He shows that the taking of opium inextricably linked De Quincey's brand of Romantic autobiography with the discourses and images of Empire: 'the turbaned "Malay"...; the imagery of Hindu theology; the Hindu caste system; the vastness of space and time in India and China...all these came together to form, in De Quincey's head, an eclectic visual style he described as the "barbaresque" ' (*The Infection of Thomas De Quincey* (1991), p. 6). Woolf's own description of the state of altered consciousness brought about by illness can in fact be read as a revision of De Quincey's own opium-fuelled dreams, especially in *The Voyage Out* (1915), where the feverish dreams of Rachel Vinrace's final illness are preceded by the slightly unreal, hallucinatory experience of the voyage upstream. On the distortion of perceptions brought about by illness see also her essay 'On Being Ill' (1926; *CD*, 43–53).
3   For Woolf's own use of and reflections on the form of the sketch in her autobiographical writings see below, Chapter 4.

4 Woolf's definition of the characteristics of biography match precisely Lukács's view of the essay as an essentially synthetic genre bringing together art and science, lived experience and cognition; see *Soul and Form* (1911) and the discussion of critical views of the essay in the Introduction above.

5 The phrase is Woolf's own way of articulating the alternation between sudden, epiphanic revelations and the more mundane, everyday quality of experience. See her account of the distinction between the two in 'A Sketch of the Past' (*MB*, 70–1). For a study of the notion of the moment in Woolf's work see Jane Goldman, *The Feminist Aesthetics of Virginia Woolf* (1998), pp. 25–38.

6 In '*Jacob's Room* and the Eighteenth Century' (1981), Roger Moss has shown that Woolf's third novel, which is often considered to be her first experimental one, uses the form of the essay or commentary to interrupt the smooth progression of the psychological novel and question its validity as if it were a piece of internal criticism. For another example of 'essayism' in Woolf's fiction see also 'The Mark on the Wall' (1917; *SF*, 83–9), which frames a long philosophical meditation in fictional terms. For more on Woolf's early short stories see above, Chapter 1.

7 Samuel Johnson, *The Lives of the English Poets* (1779–81), p. 441.

8 See, most famously, *A Room* (1929) and 'Professions for Women' (1931; *CD*, 101–6). For a discussion of Woolf's developing ambivalence towards the idea of writing for money see below, Chapter 3.

9 For an in-depth analysis of the intertextual relation between Woolf and Johnson see Beth Carole Rosenberg, *Virginia Woolf and Samuel Johnson* (1995), which focuses on the dialogic character of the idea of the common reader.

10 This image of the 'more than maternal tie' has been used by Rachel Bowlby to signify the strong relation of interdependence that characterises Woolf's position *vis-à-vis* the tradition of essay-writing, but also the link between her feminist and modernist commitments as well as the connection between her fictional and her critical work (*WE*, xiv).

11 The publication history of 'Reviewing' offers a microcosmic representation of this tension between public and private. It was originally published as a Hogarth Press pamphlet on 2 November 1939, eliciting an immediate response from the *TLS* ('a tart & peevish leader' according to Woolf (*D* 5, 245)) and then, the following Saturday, from the *New Statesman & Nation*. Woolf wrote a reply to the *NS&N* entitled 'Reviewers' which was published a week later. In a diary entry for 9 November, she remarked: 'Why an answer should always make me dance like a monkey at the Zoo, gibbering it over as I walk, & then re-writing, I dont know. It wasted a day. I suppose its all pure waste: yet if one's an outsider, be an outsider – only dont for God's sake attitudinise & take up the striking the becoming attitude' (*D* 5, 245). The reference to 'outsiders' underscores the connection between 'Reviewing' and *Three Guineas*, on which see below and Chapter 3.

12 When invited to give the first Clark lectures in 1883, Leslie Stephen chose for his topic the eighteenth century. In 1932, when she was already collecting her 'explosive' material for *Three Guineas*, Woolf was invited herself to give the Clark lectures at Cambridge. She registered in her diary how her thoughts went out to her father, who 'would have blushed with pleasure could I have

told him 30 years ago, that his daughter – my poor little Ginny – was to be asked to succeed him: the sort of compliment he would have liked' (*D* 4, 79). Woolf promptly refused the invitation on grounds both of principle and of practical considerations, but a few days later she found herself plagued by the temptation to give in to 'the devil [who] whispered, all of a sudden, that I have six lectures written in Phases of Fiction; & could refurbish them up and deliver the Clark lectures, & win the esteem of my sex, with a few weeks work' (79). On 'Phases of Fiction' and *A Room*, see below, Chapter 5.

3. Professing Literature

1   As it has often been remarked, the situation of the narrator in *A Room* reflects Woolf's own position in real life. Her paternal aunt Caroline Emelia Stephen ('the Nun') left her a considerable legacy upon her death in 1909 at the expense of Vanessa and Adrian, who received very little. The legacy was meant to encourage Woolf to write 'a solid historical work' rather than the journalism of which Caroline Stephen disapproved (*L* 1, 202). The aunt of *A Room*, though, seems to be a fictional mix between 'the Nun' and Julia Margaret Cameron, the Victorian photographer and Woolf's maternal great-aunt, who went to live in India towards the end of her life, taking with her a coffin 'laden with family china' in case proper coffins could not be had there (see 'Julia Margaret Cameron', 1926, *E* 4, 375–83). Like Annie Thackeray Ritchie, another aunt-like figure in Woolf's life, Cameron represented for Woolf the prototype of the eccentric, for more on which see above, Chapter 1.

2   Abel, *Virginia Woolf*, p. 100.

3   Ibid., p. 101.

4   Ibid., p. 86.

5   For Katharine Hilbery and Mary Datchet see especially *Night and Day*, pp. 226–35; for Woolf's description of the contest between Clarissa and Miss Kilman see *Mrs Dalloway*, pp. 136–7.

6   Woolf, [Speech Before the London/National Society for Women's Service, January 21 1931], in *The Pargiters*, ed. Mitchell A. Leaska, p. xli.

7   Ibid., p. xlii.

8   *Three Guineas* uses in fact the same example of women servants trespassing onto the realm of their masters, but with a markedly different emphasis. Instead of the ironic, amused tone that characterises the passage in 'Professions for Women', in the later essay the comparison is marked by heavy satire and more than a tinge of that anger which in 'Professions' Woolf herself exhorts her audience to avoid. Answering the third of the letters that form the background of *Three Guineas*, Woolf remarks that for men to ask women for their help in protecting 'culture and intellectual liberty' is as 'surprising' as it would be for 'the Duke of Devonshire, in his star and garter' to ask 'the maid who was peeling potatoes' in the kitchen: ' "Stop your potato peeling, Mary, and help me to construe this rather difficult passage in Pindar" '. Whereas in 'Professions' it is the master of the house who is caught off-guard by the household servants' behaviour, in *Three Guineas* it is the kitchen maid herself who is pictured 'run[ning] screaming to Louisa the cook, "Lawks, Louie, Master must be mad!" ' (*TG*, 277–78).

9 Woolf, [Speech of January 21 1931], p. xl.
10 Ibid., p. xli.
11 Ibid., p. xliv.
12 I gratefully acknowledge Rachel Bowlby's insight on the androgynous character of Woolf's representation of the Guild women. For Bowlby's reading of 'Memories' see *WE*, pp. xxvii–xxviii.
13 In this sense, the working women of the Guild function in the same way as the obscure by giving Woolf the opportunity of penetrating a past and a life that would otherwise remain inaccessible to her. On the obscure see above, Chapter 1 and below, Chapter 5.
14 For an analysis of the relationship between the androgynous ideal and the writing of history in *A Room* see below, Chapter 4.
15 For the early reception of *Three Guineas* see *Virginia Woolf* (1975) ed. Robin Majumdar and Allen McLaurin, pp. 400–19, and *Virginia Woolf* (1994), ed. Eleanor McNees, vol. ii, pp. 267–81.
16 See Jane Marcus, *Art and Anger* (1988), pp. 101–21; Susan Squier, *Virginia Woolf and London* (1985), pp. 180–89; Brenda Silver, 'The Authority of Anger' (1991).
17 See Jane Marcus, *Virginia Woolf and the Languages of Patriarchy* (1987), pp. 163–213.
18 For a biography of Bell that analyses his personal and intellectual relationship to the pacifist/liberal ethics of Bloomsbury see Peter Stansky and William Abrahms, *Journey to the Frontier* (1966).
19 The essay was posthumously published in his *Essays, Poems and Letters* (1938), pp. 335–90. Given the near- incestuous character of Bell's relationship to his mother as inscribed in his letters, it is interesting that *Three Guineas* should be so concerned with the question of the fathers' infantile fixation on their daughters, in a way which reverses and, therefore, silences Julian's attachment to his mother. For Woolf's memoirs of Bell, see Quentin Bell, *Virginia Woolf* (1972–73), vol. ii, appendix C.
20 In 'Demythologizing Facts and Photographs' (1996) Julia Duffy and Lloyd Davis argue that the use of photographs in *Three Guineas* offers a critique rather than a reinforcement of the belief in the power of photography to sanction objective reality. Their argument, though, is based on an analysis of the actual plates of generals, judges, heralds, etc. reproduced within Woolf's essay rather than of the ways in which the Spanish photographs work at a rhetorical level. As I argue in 'The Art of Propaganda' (1999), the two sets of photographs, the ones which are described and the ones which are reproduced, stand in a dialectical relationship to each other. Within the terms of the discussion carried out by Woolf in *Three Guineas*, the critique of photography as a historical document that is symbolised by the photographs of British patriarchs reproduced in the text is dependent upon and reinforces the association of photography with objective reality which is instituted by the *rhetorical* use of the Spanish pictures described in the text.
21 In her diary, Woolf famously described the amount of references and quotes she collected in preparation for the writing of *Three Guineas* as 'enough powder to blow up St Pauls' (*D* 4, 77).
22 Jane Marcus, *Art and Anger* (1988), p. 121.
23 Ibid., p. 120.

24 Ibid., p. 108.
25 This returning contradiction has also been perceived by Susan Squier, who tries to resolve it by converting the pacifism of *Three Guineas* into 'an aggressive redefinition of the concepts of militancy and patriotism to include the feminist fight against male oppression of women and outsiders'. *Virginia Woolf and London*, p. 205, n. 4.

4. Sketching the Past, or the Fictions of Autobiography

1 For the use of metaphors in Woolf's essay-writing see Edward L. Bishop, 'Metaphor and the Subversive Process of Virginia Woolf's Essays' (1987).
2 In *The World Without a Self* (1973), James Naremore describes Woolf's 'love of the sketch' as 'one of the basic characteristics of her personality... a quality that can be felt at the most elementary level of her prose' (p. 100) and which 'is analogous to her whole approach in her more experimental fiction' (p. 101). For Naremore, though, the sketch is not so much related to questions of memory and vision in Woolf's work as to the effort of representing consciousness without itemising its contents, as is the case in the stream of consciousness.
3 For a clear example of this unreflective, almost automatic use of the sketch in Woolf's writing see *Mrs Dalloway* (1925), pp. 85–86, where Peter Walsh is thinking about Clarissa and, in a parenthetical remark, reflects that 'it was a mere sketch, he often felt, that even he, after all these years, could make of Clarissa'. I thank Rachel Bowlby for pointing out this passage to me.
4 In *Virginia Woolf and the Madness of Language* (1990), Daniel Ferrer analyses this passage in the context of his discussion of the theme of the double in *Mrs Dalloway*, arguing that Woolf's focus upon the question of character both in fiction and in her memoirs is related to the return of the repressed or the 'uncanny' (pp. 12–16). Ferrer's reading of Woolf's work tends to assimilate it to the theories of enunciation and psychic structures elaborated by Lacan, who in his turn relies on Freud. As I discuss later on in this section, the analogy with Freud is indeed invited by Woolf herself during the course of her autobiography. But her reflections on the workings of memory and literature in relation to scenes differ quite fundamentally from Freud's in ways which are important if we are to understand Woolf's own contribution to the analysis of narrative both as a historiographic structure and as a fictional one.
   Woolf's discussion of the Dickensian character in terms of outlines ('three strokes of the pen') also recalls E. M. Forster's distinction between 'flat' and 'rounded' characters in *Aspects of the Novel* (1927). What is surprising is that while for Forster it is 'round' characters that have 'the incalculability of life about [them] – life within the pages of a book' (p. 106), for Woolf vitality attaches itself to the 'flat' ones and makes them unforgettable. Forster's book was reviewed by Woolf, who unfavourably compared his approach to fiction to Roger Fry's lectures on modern painting ('Is Fiction an Art?', 1927; *E* 4, 462).
5 Sigmund Freud, 'The Wolf Man', p. 284.
6 Ibid., p. 295.

7 The question of the reality of the primal scene in Freud's theory has often been the target of ferocious attacks from his critics, who claim that Freud devised this notion as a substitute for the scenes of seduction by parents or carers of children which he had uncovered in his early work on hysterical patients; see e.g. Jeffrey Masson, *The Assault on Truth* (1992). Freud's alleged cover-up has in recent times been reversed by the notion of so-called 'false memory syndrome', where therapists are indicted with 'implanting' false memories of abuse in their patients. For an account of the issues of representation, memory and vision entangled with the issue of 'false memory syndrome' see Celia Lury, *Prosthetic Culture*, (1998) pp. 105–33. The question of the reality and/or fictionality of either the primal scene or the scene of seduction is of course particularly relevant to Woolf's memoirs, which have often been read as offering irrefutable evidence of her experience of sexual abuse by the Duckworth brothers. Louise DeSalvo's *Virginia Woolf: The Impact of Childhood Sexual Abuse* (1989) relies heavily on the evidence provided by the memoirs to support her claims of the ways in which the abuse shaped Woolf's view of the world and, consequently, her work. But in treating this text like a collection of symptoms to be interpreted by the critic/analyst, DeSalvo erases from view precisely the question of the reliability of the memoirs as a faithful record of the past that is at the centre of Woolf's reflections on the form of the scene.

8 Peter Brooks, *Reading for the Plot* (1984), p. 277.

9 For an analysis of the shifting boundaries between art and life in Woolf's fiction, see also C. Ruth Miller, *Virginia Woolf: the Frames of Art and Life* (1988).

10 *Orlando* is also the only one of Woolf's books to return to that connection between eccentricity, aristocracy and literary historiography that is at the centre of some of her earlier critical projects, on which see above, Chapter 1.

11 The 'and/or' tag has been described as the constitutive structure of *Orlando* by Rachel Bowlby in *Feminist Destinations* (1997), pp. 43–53.

12 In this sense, *Orlando* fits Tzvetan Todorov's definition of the fantastic as a 'hesitation', a state of suspension between 'the real and the imaginary', *The Fantastic* (1970), p. 25.

13 Vita Sackville-West to Harold Nicolson, 12 October 1928; a shorter version of this letter is also quoted by Madeline Moore in *The Short Season* (1984), p.107.

14 For a compelling analysis of the conventions that characterise the *Bildungsroman* in both its Continental and English varieties see Franco Moretti, *The Ways of the World* (1987), especially pp. 15–73 and 181–228.

15 Sigmund Freud, 'Family Romances' (1908), p. 228.

16 In 'Posing *Orlando*' (1994), Talia Schaffer traces the history of 'deliberate mistakes, mistreatments, and misrepresentations' through which Angelica's photograph came to stand in for Sackville-West's first lover, Violet Trefusis (p. 34). She also stresses how the alternation between photographs and paintings in the plates that went to illustrate *Orlando* indicates Woolf's self-consciousness about the unspoken rivalry between two sets of family heritages, hers and Sackville-West's: 'photographs visibly encoded family history for Woolf; her great aunt [Julia Margaret Cameron] took them, her mother sat for them, her sister owned them. Woolf could position this artistic family

inheritance against Sackville-West's ancestral collection of priceless portraits'
(p. 48).

17 This cryptic reference to Ariosto's *Orlando Furioso* also works to underscore
the similarities of tone, atmosphere and subject-matter between Woolf's
mock biography and the Italian Renaissance poem. Some of these similarities
had already been noted by Carolyn Heilbrun in *Towards Androgyny* (1973),
where she cited *Orlando Furioso* as one of the literary classics providing
examples of androgynous literature, since it is peopled with figures whose
sexual and gender identities are constantly in question, from women who
dress like paladins (pp. 26–7) to male/female twin couples where the
exchange of roles and cross-dressing constitute the norm (pp. 40–41).
Furthermore, just as Woolf's *Orlando* was written with the ostensible aim of
celebrating the life of Vita Sackville-West and her family, so Ariosto's poem
was presented as a symbolic legitimation of the Estense family as the rightful
rulers of the city-state of Ferrara in Northern Italy. For an analysis of the
historical situation of the writing of *Orlando Furioso* see further Peter V.
Marinelli, *Ariosto and Boiardo* (1987). Juliette Dusinberre's study of Woolf's
re-reading of the Renaissance has also stressed some parallels between her
approach to the body and comedy and the work of Sir John Harington,
Ariosto's English translator (*Virginia Woolf's Renaissance*, pp. 206–17).

5. Images of History

1 See Virginia Woolf, *Women and Fiction*, ed. S. P. Rosenbaum (1992). The text
of the published article 'Women and Fiction' is reprinted in *Granite and
Rainbow* (1958), pp. 76–84; *CE* 2, 141–8; and *Women and Writing*, ed. Michèle
Barrett, pp. 43–52.

2 Rosenbaum, pp. xxi-xxii.

3 Ibid., p. xxxv.

4 The same indictment of the tendency to destroy past conventions for its own
sake appears in 'Mr Bennett and Mrs Brown' (1924), where Woolf describes
Georgian literature as intent on 'smashing and crashing' the Edwardian
novel. Among those involved in these destructive mission to save the future
of English literature Woolf singles out Joyce, whose 'indecency' appears to
her as 'the conscious and calculated indecency of a desperate man who feels
that in order to breathe he must break the window....what a waste of
energy...' (*E* 3, 433–4).

5 For a reading of *A Room* centred around the inscription of lesbian relationships in its narrative strategies see Jane Marcus, *Virginia Woolf and the Languages of Patriarchy* (1987), pp. 163–213.

6 For McNeillie's comments see *E* 4, xii-xiii. McNeillie also notes that the
relation between Woolf's essayistic practice and her father's interest in biography was far from being one of direct opposition, as they both shared an
interest in the lives of marginal figures which Woolf chose to rewrite in terms
of the relationship between women and history. Rachel Bowlby also makes
this point in her introduction to *A Woman's Essays*, pp. xxiv-xxvi. For a
sample of Stephen's own pronouncements on the issue of marginality and
biography see his essay 'Autobiography' (1907).

7 Homer, *The Odyssey*, x.488–574; the episode of the actual encounter with the dead is in book XI and was also echoed by Virgil in book vi of the *Aeneid*. I thank Rachel Bowlby for pointing out these allusions.

8 Except of course in the famous passage about 'tea-table training' in her memoirs, where this 'sidelong approach' is traced back to the sexual politics of the late Victorian household (*MB*, 150); for a discussion of this passage in relation to Woolf's essayistic practice see above, Chapter 1.

9 The obvious reference in this respect is to *Between the Acts* (1941) and in particular to the much-discussed scene of the toad and the snake being squashed by Giles that is echoed in the final scene, which stages the sexual encounter between Isa and Giles as a form of violent animal struggle (pp. 61, 129–30). Another reference is the scene of the killing of the fish on the boat taking the surviving members of the Ramsay family to the lighthouse, where the violence of the scene resonates with the violence of war that has been all but expurgated from the middle section and its lyrical interludes (*To the Lighthouse* (1927), pp. 196, 145). For similarly violent primal scenes in 'A Sketch of the Past' see above, Chapter 4.

10 On this see Rachel Bowlby's discussion of questions of historiography in relation to *A Room* in *Feminist Destinations* (1997), pp. 30–2.

11 For a detailed analysis of the professional relationship between the two sisters and its psychological significance, see Diane Filby Gillespie, *The Sisters' Arts* (1988).

12 In the hallucinatory world of *Mrs Dalloway* the process enacted is exactly the opposite to the one described in 'The Royal Academy', as the darkened car passing by the florist shop is seen as an embodiment of the mystique and threat of Imperial power in the aftermath of the Great War (p. 15). On this, see Gillian Beer, *The Common Ground* (1996), pp. 149–78.

13 Here Woolf's reading of the Academy pictures shows clearly the influence of the early critical attitudes developed under the guidance of her father. In 'Impressions of Sir Leslie Stephen', the essay Woolf wrote for inclusion in Fred Maitland's biography of her father, Woolf recalls her father's disappointment and frustration when any of her children expressed identification with the good character rather than the villain in Walter Scott's novels (1906; *E* 1, 127–30).

14 The same anecdote is sarcastically reported by Edith Sitwell in her *English Eccentrics* (1933; pp. 216–17), an idiosyncratic collection of lives which includes some of the figures which Woolf herself had listed as promising material for her projected but never realised book on the eccentrics, on which see above, Chapter 1.

15 Terry was part of that pre-Raphaelite circle that gathered around the Pattle sisters, of which Woolf's maternal grandmother was one. For a discussion of 'Pattledom' and Julia Margaret Cameron see above, Chapter 1.

16 For Eliot's obituary see Robin Majumdar and Allen McLaurin (eds), *Virginia Woolf: The Critical Heritage* (1975), pp. 429–31.

Postscript: Angles and Harpies

1 Walter Benjamin, *Illuminations*, p. 249.

2 For a study of the intersection of 'Messianism' and Marxism in Benjamin's philosophy of history, see Michael Jennings, *Dialectical Images* (1987), pp. 42–81.

3 Franco Moretti, *Signs Taken for Wonders*, p. 41.

4 Margaret Anne Doody, *The True Story of the Novel*, pp. 493–4.

Bibliography

Abel, Elizabeth. *Virginia Woolf and the Fictions of Psychoanalysis*. Chicago: U of Chicago P, 1989.

Adorno, Theodor W. 'The Essay as Form', in *Notes to Literature*, 1958, trans. Shierry Weber Nicholsen, vol. i. New York: Columbia UP, 1991: 3–23.

——and Max Horkheimer. *Dialectic of Enlightenment*, 1944, trans. John Cumming. 2nd edn London: Verso-NLB, 1979.

Ariosto, Ludovico. *Orlando Furioso*, 1502–32, a cura di Cesare Segre. 2 vols, Milan: Mondadori, 1990.

Barrell, John. *The Infection of Thomas De Quincey: A Psychopathology of Imperialism*. New Haven: Yale UP, 1991.

Barrett, Michèle. Introduction to *Women and Writing*, by Virginia Woolf. London: Women's Press, 1979: 1–39.

——Introduction to *A Room of One's Own; Three Guineas*, by Virginia Woolf. Harmondsworth: Penguin, 1993: ix–liii.

Bazin, Nancy Topping. *Virginia Woolf and the Androgynous Vision*. New Brunswick: Rutgers UP, 1973.

Beer, Gillian. *Arguing with the Past: Essays in Narrative from Woolf to Sidney*. London: Routledge, 1989.

——*Virginia Woolf: The Common Ground. Essays*. Edinburgh: Edinburgh UP, 1996.

Bell, Julian. *Essays, Poems and Letters*, ed. Quentin Bell. London: Hogarth, 1938.

Bell, Quentin. *Virginia Woolf: A Biography*. 2 vols, London: Hogarth, 1972–73.

Benjamin, Walter. *Illuminations*, 1955. Ed. Hannah Arendt, trans. Harry Zohn. London: Fontana-HarperCollins, 1992.

Bennett, Arnold. 'Is the Novel Decaying?'. *Cassell's Weekly*, 28 March 1923: 47. Reprinted in *Virginia Woolf: The Critical Heritage*, ed. Robin Majumdar and Allen McLaurin. London: Routledge, 1975: 113; and in *Virginia Woolf: Critical Assessments*, ed. Eleanor McNees, vol. i. Mountfield: Helm Information, 1994: 184.

Benveniste, Émile. *Problems in General Linguistics*, 1966, trans. Mary Elizabeth Meek. Coral Gables: U of Miami P, 1971: 205–22.

Bishop, Edward L. 'Metaphor and the Subversive Process of Virginia Woolf's Essays', *Style* 21: 4 (1987): 573–89.

Bowlby, Rachel. *Feminist Destinations and Further Essays on Virginia Woolf*. Edinburgh: Edinburgh UP, 1997.

Brewster, Dorothy. *Virginia Woolf*. New York: New York UP, 1962.

Brooks, Peter. *Reading for the Plot: Design and Intention in Narrative*. Oxford: Clarendon, 1984.

Brosnan, Leila. *Reading Virginia Woolf's Essays and Journalism*. Edinburgh: Edinburgh UP, 1997.

Cannadine, David. *Aspects of Aristocracy: Grandeur and Decline in Modern Britain*. New Haven: Yale UP, 1994.

Childers, Mary M. 'Virginia Woolf on the Outside Looking Down: Reflections on the Class of Women'. *Modern Fiction Studies* 38.1 (1992): 61–79.

Cixous, Hélène. 'The Laugh of the Medusa', 1975, trans. Keith Cohen and Paula Cohen, in *New French Feminisms: An Anthology*, ed. Elaine Marks and Isabelle de Courtivron. Brighton: Harvester, 1981: 245–64.

Daiches, David. *Virginia Woolf*. New York: New Directions, 1942.

de Obaldia, Claire. *The Essayistic Spirit: Literature, Modern Criticism and the Essay*. Oxford: Clarendon, 1995.

DeSalvo, Louise A. 'Shakespeare's "Other" Sister', in *New Feminist Essays on Virginia Woolf*, ed. Jane Marcus. London: Macmillan, 1981: 61–81.

—— *Virginia Woolf: The Impact of Childhood Sexual Abuse on Her Life and Work*. Boston: Beacon, 1989.

DiBattista, Maria. *Virginia Woolf's Major Novels: The Fables of Anon*. New Haven: Yale UP, 1980.

Dobrée, Bonamy. *English Essayists*. London: Collins, 1946.

Doody, Margaret Anne. *The True Story of the Novel*, 1996. London: Fontana-HarperCollins, 1997.

Dubino, Jeanne. 'Virginia Woolf: From Book Reviewer to Literary Critic, 1904–918', in *Virginia Woolf and the Essay*, ed. Beth Carole Rosenberg and Jeanne Dubino. London: Macmillan, 1997: 25–40.

Duffy, Julia and Lloyd Davis. 'Demythologizing Facts and Photographs in *Three Guineas*', in *Photo-Textualities. Reading Photographs and Literature*, ed. Marsha Bryant. Newark: U of Delaware P and London: Associated UP, 1996. 128–40.

DuPlessis, Rachel Blau. 'For the Etruscans', in *The New Feminist Criticism. Essays on Women, Literature and Theory*, ed. Elaine Showalter. New York: Pantheon-Random, 1985: 271–91.

Dusinberre, Juliet. *Virginia Woolf's Renaissance: Woman Reader or Common Reader?* London: Macmillan, 1997.

Ezell, Margaret J. M. *Writing Women's Literary History*. Baltimore: Johns Hopkins UP, 1993: 39–65.

Ferrer, Daniel. *Virginia Woolf and the Madness of Language*, trans. Geoffrey Bennington and Rachel Bowlby. London: Routledge, 1990.

Forster, E. M. *Aspects of the Novel*. London: Arnold, 1927.

Foucault, Michel. 'What Is an Author?', 1969. Reprinted in *The Foucault Reader*, ed. Paul Rabinow. New York: Pantheon, 1984: 101–20.

Freud, Sigmund. 'Family Romances', 1909. Trans. James Strachey. *The Standard Edition of the Complete Psychological Works of Sigmund Freud*, vol. 9. London: Hogarth, 1959: 235–41.

—— 'From the History of an Infantile Neurosis (The "Wolf Man")', 1918. Reprinted in *Case Histories II. The 'Rat Man', Schreber, the 'Wolf Man', A Case of Female Homosexuality*, Penguin Freud Library, trans. James Strachey, vol. 9. Harmondsworth: Penguin, 1990: 227–366.

Fuss, Diana. 'Getting Into History'. *Arizona Quarterly* 45.4 (1989): 95–108.

Gillespie, Diane Filby. *The Sisters' Arts: The Writing and Painting of Virginia Woolf and Vanessa Bell*. Syracuse: Syracuse UP, 1988.

Goldman, Jane. *The Feminist Aesthetics of Virginia Woolf: Modernism, Post-Impressionism and the Politics of the Visual*. Cambridge: Cambridge UP, 1998.

Goldman, Marc. *The Reader's Art: Virginia Woolf as Literary Critic*. The Hague: Mouton, 1976.

Good, Graham. *The Observing Self: Rediscovering the Essay*. London: Routledge, 1988.

Greenblatt, Stephen. *Renaissance Self-Fashioning: From More To Shakespeare.* Chicago: U of Chicago P, 1980.

Gross, John. *The Rise and Fall of the Men of Letters: Aspects of English Literary Life since 1800,* 1969. Reprinted Harmondsworth: Penguin, 1991.

Gualtieri, Elena. 'The Art of Propaganda: *Three Guineas* and the Photograph', in *Women Writers of the 1930s: Gender, Politics, History,* ed. Maroula Joannou. Edinburgh: Edinburgh UP, 1999, pp. 165–78.

Guiguet, Jean. *Virginia Woolf and Her Works,* trans. Jean Stewart. London: Hogarth, 1965.

Heilbrun, Carolyn. *Towards Androgyny: Aspects of Male and Female in Literature,* 1964. 2nd edn, London: Gollancz, 1973.

Homer. *The Odyssey,* trans. and intro. Richmond Lattimore. New York: Harper Perennial, 1991.

Jennings, Michael W. *Dialectical Images: Walter Benjamin's Theory of Literary Criticism.* Ithaca: Cornell UP, 1987.

Joeres, Ruth-Ellen Boetcher and Elizabeth Mittman, eds. *The Politics of the Essay: Feminist Perspectives.* Bloomington: Indiana UP, 1993.

Johnson, Samuel. *Lives of the English Poets,* 1779–81. Ed. George Birkbeck Hill. Oxford: Clarendon, 1905.

Kauffman, Michael. 'A Modernism of One's Own: Virginia Woolf's *TLS* Reviews and Eliotic Modernism', in *Virginia Woolf and the Essay,* ed. Beth Carole Rosenberg and Jeanne Dubino. London: Macmillan, 1997: 137–55.

Lacoue-Labarthe, Phillipe. *Heidegger, Art and Politics: The Fiction of the Political,* trans. Chris Turner. Oxford: Blackwell, 1990.

Leavis, Q. D. 'Caterpillars of the World Unite!', *Scrutiny,* 1938: 203–14. Reprinted in *Virginia Woolf: The Critical Heritage,* ed. Robin Majumdar and Allen McLaurin. London: Routledge, 1975: 409–19; and in *Virginia Woolf: Critical Assessments,* ed. Eleanor McNees, vol. ii. Mountfield: Helm Information, 1994: 272–81.

Lee, Hermione. *Virginia Woolf.* London: Chatto, 1996.

London, Bette. *The Appropriated Voice: Narrative Authority in Conrad, Forster and Woolf.* Ann Arbor: U of Michigan P, 1990.

—— 'Guerrilla in Petticoats or Sans-Culotte? Virginia Woolf and the Future of Feminist Criticism', *Diacritics: A Review of Contemporary Criticism* 21.2–3 (1991): 11–29.

Lukács, Georg. 'On the Nature and Form of the Essay: A Letter to Leo Popper', 1910. *Soul and Form,* 1911. Trans. Anna Bostock. London: Merlin, 1974: 1–18.

Lury, Celia. *Prosthetic Culture: Photography, Memory and Identity.* London and New York: Routledge, 1998.

Majumdar, Robin and Allen McLaurin, eds. *Virginia Woolf: The Critical Heritage.* London: Routledge, 1975.

Marcus, Jane. 'Thinking Back Through Our Mothers', in *New Feminist Essays on Virginia Woolf,* ed. Jane Marcus. London: Macmillan, 1981: 1–30.

—— *Virginia Woolf and the Languages of Patriarchy.* Bloomington: Indiana UP, 1987.

—— *Art and Anger: Reading Like a Woman.* Columbus: Ohio State UP, 1988.

—— 'Pathographies: The Virginia Woolf Soap Operas', *Signs: A Journal of Women in Culture and Society* 17 (1992): 806–19.

Marder, Herbert. *Feminism and Art: A Study of Virginia Woolf.* Chicago: U of Chicago P, 1968.

Marinelli, Peter V. *Ariosto and Boiardo: The Origins of* Orlando Furioso. Columbia: U of Missouri P, 1987.

Masson, Jeffrey. *The Assault on Truth: Freud and Child Sex Abuse,* rev. edn. London: Fontana, 1992.

McNees, Eleanor, ed. *Virginia Woolf: Critical Assessments.* 4 vols, Mountfield: Helm Information, 1994.

Meisel, Perry. *The Absent Father: Virginia Woolf and Walter Pater.* New Haven: Yale UP, 1980.

Miller, C. Ruth. *Virginia Woolf: The Frames of Art and Life.* London: Macmillan, 1988.

Moi, Toril. *Sexual/Textual Politics: Feminist Literary Theory.* London: Methuen, 1985.

Moore, Madeleine. *The Short Season Between Two Silences: The Mystical and the Political in Virginia Woolf.* Boston: Allen, 1984: 93–115.

Moretti, Franco. *The Way of the World: The Bildungsroman in European Culture.* London: Verso-NLB, 1987.

——*Signs Taken for Wonders: Essays in the Sociology of Literary Forms,* 1987, trans. Susan Fischer, David Forgacs and David Miller. 2nd edn, London: Verso-NLB, 1988.

Moss, Roger. 'Jacob's Room and the Eighteenth Century: From Elegy to Essay'. *Critical Quarterly* 23.3 (1981): 39–54.

Musil, Robert. *The Man Without Qualities,* 1930–42. Trans. Sophie Wilkins and Burton Pike, London: Picador, 1995.

Naremore, James. *The World Without a Self: Virginia Woolf and the Novel.* New Haven: Yale UP, 1973.

Otway, Thomas. *Venice Preserved,* 1682. Ed. Malcolm Kelsall, London: Arnold, 1969.

Pinkney, Makiko Minow. *Virginia Woolf and the Problem of the Subject.* Brighton: Harvester, 1987.

Poole, Roger. *The Unknown Virginia Woolf,* 1978. 2nd edn, Brighton: Harvester, 1982.

Ricoeur, Paul. *Time and Narrative,* trans. Kathleen McLaughlin and David Pellauer. 3 vols, Chicago: U of Chicago P, 1984–88.

Rose, Gillian. *The Melancholy Science: An Introduction to the Thought of Theodor W. Adorno.* New York: Columbia UP, 1978.

Rosenberg, Beth Carole. *Virginia Woolf and Samuel Johnson: Common Readers.* London: Macmillan, 1995.

—— and Jeanne Dubino, eds. *Virginia Woolf and the Essay.* London: Macmillan, 1997.

Sackville-West, Vita. Letter to Harold Nicholson, 12 October 1928, printed in *Twentieth Century Literature.* 25.3-4 (1979): 349.

Sandbach-Dahlström, Catherine. ' "Que scais-je?"': Virginia Woolf and the Essay as Feminist Critique', in *Virginia Woolf and the Essay,* ed. Beth Carole Rosenberg and Jeanne Dubino. London: Macmillan, 1997: 275–93.

Schor, Naomi. 'Introducing Feminism', in *Paragraph 8.* Oxford: Oxford UP, 1986: 94–101.

Schaffer, Talia. 'Posing *Orlando*', in *Sexual Artifice: Persons, Images, Politics,* ed. Ann Kibbey, Kayann Short and Abouali Farmanfarmaian. New York and London: New York UP, 1994: 26–63.

Sharma, Vijay L. *Virginia Woolf as Literary Critic: A Revaluation*. New Delhi: Arnold-Heinemann, 1977.

Showalter, Elaine. *A Literature of Their Own: British Women Novelists From Brontë to Lessing*. London: Virago, 1979.

Silver, Brenda. *Virginia Woolf's Reading Notebooks*. Princeton: Princeton UP, 1983.

—— 'The Authority of Anger: *Three Guineas* as Case-Study', *Signs: A Journal of Women in Culture and Society* 16.2 (1991): 340–70.

Sitwell, Edith. *English Eccentrics*. 1933. New edn, London: Dobson, 1959.

Snyder, John. *Prospects of Power: Tragedy, Satire, the Essay and the Theory of Genre*. Lexington: UP of Kentucky, 1991.

Squier, Susan. *Virginia Woolf and London: The Sexual Politics of the City*. Chapel Hill: U of North Carolina P, 1985: 180–89.

Stansky, Peter, and William Abrahms. *Journey to the Frontier: Julian Bell and John Cornford: Their Lives and the 1930s*. London: Constable, 1966.

Stephen, Leslie. *English Literature and Society in the Eighteenth Century*. London: Duckworth, 1904.

—— 'Autobiography', in *Hours in A Library*, vol. 4. London: Duckworth, 1907: 185–231.

Todd, Janet. *Feminist Literary History*. New York: Routledge, 1988.

Todorov, Tzvetan. *The Fantastic: A Structural Approach to a Literary Genre*, 1970. Trans. Richard Howard, foreword Robert Scholes, Ithaca: Cornell UP, 1975.

White, Hayden. *Tropics of Discourse: Essays in Cultural Criticism*. Baltimore: Johns Hopkins UP, 1978: 27–50.

—— *The Content of the Form: Narrative Discourse and Historical Representation*. Baltimore: Johns Hopkins UP, 1989. 1–25.

Williams, Orlo. *The Essay*. London: Secker, n.d.

Williams, Raymond. *Keywords: A Vocabulary of Culture and Society*. 1976. London: Fontana, 1983.

Woolf, Leonard. *Autobiography*. 5 vols, New York: Harvest- Harcourt, 1960–69.

Woolf, Virginia. *The Voyage Out*. 1915. Ed. and intro. Jane Wheare, Harmondsworth: Penguin, 1992.

—— *Night and Day*. 1919. Ed. and intro. Julia Briggs, Harmondsworth: Penguin, 1992.

—— *Jacob's Room*. 1922. Ed. and intro. Kate Flint, Oxford: World's Classics-Oxford UP, 1992.

—— *Mrs Dalloway*. 1925. Ed. Stella McNichol, intro. and notes Elaine Showalter, Harmondsworth: Penguin, 1992.

—— *The Common Reader. First Series*. 1925. Ed. and intro. Andrew McNeillie, London: Hogarth, 1984.

—— *To the Lighthouse*. 1927. Ed. Stella McNichol, intro. and notes Hermione Lee, Harmondsworth: Penguin, 1992.

—— *Orlando. A Biography*. 1928. Ed. and intro. Rachel Bowlby, Oxford: World's Classics-Oxford UP, 1992.

—— *A Room of One's Own*. 1929. Ed. and intro. Morag Shiach, Oxford: World's Classics-Oxford UP, 1992.

—— *The Waves*. 1931. Ed. and intro. Gillian Beer, Oxford: World's Classics-Oxford UP, 1992.

—— *The Common Reader. Second Series*. 1932. Ed. and intro. Andrew McNeillie, London: Hogarth, 1986.

—— *The Years*. 1937. Ed. and intro. Hermione Lee, notes Sue Asbee, Oxford: World's Classics-Oxford UP, 1992.

—— *Three Guineas*. 1938. Ed. and intro. Morag Shiach, Oxford: World's Classics-Oxford UP, 1992.

—— *Roger Fry. A Biography*. London: Hogarth, 1940.

—— *Between the Acts*. 1941. Ed. and intro. Gillian Beer, Harmondsworth: Penguin, 1992.

—— *The Death of the Moth, and Other Essays*. London: Hogarth, 1942.

—— *The Moment, and Other Essays*. London: Hogarth, 1947.

—— *The Captain Death's Bed, and Other Essays*. London: Hogarth, 1950.

—— *Granite and Rainbow. Essays*. London: Hogarth, 1958.

—— *Contemporary Writers*. London: Hogarth, 1965.

—— *Collected Essays*, ed. Leonard Woolf. 4 vols, London: Hogarth, 1966–67.

—— *The Letters of Virginia Woolf*, ed. Nigel Nicolson and Joanne Trautmann. 6 vols, London: Hogarth, 1975–84.

—— *Moments of Being: Unpublished Autobiographical Writings of Virginia Woolf*. 1976, ed. Jeanne Schulkind. 2nd edn, New York: Harvest-Harcourt Brace, 1985.

—— *The Pargiters by Virginia Woolf: The Novel- Essay Portion of* The Years, ed. and intro. Mitchell A. Leaska. London: Hogarth, 1978.

—— '"Anon" and "The Reader": Virginia Woolf's Last Essays', ed. and intro. Brenda R. Silver. *Twentieth Century Literature* 25.3–4 (1979): 356–441.

—— *The Diary of Virginia Woolf*, 1977–84, ed. Anne Olivier Bell and Andrew McNeillie, intro. Quentin Bell. 5 vols, Harmondsworth: Penguin, 1979–85.

—— *The Complete Shorter Fiction of Virginia Woolf*, ed. Susan Dick. New York: Harvest-Harcourt Brace, 1985.

—— *The Essays of Virginia Woolf*, ed. Andrew McNeillie. 4 vols to date, London: Hogarth, 1986– .

—— *A Woman's Essays: Selected Essays*, vol. i, ed. and intro. Rachel Bowlby. Harmondsworth: Penguin, 1992.

—— *Women and Fiction: The Manuscript Versions of* A Room of One's Own, ed. S. P. Rosenbaum. Oxford: Blackwell, 1992.

—— *The Crowded Dance of Modern Life: Selected Essays*, vol. ii, ed. and intro. Rachel Bowlby. Harmondsworth: Penguin, 1993.

—— *Killing the Angel in the House: Seven Essays*, ed. Rachel Bowlby. Penguin 60s Series. Harmondsworth: Penguin, 1995.

Index

sketch, the, 19, 55, 56, 94–5, 96, 97, 102, 104, 125, 128, 129–30, 132, 162 n. 2, 162 n. 3; *see also* essay and fiction, the; essay and photography, the
Smith, R., 24
Snyder, J., 9–11
Spanish Civil War: *see* Bell, J.; Woolf, V., *Three Guineas*
Squier, S., 162 n. 25
Stansky, P., 161 n. 18
Stephen, C.E., 23, 160 n. 1
Stephen, J., 41, 98–9, 101, 143
Stephen, L., 24, 25, 67, 100, 155 n. 16, 159 n. 12, 164 n. 6, 165 n. 13; *see also Dictionary of National Biography*
Stephen, V., 23–5, 29–32; *see esp.* 153 n. 2, 155 n. 19
  essays: 'An Andalusian Inn', 156 n. 20; 'Art and Life', 32; 'Château and Country Life', 31; 'The Duchess of Newcastle', 38, 39, 40; 'The Duke and Duchess of Newcastle', 31; 'John Delane', 24; 'The Journal of Elizabeth Lady Holland', 24; 'Lady Fanshawe's Memoirs', 26; 'Lady Hester Stanhope', 37–9, 40; 'Letters of Christina Rossetti', 24; 'The Letters of Jane Carlyle', 155 n. 16; 'Louise de la Vallière', 24; 'The Memoirs of Lady Dorothy Neville', 24, 31; 'The Novels of George Gissing', 24; 'Philip Sidney', 24; 'A Priory Church', 156 n. 20; 'Shelley and Elizabeth Hitchener', 24; 'The Sister of Frederic the Great', 26; 'Social England', 153 n. 1; 'The Son of Royal Langbirth', 153 n. 1; 'Street Music', 24, 29; 'The Value of Laughter', 29; 'A Vanished Generation', 43; 'A Walk By Night', 156 n. 20; 'A Week at the White House', 24; 'Wordsworth and the Lakes', 24
  fiction: ['A Dialogue upon Mount Pentelicus'], 31, 34, 156 n. 22; ['The Journal of Mistress Joan Martyn'], 31, 42–3, 157 n. 32; *Melymbrosia*, 31, 32; *see also The Voyage Out*; 'Memoirs of a Novelist', 24, 33; ['The Mysterious Case of Miss V.'], 31; ['Phyllis and Rosamond'], 31
  journals, 30, 155 n. 19
  on Platonic dialogues, 31–2, 156 n. 22; *see also* Plato
Stevenson, R.L., 54

Todd, J., 152 n. 22
Tennyson, A., 41

Watt, I., 6
Watts, G.F., 41, 142
Wells, H.G., 30
White, H., 156 n. 21
Williams, O., 151 n. 4
Williams, R., 157 n. 35
Winchelsea, L., 45
Woolf, L., 3, 12, 25, 32, 66–7, 75, 154 n. 5
Woolf, V.,
  autobiography/biography: *Moments of Being*, 28, 39–40, 95–6; 'Old Bloomsbury', 155 n. 8; *Orlando*, 17, 19, 20, 36, 39, 40, 94, 104–15, 116, 120, 150; 'A Sketch of the Past', 19, 20, 28, 94–102, 103–4, 105, 113, 142–3, 159 n. 5, 165 n. 8
  essays: ' "Anon" and "The Reader" ', 46–8; 'The Art of Biography', 56; 'Bad Writers', 62; 'A Book of Essays', 63; 'Byron & Mr Briggs', 33–4; 'The Common Reader', 58–9; *Common Reader: First Series*, 32, 33, 35–6, 43, 44, 94, 122, 156 n. 27; *see also* titles of individual essays; *The Death of the Moth*, 75, 129; 'The Decay of Essay-writing', 24, 49–50; 'De Quincey's Autobiography', 55–6; 'The Eccentrics', 38, 40, 43; 'The Elizabethan Lumber Room', 51–2; 'Ellen Terry', 141–3; 'The English Mail Coach', 54–5; 'Foreword to